# ACT NOW

## Action Steps that will Change Your Life Forever

### LINTON THOMAS

WESTBOW
PRESS®
A DIVISION OF THOMAS NELSON
& ZONDERVAN

This book is a work of non-fiction. Unless otherwise noted, the author and the publisher make no explicit guarantees as to the accuracy of the information contained in this book and in some cases, names of people and places have been altered to protect their privacy.

WestBow Press books may be ordered through booksellers or by contacting:

WestBow Press
A Division of Thomas Nelson & Zondervan
1663 Liberty Drive
Bloomington, IN 47403
www.westbowpress.com
844-714-3454

ISBN: 979-8-3850-2253-3 (sc)
ISBN: 979-8-3850-2254-0 (e)

Library of Congress Control Number: 2024906350

Print information available on the last page.

WestBow Press rev. date: 4/10/2024

# CONTENTS

# DEDICATION

First, this book is affectionately dedicated to Bishop Gary Thomas and the esteemed members and leadership of the New Birth Federation of Churches. It was the gracious invitation extended to me to speak at their 2023 Convention, themed "Act Now," that served as the catalyst for the creation of this book.

Time is a precious, priceless resource that cannot be bottled. We must use it wisely. This book is dedicated to those who have faced formidable foes that hinder progress. It is for the brave souls who have grappled with the tyranny of procrastination, the weight of a lack of motivation, the paralyzing grip of fear of failure, and the uncertainty bred by a lack of planning. It is for those who've tasted the bittersweet sting of overambition and navigated through the maze of distractions in the modern world.

To the warriors who have battled against the clock due to a lack of time management and contended with the relentless onslaught of negative self-talk, this dedication is for you. You, who have trodden the path alone, seeking to achieve your dreams, even when lacking the support and encouragement of those around you. For the indomitable spirits who muster the strength to persevere in the face of health challenges and for those whose dreams have been deferred due to financial constraints. To the resilient souls who, against all odds, have remained steadfast despite the unpredictable storms of external circumstances.

May this book serve as a beacon of hope, a wellspring of guidance, and a source of inspiration. In its pages, may you find the tools, wisdom, and encouragement to conquer these adversaries and forge ahead toward your goals. May it be a reminder that your struggles are not in vain and that there is a path forward, even in the darkest times. To all those who have faced these challenges, this book is dedicated to you. Your strength, resilience, and determination are unquestionable proof that we can still find our way to the light in the face of adversity.

# The Unyielding Imperative of this Moment

It is with deep gratitude that I accept the opportunity to pen the foreword for the remarkable book Act Now. In an era, devoid of such profound insights, this book stands as a beacon, shedding light on issues frequently overlooked in our societal fabric – within our homes, places of worship, or workplaces. Authored by the venerable Linton Thomas, Act Now draws upon a wealth of Christian ministry experience, teaching, and a heartfelt commitment to sharing the boundless love of God.

Having known Linton Thomas for over two decades, I can attest to his unwavering dedication to education. His written words embody clarity, conciseness, and an undeniable ability to captivate the reader's attention. As both a pastor and educator, Linton is a rare gem, characterized by humility, integrity, and a profound spirituality that permeates his every endeavor. My appreciation for this book knows no bounds – while few works can rightfully claim the status of 'classic,' Act Now unquestionably earns such distinction.

I am confident that the influence of this book will only burgeon with time as its message resonates with an ever-expanding audience. As an anthropologist and historian, I firmly believe that Act Now will be vital in fostering cross-cultural understanding within academic spheres. Moreover, I am convinced that its impact will extend far beyond, shaping the perspectives of a new generation on a global scale.

For those seeking to propel their lives forward, the invitation to embark upon the transformative journey outlined in Act Now is not one to be declined. Within its pages lie the keys to unlocking powerful possibilities in every facet of life – from personal growth to familial harmony and spiritual enrichment to community engagement. Without hesitation, I wholeheartedly endorse this book to all who seek inspiration and empowerment.

Gary A. Thomas, Author
Bishop, New Birth Federation of Churches

# CHAPTER 1

# Act Now: Examine Your Friendships!

*Time is fleeting, moments are limited; cherish every
connection and make each second count!*

## THE JOURNEY OF LIFE

Where are you now?
In which stage of life do you now reside?
Are you in your tender teens, sweet and wide-eyed?
Are you navigating the teachable twenties to learn and grow?

Or are you in your tireless thirties, where rest is vital to know?
Perhaps you've reached the fiery forties,
where ambition's your guide?
Are you in your forceful fifties, maintaining
your vim, vigor, and vitality?
Have you entered the serious sixties, a time to move and exercise?

Or have you entered the sacred seventies,
where each day's a precious prize?
Maybe you are in your aching eighties, and you
might be experiencing shortness of breath,
Take one day at a time; ease your fear.
And if you've entered the nervous nineties,
please don't dread it! Don't be afraid!
Eternity awaits just ahead.

No matter your place in this journey, it's true to say,
Life's fleeting, with limited time each day.
So, cherish every moment, make each second count,
For this is it: it is the journey of our lives!

## FRIENDSHIPS

Friends are like stars!
You may not always see them, but you know
they're there, shining in the darkness of life.
Friends are like a warm blanket!
They provide comfort and security during
the chilliest moments of life.
Friends are like a lighthouse!
They guide you through stormy seas and
help you find your way when lost.
Friends are like a cup of tea!
They soothe your soul, offering warmth and calm in times of need.
Friends are like a jigsaw puzzle!
Each one is a unique piece that, when put
together, forms a beautiful picture of life.
Friends are like a garden!
They require nurturing and care to flourish, and
their presence adds beauty to the world.

Friends are like a favorite book!
You can revisit them time and time again to find
comfort and familiarity in their pages.
Friends are like a rainbow!
A beautiful, fleeting moment in your life
that brings joy and wonder.
Friends are like a compass!
They provide direction and guidance when
you're unsure which path to take.
Friends are like a song!
They add melody and harmony to the soundtrack of life!

On the contrary, friendships can change over time. People may move away, change interests, or grow apart. Maintaining close friendships requires effort and communication; even then, they can evolve or diminish. Some friendships, like milk, can expire. Milk has a finite period during which it remains fresh and suitable for consumption. Friendships may have a natural lifespan, too. Like many other aspects of life, friendships can change over time due to evolving circumstances, interests, or personal growth.

People step onto our stage for various purposes and durations. They are the actors in the intricate play of existence, each playing a unique role. In this chapter, we delve into the profound complexities of why people come into your life, with a reminder that not all friends are destined to be permanent fixtures.

## Guiding Lights

Some individuals enter our lives as guiding lights. They wear many hats, serving as motivators, counselors, role models, advisors, and door openers. Their presence in our journey is often deliberate, designed to steer us toward self-discovery, growth, and understanding. They teach us invaluable lessons and stand by us during challenging times.

These friends walk beside us when we most need them, casting a guiding glow on our path. Some friends are destiny helpers; others are destiny destroyers! Know the difference.

For instance, consider John Mark, whose initial purpose was as a helper. He briefly left the apostle Paul but returned later as a faithful assistant, reinforcing that friendships can ebb and flow like seasons in a year. Eleanor Roosevelt, former First Lady of the United States, was a prominent figure in history and an inspirational friend to many. She was a guiding light through her wisdom, compassion, and advocacy for social justice and human rights. One of Eleanor Roosevelt's notable friends and an inspirational figure in her life was Marion Dickerman. Marion Dickerman was an American educator, reformer, and a close friend of Eleanor Roosevelt. Their friendship was deeply rooted in shared values and a commitment to social justice and human rights. Both women collaborated in establishing a progressive, experimental school called Todd School for Boys and Girls in North Tarrytown, New York (now known as Sleepy Hollow). This school was founded in 1928 and was innovative for its time, promoting holistic education and focusing on developing each child's unique potential. Eleanor Roosevelt and Marion Dickerman believed in the importance of nurturing young minds and providing children with an environment that encouraged critical thinking, creativity, and a deep sense of social responsibility. Their friendship and shared educational vision were crucial to the school's success.

Harriet Tubman, known for her role in the Underground Railroad, Tubman was a guiding light to countless individuals who escaped slavery. Her selflessness and determination to lead others to freedom serve as a powerful example of friendship and support in times of need. Harriet Tubman's legacy primarily involves her courageous efforts to guide enslaved individuals to freedom through the Underground Railroad, a network of safe houses and secret routes.

Fred Rogers (Mister Rogers), a beloved children's television host, was a guiding light for generations of young viewers. His kindness, patience, and message of unconditional acceptance and friendship continue to inspire people of all ages. His impact extended far beyond the realm of entertainment, and he exemplified the qualities of kindness, patience, and the message of unconditional acceptance and friendship. Fred Rogers' on-screen persona was marked by his genuine kindness and patience. He had a unique ability to connect with young children, often addressing them directly through the camera, making them feel seen and valued. His calm and gentle demeanor reassured the children and provided a sense of emotional safety. Although he primarily targeted children, Mister Rogers' authenticity and wisdom resonated with people of all ages. He created content that spoke to the core of human emotions and aspirations, making him a beloved figure for kids, their parents, and even grandparents. Mister Rogers' impact transcended his television show. His words and philosophy continue to inspire people of all generations. His life's work is a testament to the idea that kindness and friendship know no age or demographic boundaries. His influence can still be seen in initiatives and organizations that aim to foster the values he cherishes.

Through her diary, Anne Frank became a symbol of hope and friendship in the darkest of times. Her words have touched the hearts of readers worldwide and offered a glimpse into the enduring power of human connection, even in the face of adversity. Anne Frank's diary stands as a testament to the extraordinary friendship she developed with readers worldwide. Her words and her spirit continue to touch the hearts of people, offering a glimpse into the indomitable power of hope and the enduring bonds of human connection, even in the face of the darkest adversity. She's a literary friend.

## Seasonal Friends

Some friends are like seasons – they may be brief, lasting only a short time, or extend into many years. These relationships may have a specific purpose during a particular chapter of our lives. They offer companionship, share experiences, and contribute to our story. However, like the changing seasons, they may eventually fade as circumstances and personal journeys evolve. The story of Barnabas, who supported Saul and embarked on missionary journeys before parting ways due to conflicts, exemplifies the transient nature of certain friendships. Barnabas and Saul had a close and supportive friendship. Barnabas played a pivotal role in the early Christian community by introducing Saul to the Jerusalem church. At the time, Saul, who had previously persecuted Christians, was not trusted by the believers, but Barnabas vouched for him, and their friendship grew. Barnabas and Saul embarked on significant missionary journeys, spreading the Christian message to various regions. Their partnership was marked by a shared commitment to their faith and a joint mission to share it with others. During this time, their friendship was deepened by their common purpose and shared experiences. However, conflicts arose between Barnabas and Saul, particularly related to their choice of a companion for a subsequent journey. The disagreement led to a separation, with Barnabas and Saul choosing to go their separate ways. This parting of paths clearly indicated the transient nature of friendship.

## Treasonable Friends

Not all who cross our path come with noble intentions. There are those who, with treachery in their hearts, aim to hurt, rob, abuse, or take advantage of us. Their presence often leaves scars, a reminder that in the complexity of human connections, not everyone is a true friend. There have been several individuals who are notorious for their acts of betrayal and treachery. "Treasonable friends" are those who pretended to be allies but harbored ulterior motives to hurt or betray others. Among these infamous traitors, Judas Iscariot. Judas is perhaps the most iconic traitor in history due to his role in the betrayal of Jesus Christ. He was one of Jesus' twelve disciples and appeared to be a loyal follower. Judas' motive was to receive thirty pieces of silver in exchange for his betrayal. His actions led to Jesus' crucifixion, and his name has since become synonymous with treachery and betrayal. Judas serves as a chilling reminder of the treacherous friend archetype. His story exemplifies how someone who appears trustworthy and close can have malicious intentions, causing profound harm to those who place their trust in them. This historical example underscores the importance of discernment and caution in evaluating the true nature of our relationships, as not all who present themselves as friends have noble intentions.

Benedict Arnold was an American military officer during the American Revolutionary War. Arnold initially fought for the Continental Army and played a vital role in the American cause. However, driven by a mix of personal grievances and financial desperation, he conspired to betray his own side. In 1780, he planned to hand over the strategically important fortress of West Point to the British. Although the plot was foiled, Arnold's name became synonymous with betrayal in American history. His actions revealed the depths to which some individuals might descend when motivated by personal gain or vendettas, and his legacy stands as a cautionary tale of treachery in the face of trust and loyalty.

## Post Seasonal Friends (David and Jonathan)

Along with transient and treacherous friends, lifelong bonds exist beyond the regular season of friendships. These are the connections that persist long after others have departed. These friendships weather the storms and stand the test of time. They are the true treasures of our lives, for they remain with us through thick and thin. The enduring friendship of David and Jonathan, marked by their deep bond and unwavering loyalty, epitomizes the beauty of relationships that endure throughout the "postseason" of life.

The friendship between David and Jonathan, as described in the Bible, serves as a powerful example of enduring and selfless love. Their relationship was marked by unwavering loyalty and deep emotional connection, extending beyond Jonathan's lifetime, influencing their respective families, particularly Jonathan's son, Mephibosheth.

David and Jonathan made a covenant, a solemn promise of loyalty and friendship, as described in the Bible (1 Samuel 18:3). This covenant was a sacred agreement that went beyond their individual lives, signifying their deep commitment to each other. After Jonathan's death, David took it upon himself to protect Jonathan's surviving family members. This included his son Mephibosheth. Mephibosheth was disabled, and David showed kindness by providing for him and ensuring his safety. This act exemplified David's commitment to fulfilling his covenant with Jonathan and extending that loyalty to Jonathan's son. Mephibosheth was living in exile and poverty due to the political turmoil following the deaths of Saul and Jonathan. When David learned of Mephibosheth's existence, he ordered for him to be brought to the palace and gave him a place at the royal table (2 Samuel 9:7). This not only provided Mephibosheth with security and sustenance but also elevated him to a place of honor and respect in the royal court.

David's actions toward Mephibosheth demonstrated forgiveness and generosity. Mephibosheth was the grandson of King Saul, David's predecessor and occasional adversary. Despite this, David didn't hold a grudge. He showed kindness, illustrating his commitment to his friendship with Jonathan and his desire for reconciliation and unity. The enduring nature of their friendship can be seen in how

David continued to remember Jonathan and honor his memory. In 2 Samuel 1, David mourned the deaths of Jonathan and Saul, expressing deep sorrow and celebrating their bravery in battle. This ongoing remembrance of Jonathan and the deep emotions displayed by David were a testament to the lasting impact of their friendship. Their profound friendship and covenant resulted from David's love and courtesy extended to Jonathan's family, particularly his son Mephibosheth. David's actions demonstrated not only his loyalty and commitment but also his capacity for forgiveness, generosity, and the ability to see beyond political and familial rivalries to honor the memory of a dear friend. Their story in the Bible serves as a timeless example of enduring friendship and the power of love and kindness in human relationships.

Eleanor Roosevelt wisely noted, "Many people will walk in and out of your life, but only true friends will leave footprints in your heart." The friends who enter our lives for a reason, season, treason, or the postseason all play a crucial part in shaping our journey. Not all friendships are destined to be lifelong, and that's not a reflection of personal worth. It's a reminder that life is woven with a diverse array of individuals, each contributing their unique thread to the pattern of our existence. Not all friendships are meant to last forever, and it's natural for some to change or "expire" over time. It serves as a reminder that it's okay to outgrow certain relationships and make room for healthier, more mutually beneficial connections.

# CHAPTER 2

# Act Now: Step Off the Boat!

*"Courage is not the absence of fear, but the choice to act despite it. Stepping off the boat is a declaration of faith in the transformative power of change and the unwavering spirit within us all."*

In the tranquil waters of the known, the boat sits—a vessel of comfort and familiarity. It's a tempting place to remain, shielded from the storms that rage beyond its wooden hull. But as the tides of time beckon us forward, we must recognize that the boat, once a haven, can become a prison of complacency. The call to action is a call to step off the boat, embrace the uncharted waters, and redefine courage in the face of uncertainty.

Stepping out of one's comfort zone and embracing change can lead to personal growth and new opportunities. We must step off the boat of routine. The safety of routine can lead to stagnation. Stepping off this boat means breaking free from monotony and embracing new experiences. Experiences that challenge your status quo. The boat of fear is a prison from which we need liberation. Fear can confine you to a limited perspective. Stepping off this boat involves confronting your fears, pushing your boundaries, and discovering your hidden potential. We do not need the Boat of Negative Relationships. Unhealthy relationships can hold you back and drain your energy. Stepping off this boat means recognizing toxic dynamics and choosing to surround yourself with people who uplift and support you. The Boat of Past Regrets keeps us looking in the rearview mirror. Dwelling on past mistakes can hinder progress. Stepping off this boat involves forgiving yourself, learning from your experiences, and moving forward with a positive outlook. Let's go! Please do it! A job could keep you from your career or calling. There is the boat of comfortable employment. Staying in a job or career that no longer challenges you can hinder professional growth. Stepping off this boat means exploring new opportunities, pursuing your passions, and embracing change in your professional life. Once, I found solace in my role as a library assistant, nestled within the walls of the Kingston and St. Andrew Parish Library in Jamaica. My days were spent in the reference section, guiding patrons through the labyrinth of knowledge. However, an awakening came to me—an epiphany that shifted the very ground beneath my feet. It dawned on me that I was diligently aiding others in their pursuit of degrees while I, myself, lacked one. So, I resigned and entered tertiary education.

The boat of self-doubt is familiar, but negative self-talk can undermine your confidence. Stepping off this boat involves recognizing your worth, believing in your abilities, and pursuing your goals with self-assurance. The boat of fixed mindset keeps us in one place. A fixed mindset limits your growth potential. Stepping off this boat means adopting a growth mindset, embracing challenges, and viewing failures as opportunities for learning and improvement. Stepping off these boats doesn't mean discarding all elements of familiarity and comfort. It's about recognizing when those elements are holding you back and actively seeking new horizons that align with your personal growth and aspirations. You need a vision for your future. Without it, you will live in inertia or revert to the shadows of your past.

## The Temptation of the Familiar: Icons to Admire

The boat represents the allure of the familiar—the comfort zones that envelop us in the safety of routine. Yet, while the familiar may offer shelter, it can also stifle growth. Remaining seated in the boat means adhering to the status quo, even when it no longer serves our collective progress. The true challenge lies not in staying put but in mustering the courage to set sail.

We have icons to look at. Steve Jobs, co-founder of Apple Inc., left college and a traditional job to build a company that revolutionized technology and design. J.K. Rowling, author of the immensely popular Harry Potter series, was a struggling single mother before she pursued her dream of writing, eventually becoming one of the best-selling authors in history. Elon Musk had success in the tech industry with companies like PayPal, but he left his comfortable career to focus on SpaceX, Tesla, and other ventures that align with his vision for the future. Julia Child was a public relations executive before discovering her passion for cooking and becoming a renowned chef and cookbook author. Oprah Winfrey left her traditional broadcasting job to launch her own talk show, which eventually led to a media empire including television, film, and philanthropic endeavors. Originally a newspaper cartoonist, Walt Disney left his job to create an animation studio, which eventually grew into The Walt Disney Company, one of the most iconic entertainment companies in the world. Colonel Sanders, founder of KFC, pursued his passion for cooking and entrepreneurship in his later years, creating the world-famous fried chicken recipe. Chris Gardner left a job as a medical equipment salesman to become a stockbroker and eventually shared his inspiring life story in the book and film "The Pursuit of Happyness." Angela Duckworth left her career in management consulting. Duckworth pursued her interest in psychology and education, becoming a psychologist and author known for her work on grit and success. Sara Blakely, founder of Spanx, started her career in sales but left to invent a revolutionary undergarment that reshaped the fashion industry. Brandon Stanton left his bond trading job to start Humans of New York, a photography project that turned into a worldwide phenomenon, sharing stories of people from all walks of life. Marie Curie, though trained as a physicist, Curie followed her passion for scientific research, making groundbreaking contributions to the fields of radioactivity and winning two Nobel Prizes. Warren Buffett began in finance, transitioned into investment, and built Berkshire Hathaway, becoming one of the world's most successful and respected investors. Richard Branson left school to start his own magazine and record store before founding the Virgin Group, a conglomerate of over 400 companies. Despite facing challenges in his acting career, Sylvester Stallone wrote and starred in the iconic "Rocky" film series, launching his successful journey in the entertainment industry.

Stepping off the boat is a declaration of faith—a recognition that change is integral to life. The uncharted horizons hold promise but demand adaptability, resilience, and the willingness to learn. By stepping into the unknown, we embrace the transformative potential of change, realizing that growth resides at the intersection of discomfort and discovery.

## The Evolution of Courage

Courage is often misconstrued as the absence of fear. But true courage lies not in the absence of fear but in the decision to act despite it. To step off the boat is to rewrite the narrative of courage, recognizing that every leap into uncertainty is a triumph over apprehension. It's a testament to the indomitable spirit that resides within us all. Like the winds that shape the sea, change is a force beyond our control. Yet, we possess the power to hoist our sails and navigate its currents. Stepping off the boat is a gesture of empowerment—an affirmation that we are not mere passengers but captains of our destinies. It's an invitation to harness change and shape it to our advantage.

## Building Resilience Amidst Uncertainty

The boat may represent security, but it cannot shield us from life's inevitable storms. Stepping off the boat acknowledges that life's challenges cannot be avoided—they can only be faced. It's a call to build resilience, weather the storms with determination, and emerge from adversity stronger than before. Every individual who steps off the boat echoes a message of empowerment that reverberates through time and space. By taking that courageous step, we inspire others to do the same. Each act of bravery becomes a beacon that illuminates the path for those who seek change but hesitate on the edge of the boat. Consider the boat in your own life. What have you clung to out of familiarity? What uncharted waters await your exploration? The call to step off the boat extends to all—regardless of background, age, or circumstance. It's a universal call to embrace the unknown, adapt to change, and cultivate resilience within each of us. Carve out your path in the waves of change. A cloud of witnesses surrounds us, those who have been there and done that! They are your cheerleaders who dare you to step off the boat—individuals who embraced the unknown and forged their paths in the waves of change. Let their stories remind you that the boat is not your destination—it's merely a vessel that carries you to the precipice of transformation. The time has come to step off the boat and embark on a journey of courage, growth, and limitless possibility.

A Biblical Perspective

The power of good examples is undeniable, as they possess the ability to shape minds, inspire actions, and pave the way for positive change. A single individual who embodies qualities of integrity, compassion, and resilience can ignite a ripple effect that transcends boundaries.

Such examples showcase the potential for growth, transformation, and the triumph of the human spirit. Whether on a global scale or within our immediate circles, these beacons of light remind us that even in the face of adversity, kindness, determination, and empathy can uplift, motivate, and create a better world for all. There are several biblical examples of individuals who left their previous occupations or circumstances to pursue their calling or a higher purpose.

Originally a prince in Egypt, Moses fled and spent years in the wilderness. He eventually returned to lead the Israelites out of slavery and became a significant figure in religious history. David was a shepherd who became a king. He left his humble occupation to fulfill his destiny as the second king of Israel and a revered figure in the Bible. Fishermen Peter, James, and John left their fishing boats to become disciples of Jesus Christ, ultimately becoming key figures in the early Christian church. Paul (formerly Saul) was a zealous persecutor of Christians before a transformative experience led him to become the apostle Paul. He went from persecutor to preacher, playing a pivotal role in spreading Christianity. Abraham left his homeland in response to a divine call and became the father of many nations according to biblical tradition. Ruth left her own people to follow her mother-in-law, Naomi, and eventually became a central figure in the lineage, leading to King David and Jesus Christ. Elijah left his farming life to become a prophet under the guidance of Elijah, carrying on his prophetic work after Elijah's departure. Gideon, initially a farmer, Gideon was called by God to lead the Israelites against their enemies, demonstrating how God can use unlikely individuals for significant purposes. Mary and Joseph followed a divine plan when they accepted their roles in the birth of Jesus, demonstrating their willingness to leave behind their previous lives for a higher calling. These biblical examples reflect themes of faith, obedience, and the willingness to leave behind familiar circumstances in pursuit of a higher purpose or calling.

# CHAPTER 3

# Breaking Chains of Mental Slavery

*"Emancipate yourself from mental slavery; none but ourselves can free our minds." - Bob Marley.*

In a world where information flows freely and opportunities abound, it might seem paradoxical that mental slavery still persists. Yet, the chains that bind our minds are often invisible, woven from societal expectations, self-doubt, and limiting beliefs. Just as physical chains once held people captive, mental chains can imprison us within the confines of our thoughts. But fear not, history has shown, emancipation is possible. The journey to freeing our minds requires courage, introspection, and a commitment to self-liberation.

## Recognizing the Chains

The first step towards liberation is to recognize the chains that have entangled your mind. These chains manifest as negative self-talk, fixed mindsets, and conformity to societal norms that stifle your individuality. Begin by identifying thoughts that hold you back, such as *"I'm not good enough"* or *"I can't do that."* Acknowledge the areas of your life where you've accepted limitations and restrictions without question. By shedding light on these chains, you're taking the crucial first step towards breaking them. Negative self-talk involves our internal dialogue with ourselves, where we often criticize, doubt, or belittle our abilities and worth. These self-deprecating thoughts can hinder our confidence and undermine our efforts to achieve our goals. For instance, if someone constantly tells themselves, "I'm not good enough," they are chaining their mind to a belief. It is one that limits their potential and prevents them from taking risks or pursuing opportunities.

Fixed mindsets are another aspect of mental chains. A fixed mindset is the belief that our abilities and intelligence are static traits that cannot be changed. People with fixed mindsets often shy away from challenges or new experiences out of fear of failure or the belief that they're not naturally talented. This fixed mindset chains individuals to their comfort zones and prevents them from embracing growth and learning.

Conforming to societal norms can also act as a mental chain. Society often imposes expectations and standards on individuals regarding how they should look, behave, and succeed. This pressure to fit in or meet certain standards can stifle individuality and authenticity. It chains people to a predefined path that might not align with their true desires and passions. Breaking these chains of mental slavery involves recognizing and challenging these negative thought patterns, fostering a growth mindset that encourages learning and development, and daring to express oneself authentically, even in the face of societal expectations. Ultimately, breaking free from mental chains allows individuals to cultivate a stronger sense of self-worth, as a result, they can confidently pursue their aspirations, and shape their own narrative of success and fulfillment.

## Cultivating Self-Awareness

Self-awareness is the cornerstone of emancipation. Self-awareness acts as the cornerstone of emancipation because it empowers individuals to break free from the chains of limiting beliefs and societal pressures.

It opens the door to personal growth, authenticity, and pursuing one's own path. Through self-awareness, individuals gain the insights and tools needed to actively shape their lives in ways that align with their true selves and aspirations. Spend time reflecting on your thoughts, feelings, and behaviors. Question their origins – are they based on your true desires or imposed expectations? Journaling, meditation, and seeking therapy can help you delve deep into your psyche, uncovering the layers of conditioning that have shaped your mental landscape. As you become more attuned to your inner world, you'll gain the power to challenge and reshape your beliefs.

## Challenging Limiting Beliefs

To break free from mental slavery, you must challenge your limiting beliefs. Replace *"I can't"* with *"I will try."* Transform *"I'm not capable"* into *"I am learning and growing."* This shift in language reflects a shift in mindset – from fixed to growth-oriented. Engage in positive self-affirmations daily, reinforcing your newfound belief in your potential. Surround yourself with supportive individuals who uplift and encourage your aspirations. Remember, it's through adversity that strength and resilience are forged. Knowledge is the antidote to mental slavery. Embrace a lifelong journey of learning and exploration. Curiosity fuels creativity and broadens your perspectives. Dive into books, podcasts, courses, and experiences that challenge your existing beliefs. Engage in conversations with people from diverse backgrounds – their insights might reveal unexplored horizons. By continually expanding your mind, you fortify your mental liberation.

## Nurturing Resilience

Emancipation is not a linear path. Setbacks and challenges will test your resolve. But every obstacle is an opportunity to demonstrate resilience – the ability to bounce back from challenges, setbacks, or adversity, and to adapt positively in the face of difficult situations. It involves emotional strength, mental fortitude, and the capacity to navigate through adversity without being overwhelmed.

When faced with adversity, remind yourself of your journey towards mental freedom. Draw strength from the progress you've made and the battles you've won. Adaptability and perseverance are your allies in this ongoing quest. As you break free from mental slavery, take control of your narrative. You are the author of your life story. Rewrite the script, emphasizing your strengths, passions, and aspirations. Visualize your ideal self and the life you wish to lead. Create a vision board to serve as a daily reminder of your goals. You shape your reality and manifest your dreams by crafting a compelling narrative. Imagine a person who loses their job unexpectedly. Initially, they may feel a sense of shock, disappointment, and stress. However, a resilient individual would assess the situation, acknowledge their emotions, and then actively seek new opportunities or ways to cope. They might update their resume, network with contacts, and explore different career paths. Instead of succumbing to despair, they demonstrate resilience by adapting to the change, learning from the experience, and ultimately finding a way forward despite the initial setback.

## The Essence of Liberation

Liberation from the penalty of sin is grounded in the biblical teaching of justification through faith in Jesus Christ. Romans 3:23-24 states, "for all have sinned and fall short of the glory of God, and all are justified freely by his grace through the redemption that came by Christ Jesus." Justification is the act of God declaring a sinner righteous based on their faith in Jesus. This liberation from penalty is made possible through the atoning sacrifice of Jesus on the cross. Believers are no longer condemned but are justified before God through faith in Christ (Romans 8:1).

The liberation from the power of sin is connected to the process of sanctification. Romans 6:14 affirms, "For sin shall no longer be your master, because you are not under the law, but under grace." Sanctification is the ongoing process by which believers, empowered by the Holy Spirit, are set apart and transformed to become more like Christ. The believer is no longer enslaved to the power of sin but is given the ability to live a life pleasing to God (Galatians 5:16). This process continues throughout the believer's earthly life. The anticipation of liberation from the presence of sin finds its fulfillment in the concept of glorification. Revelation 21:4 describes the future state: "He will wipe every tear from their eyes. There will be no more death or mourning or crying or pain, for the old order of things has passed away." Glorification is the final stage of the believer's journey, occurring in the presence of God in the new heavens and new earth. In this state, believers will be completely freed from the presence of sin. The culmination of God's redemptive plan is the restoration of a perfect and sinless existence for those who have been justified and sanctified through Christ (1 Corinthians 15:51–54).

*"Emancipate yourself from mental slavery"* – Bob Marley's words echo through time, reminding us that liberation form the shackles of slavery, colonialism and racism begins within. To free our minds from the shackles of mental slavery, we must embark on a journey of self-discovery. Who are we? Where are we from? Why are we here? How do we move forward?

## Spiritual Liberation: Breaking Mental Chains from a Religious Perspective

*"And you will know the truth, and the truth will set you free."* – John 8:32

In spirituality, the concept of emancipation from mental slavery takes on a profound dimension. Many religious teachings emphasize the liberation of the soul and mind as a path toward deeper connection, purpose, and fulfillment. One of the cornerstones of religious practice is seeking guidance from a higher power. Whether you follow Christianity, Islam, Buddhism, Hinduism, or any other faith, connecting with the divine can provide solace, clarity, and strength. You create a channel for communication with the transcendent through prayer, meditation, or rituals. By surrendering your fears, doubts, and limitations to this higher wisdom, you begin the process of freeing your mind from the chains of worry and insecurity. Many religious teachings emphasize the importance of loving oneself and extending that love to others. Recognizing your inherent worth as a creation of the divine can shatter the chains of self-doubt and self-criticism. Practice self-compassion as an expression of gratitude for the life you've been gifted. Just as your faith teaches you to love your neighbor, love yourself with the same tenderness and care.

## Transcending Material Attachments

Most religions emphasize the temporal nature of material possessions and the pursuit of spiritual wealth. Embracing detachment from materialism can liberate your mind from the endless desire, comparison, and competition cycle. Focus on cultivating qualities such as gratitude, generosity, and contentment, and you'll find yourself less bound by the illusion of material success. Success cannot be adequately defined as the accumulation of "things", but rather, the fulfilment of one's purpose in life. "Don't copy the behavior and customs of this world, but let God transform you into a new person by changing the way you think. Then you will learn to know God's will for you, which is good and pleasing and perfect" (Rom 12:2, NLT).

Meditation, deeply rooted in many spiritual traditions, is a powerful tool for breaking mental chains. Engage in moments of silent reflection, where you observe your thoughts and emotions without judgment. This practice allows you to detach from negative thought patterns and gain clarity about their origins. By becoming an observer of your mind, you begin to free yourself from the grip of automatic reactions and conditioned behaviors. A renewal of the mind is an ongoing process, empowering individuals to break free from worldly influences and align their thoughts with the divine, fostering spiritual growth and maturity.

## Living in Alignment with Values

Religious teachings often provide a moral compass for living a virtuous life. Embrace these values as guideposts for your actions, decisions, and interactions. When your life is aligned with your spiritual values, you'll find a sense of purpose and authenticity that transcends societal pressures. This alignment liberates your mind from the need for approval and validation from external sources. Many religious traditions advocate for forgiveness to release emotional baggage and resentment. By forgiving those who wronged you, you unburden your heart and mind, allowing space for healing and growth. Forgiving is not just for others; it's a gift you give yourself, breaking the chains that tie you to past hurts. Religious communities offer a supportive network of like-minded individuals who share similar values and beliefs. Engaging with such a community can provide a sense of belonging, encouragement, and accountability. As you journey toward mental emancipation, these connections can offer guidance, fellowship, and the reassurance that you're not alone in your quest. Begin to incorporate these principles into your religious practice can help you break free from mental slavery and forge a deeper connection with your spirituality. By aligning your mind, heart, and actions with the teachings of your faith, you can experience true liberation and embark on a transformative journey toward self-discovery and divine connection.

## Mental Liberation for Descendants of Enslaved People

*"The scars and the history that we've inherited from our ancestors are deeply ingrained, but they do not define us. We have the power to break free and rewrite our narrative."*

The descendants of enslaved people carry a unique legacy marked by the trauma and injustices of the past. The chains of mental slavery can be particularly tenacious, woven from generations of oppression. Yet, liberation from this inherited burden is attainable through intentional efforts, healing, and empowerment. Let us explore steps that descendants of enslaved people can take to gain liberation from mental slavery.

## Acknowledge and Confront Generational Trauma

Some people are walking around with unhealed trauma. Recognition is the first step towards healing. They were not given the therapy needed to heal. Understand that the emotional and psychological scars of slavery have been passed down through generations. Confront this truth and validate the pain your ancestors endured. Acknowledging the impact of this trauma opens the door to healing for yourself and others. Celebrate your cultural heritage with pride. Your roots are a source of strength, resilience, and identity. We can connect to your ancestral traditions, languages, and practices, you reclaim a sense of belonging that counters the narratives of inferiority perpetuated by slavery. Embracing your cultural identity empowers you to rewrite the story of your lineage.

## Educate and Empower

Knowledge is a powerful tool for liberation. Educate yourself about the history of slavery, resistance movements, and the achievements of your ancestors. Learn about their resilience, strength, and contributions to society. It is powerful, hence, there has been a powerful attempt at erasure. The knowledge of your ancestral history empowers you to counter the narratives of oppression with stories of triumph. Open conversations within your family and community about generational trauma. Share experiences, emotions, and reflections. Such discussions foster understanding and support. They break the silence that often shrouds intergenerational pain. By validating each other's experiences, you collectively work towards healing. Prioritize your mental health and well-being. Seek professional help if needed, as addressing generational trauma requires therapeutic intervention. Engage in self-care practices that nurture your mind, body, and spirit. Activities such as meditation, journaling, and spending time in nature can aid healing and liberation.

## Transformative Activism

Channel your energy into transformative activism—advocate for systemic changes that address the ongoing consequences of historical injustices. Silence is not an option. Activism is faith in action which contributes to dismantling oppressive structures and creating a more just society for current and future generations. View yourself through a lens of empowerment. Recognize that you are not defined by past trauma but by your ability to transcend it. Cultivate resilience by focusing on your strengths, achievements, and dreams. Embrace a growth mindset that believes in your capacity to overcome adversity. Turn your ness into a positive message. Turn your testimony into a testament.

## Create New Narratives

Break free from narratives that perpetuate victimhood and limitation. It is the start of a transformative journey toward empowerment and self-discovery. It requires a conscious effort to challenge the stories we tell ourselves, the stories that society may impose upon us, and the stories that history might have etched into our collective psyche. Stories of the past often cast us as passive recipients of circumstances, inhibiting our potential and stifling our ability to take charge of our lives. To break these chains, we must recognize that our stories are not fixed; they are malleable, subject to our reinterpretation and redefinition. Embracing this awareness empowers us to rewrite our narratives, casting ourselves not as victims but as protagonists holding the pen to our destinies. By embracing our agency, acknowledging our strengths, and reframing challenges as opportunities for growth, we dismantle the victimhood narrative and step into the realm of boundless possibility. This journey requires courage and resilience, as well as a commitment to nurturing a story that amplifies our strengths, celebrates our triumphs, and paves the way for a future unburdened and unhindered by the limitations of the past.

Write your own story of triumph and liberation. Writing such a story is an act of empowerment that begins with embracing your unique journey. It's a narrative that captures the challenges you've overcome, the lessons you've learned, and the growth you've experienced along the way. In this story, you are the hero who navigates the twists and turns of life with unwavering determination. Amidst the pages of your story, you'll find chapters that illustrate moments of adversity — the times when life presented obstacles that seemed impossible. These chapters are not tales of defeat but rather accounts of your resilience and courage. Each challenge you face becomes an opportunity to tap into your inner strength and adaptability, allowing you to emerge stronger than before.

But your story is not solely defined by challenges; it's also a tapestry woven with threads of triumph. These moments of victory, whether large or small, signify your progress and growth. Each achievement, no matter how modest, contributes to the overarching narrative of your resilience. Your triumphs will remind you of your capability to conquer hardships and prove that setbacks do not define your path. Central to your story is the theme of liberation – the breaking of chains that once held you captive. These chains might have been self-doubt, societal expectations, or the weight of past mistakes. As you journey through your story, you cast off these shackles one by one, revealing a liberated spirit that's unafraid to chase dreams, embrace authenticity, and cultivate a life aligned with your deepest desires. Ultimately, writing your story of triumph, resilience, and liberation is an ongoing endeavor, a narrative that unfolds with every new experience and decision. It's a story that transcends the boundaries of time, inviting you to shape the plotlines, define the characters, and determine the outcomes. As you craft this story, remember that you are the author, the protagonist, and the architect of your own destiny as God guides. Embrace your power to create a narrative that inspires others, celebrates your growth, and embodies the essence of who you are meant to be, and glorify your maker.

Define your own identity and purpose beyond the confines of history. Defining your own identity and purpose beyond the confines of history is a liberating and transformative journey that requires introspection, self-discovery, and a courageous break from societal expectations. It involves peeling away the layers of inherited narratives, biases, and limitations that might have shaped your perception of who you are. This journey invites you to look within, beyond the echoes of the past, to uncover the essence of your true self. At the heart of this endeavor lies the process of self-definition. It's a deliberate act of stepping into the role of an architect, crafting a unique identity that resonates with your authentic being. You shed the labels and definitions that others might have assigned you, and instead, you embrace the freedom to explore your passions, values, and aspirations. By defining your identity on your own terms, you pave the way for a sense of self that's rich, dynamic, and unburdened by historical constraints.

Central to defining your identity is the quest for purpose. Liberating yourself from history's confines means letting go of predetermined roles and expectations. Instead, you embark on a journey to discover your purpose – the reason that ignites your soul, fuels your ambitions, and brings a sense of fulfillment. This purpose might be rooted in your passions, talents, or a deep desire to make a meaningful impact on the world. Defining your purpose becomes a guiding light, helping you navigate life's choices with intention and conviction. Breaking free from historical confines doesn't mean ignoring your roots; it's about embracing them as part of your unique story. Your history becomes a source of wisdom, resilience, and inspiration rather than a limiting force. As you forge your identity and purpose, you honor the struggles and victories of your ancestors by shaping a narrative that acknowledges the past but doesn't bind you to it. In essence, defining your own identity and purpose is an act of self-liberation. It's a declaration that you are not defined solely by what has come before but by the choices you make, the passions you pursue, and the legacy you choose to leave behind. It's a journey that requires courage, self-awareness, and a belief in your innate potential to transcend history's confines and step into a future that's uniquely yours. By crafting new narratives, you pave the way for future generations to embrace their full potential.

## Foster Solidarity and Unity

Forge connections with other descendants of enslaved people. Forging connections with other descendants of enslaved people is a meaningful and empowering endeavor that can provide a sense of community, understanding, and shared healing. It involves creating relationships with individuals who share similar historical experiences and challenges, allowing you to bond over shared narratives and journeys. Look for organizations, community groups, events, or online platforms that are specifically geared toward descendants of enslaved people. These spaces often provide a safe and understanding environment where you can connect with others who share your background. When you meet other descendants, open up about your experiences and family history. Sharing your story can create a sense of camaraderie and foster deeper connections. It's through these shared narratives that you can find common ground and build empathy. Participate in cultural events, heritage celebrations, or workshops that focus on the history and experiences of enslaved people. These events offer opportunities to meet others who are interested in preserving their heritage and connecting with fellow descendants. Utilize social media platforms, forums, and online groups dedicated to descendants of enslaved people. These virtual spaces can provide a way to connect with others regardless of geographical boundaries, enabling you to engage in discussions, share resources, and build relationships. Initiate conversations that delve into shared experiences, challenges, and the process of healing. Engaging in meaningful dialogues can lead to mutual understanding, support, and the exchange of coping strategies. Consider participating in workshops, retreats, or seminars that focus on healing, empowerment, and personal growth for descendants of enslaved people. These gatherings often provide a structured environment for introspection, connection, and learning. When connecting with other descendants, actively listen to their stories and experiences. This demonstrates respect and empathy, creating a foundation for deeper connections. Collaborative initiatives, such as research projects, art exhibitions, or community outreach efforts, can bring descendants of enslaved people together to work towards a common goal. These shared endeavors can strengthen your connections and create a sense of purpose.

Remember that even within the shared background of being descendants of enslaved people, individuals may have unique experiences and perspectives. Approach conversations with an open heart and a willingness to learn from each other. By forging connections with other descendants of enslaved people, you're creating a network of support, understanding, and solidarity. These connections can serve as a source of strength, affirmation, and shared healing as you navigate the complexities of your shared history and journey toward personal empowerment and liberation. Build a community that supports one another's healing journeys. By sharing experiences and strategies, you create a network of empowerment that amplifies the collective strength of your community. The journey to liberation from mental slavery for descendants of enslaved people is a profound and ongoing process. We must acknowledge the past, embrace cultural identity, and work towards healing and empowerment. It is only then that we can rewrite the narrative of your lineage. Remember that you have the power to break free from the chains of history and create a legacy of resilience, strength, and transformation.

## Honorable Mention

While there may not be an official "Hall of Fame" for mentally liberated historical figures, there are numerous individuals who have become icons of mental liberation due to their profound impact, resilience, and ability to break free from societal constraints. In contemporary times, Nelson Mandela's struggle against apartheid and his subsequent imprisonment exemplified mental liberation. Despite being unjustly incarcerated for 27 years, he never allowed his spirit to be broken. His ability to forgive his oppressors and work towards reconciliation after his release showcased a remarkable mental emancipation that inspired a nation and the world. Malala Yousafzai's advocacy for girls' education in Pakistan reflects a fierce determination to overcome oppressive forces. Her unwavering commitment to her cause showcases a mental liberation that empowers not only herself but countless others striving for education and equality.

A historical figure like Harriet Tubman is a perfect example of someone who was liberated from mental slavery. Tubman's escape from slavery and subsequent work as a conductor on the Underground Railroad epitomizes mental liberation. Her courage to defy societal norms repeatedly risked her life to free others and championed the abolitionist cause, which marked her as a symbol of resilience against mental enslavement. Mahatma Gandhi's philosophy of nonviolent resistance against British colonial rule in India is a testament to mental liberation. His ability to lead and inspire millions toward change while advocating for justice and freedom showcased his commitment to breaking mental chains. Frida Kahlo's art and life story embodied mental liberation. Despite facing immense physical and emotional pain due to illness and personal struggles, she channeled her pain into her artwork, using it as a medium of self-expression and liberation from emotional constraints. Maya Angelou's literary work, particularly her autobiography "I Know Why the Caged Bird Sings," spoke to her journey of mental liberation from her past traumas. Through her writing, she shared her experiences and demonstrated the power of storytelling to free the mind from the weight of history. Frederick Douglass's journey from slavery to becoming a prominent abolitionist and advocate for human rights showcases a remarkable mental liberation. His intellectual prowess, eloquence, and tireless efforts to educate others on the realities of slavery and the need for freedom reflect his commitment to breaking the chains of mental enslavement. Mental liberation is possible. We have witnesses. These historical figures serve as examples of mental liberation through their ability to rise above adversity, challenge societal norms, and inspire change. They demonstrate that mental freedom can be achieved by confronting limitations, embracing resilience, and advocating for justice and equality.

# CHAPTER 4

# Act Now: Take your Shoes off your Feet!

*"Act now—take your shoes off your feet and experience the profound connection that comes from being grounded with the Earth."*

## Spiritual Grounding

Spiritual grounding refers to the act of connecting with a sacred or spiritual place and submitting to a higher power or authority, often in a religious or spiritual context. This practice involves acknowledging the holiness of a particular place and recognizing its significance. When Moses was instructed to take off his shoes in the presence of the burning bush, he was engaging in a form of spiritual grounding. This act symbolized his recognition of God's authority and the sacredness of the moment. Moses, who would later become a significant figure in the history of the Israelites, was initially living in exile in the land of Midian. One day, while tending to his father-in-law's sheep on the slopes of Mount Horeb (also known as Mount Sinai), Moses saw a remarkable sight: a bush that appeared to be on fire but was not consumed by the flames. This unusual sight caught his attention, and he decided to approach it to investigate. As Moses approached the burning bush, God spoke to him from within the bush. God identified Himself as the God of Moses' ancestors, the God of Abraham, Isaac, and Jacob. God told Moses that He had seen the suffering of the Israelites who were enslaved in Egypt and that He intended to deliver them from their oppression and lead them to the land promised to their ancestors. The instruction to take off his shoes came as a sign of respect and reverence in the presence of God's holiness. The ground surrounding the burning bush was considered holy because it was the location where God was manifesting His presence.

Spiritual grounding is symbolic of a cleansing of the soul and spirit. It is an act of purification and Removal of Impurities. Just as physical cleansing involves removing dirt and impurities from the body, spiritual grounding can be seen as a symbolic act of purifying the soul and spirit. Removing one's shoes, as Moses did before the burning bush, represents shedding the "dirt" of worldly concerns and distractions. This act symbolizes a readiness to stand before the divine presence with a pure heart and a receptive spirit. Spiritual grounding is symbolic of submission and humility. Taking off one's shoes or engaging in any act of spiritual grounding often requires a gesture of humility and submission. By humbling oneself before a higher power or sacred space, an individual symbolically let go of ego, pride, and self-importance. This act of surrender can be seen as a cleansing of the soul from arrogance and a willingness to receive spiritual guidance and growth. It is also symbolic of an act of renewal and rebirth. Many cultures and religions associate water with purification and rebirth. Similarly, spiritual grounding can be symbolic of a fresh start and renewal of the spirit. Just as water cleanses the body, the act of spiritual grounding can be seen as a renewal of one's spiritual self, a way to wash away past mistakes and negative energies and emerge spiritually rejuvenated.

Spiritual grounding, like the one Moses experienced, is a symbol of the connection that we must have with the divine. The one who enables. It involves connecting with a sacred space or divine presence.

This connection can be symbolic of re-establishing a deep bond with the source of spiritual nourishment. In this context, spiritual grounding can be seen as a cleansing process that removes barriers and distractions, allowing the individual to connect more directly with the divine and experience a sense of spiritual clarity and closeness. It symbolizes our release of burdens. When one might physically drop heavy baggage to feel lighter, spiritual grounding can symbolize releasing burdens from the soul. By acknowledging the sacredness of space and submitting to a higher power, an individual might feel empowered to let go of emotional baggage, regrets, and negativity. This release can be seen as a form of spiritual cleansing, making space for growth and positivity. Ultimately, spiritual grounding is preparation for transformation. It symbolizes a preparatory step for undergoing transformation and change. By engaging in this practice, individuals can signify their willingness to undergo a process of inner change and growth. Just as the act itself is a gesture of preparation, it can also symbolize being ready for the transformative journey that lies ahead.

## Cross-cultural Connections

In Christian tradition, Jesus' baptism by John the Baptist in the Jordan River is seen as a form of spiritual grounding and purification. The act of being submerged in water symbolizes cleansing and renewal, as well as Jesus' submission to the divine will. This event marked the beginning of his public ministry.

Before attaining enlightenment, Siddhartha Gautama, the historical Buddha, engaged in a form of spiritual grounding by sitting under the Bodhi tree for meditation and reflection. This act symbolized his dedication to seeking spiritual truth and a deeper connection with the universe. His eventual enlightenment marked a profound transformation and renewal of his spiritual self. Mahatma Gandhi, known for his principles of nonviolence and civil disobedience, engaged in acts of spiritual grounding through humility, submission, and connection with the divine. His simple lifestyle, self-discipline, and meditation practices were symbolic of his commitment to spiritual purity and inner transformation. The 13th-century Persian poet and mystic Rumi often wrote about spiritual grounding and connection with the divine. His poetry frequently explores themes of surrender, humility, and the search for deeper spiritual meaning. Rumi's works symbolize his journey toward cleansing the soul and experiencing a profound connection with the divine presence. The former President of South Africa, Nelson Mandela, experienced a form of spiritual grounding during his 27 years of imprisonment. His time in confinement allowed him to reflect deeply on his values, humility, and commitment to justice and reconciliation. Mandela's eventual release marked a symbolic rebirth of his vision for a better South Africa. A Vietnamese Zen Buddhist monk, Thich Nhat Hanh, emphasizes mindfulness and being present in the moment as forms of spiritual grounding. His teachings encourage individuals to connect with themselves, others, and the world around them in a way that promotes inner peace and transformation.

Various indigenous cultures engage in practices that align with spiritual grounding. For instance, some Native American tribes perform rituals involving connection with the land and nature as a form of cleansing and renewal of their spiritual connection with the earth and their ancestors. These icons illustrate how individuals from diverse backgrounds have engaged in forms of spiritual grounding to seek inner transformation, purification, and a deeper connection with the divine or the universe. While the practices and contexts may vary, the underlying themes of humility, submission, renewal, and connection remain consistent. Spiritual grounding is a symbolism of cleansing the soul and spirit; it is rich and multifaceted. Through acts of humility, submission, renewal, and connection, individuals engage in practices that reflect their desire for spiritual purity, growth, and a deeper connection with the divine.

## Physical Grounding

Grounding, also known as earthing, refers to the practice of physically connecting oneself to the Earth's surface, typically through direct skin contact with the ground. Grounding can be accomplished by walking barefoot on natural surfaces like grass, soil, or sand or immersing oneself in water like oceans, lakes, or rivers. Physical grounding or earthing involves direct physical contact with the Earth's surface, typically through bare feet or hands. This practice is based on the idea that the Earth carries a subtle electrical charge that can be beneficial when absorbed by the body. Studies show that physical grounding reduces Inflammation, a natural response by the body to injury or infection, but chronic inflammation is linked to various health conditions, including heart disease and arthritis. Some proponents of grounding suggest that direct contact with the Earth's electrons might have anti-inflammatory effects. It improves sleep by influencing the body's circadian rhythms. Exposure to natural light and the Earth's electrical potential could help regulate sleep-wake cycles and improve overall sleep quality. Advocates of grounding believe that the transfer of electrons from the Earth to the body might help alleviate pain by reducing inflammation and promoting relaxation. Finally, physical grounding reduces stress. Walking barefoot on natural surfaces, such as grass or sand, is thought to offer a sense of connection to nature and promote relaxation. This connection with the Earth is believed to help reduce stress and promote a sense of well-being. The concept of grounding is based on the idea that the Earth carries a natural, subtle electrical charge. When a person makes direct contact with the Earth, they can potentially absorb electrons from the Earth's surface. Some proponents believe this interaction has potential health benefits due to the transfer of these electrons.

Advocates of grounding or earthing propose several potential benefits, including reducing Inflammation. Some believe that grounding can help reduce inflammation in the body, as inflammation is associated with various chronic health conditions. It helps people to sleep. Grounding has been suggested as a way to improve sleep by promoting relaxation and resetting the body's natural circadian rhythms. Grounding is said to alleviate pain. This free physical activity contributes to pain relief and better overall well-being. In an age of stress, grounding reduces stress. So, walking barefoot on natural surfaces is often seen as a way to connect with nature and reduce stress. It's important to note that while there are anecdotal reports and some studies suggesting potential benefits of grounding, the scientific evidence supporting these claims is not yet robust or conclusive.

Scientific research on the topic is still developing, and more rigorous studies are needed to establish a clear cause-and-effect relationship between grounding and these health benefits. However, "Multi-disciplinary research has revealed that electrically conductive contact of the human body with the surface of the Earth (grounding or earthing) produces intriguing effects on physiology and health. Such effects relate to inflammation, immune responses, wound healing, and prevention and treatment of chronic inflammatory and autoimmune diseases" (Oschman et al., 2015). Ultimately, whether through spiritual or physical grounding, individuals often seek a sense of connection, peace, and well-being. These practices can be meaningful and beneficial to many people, whether they're seeking a deeper connection with the divine or exploring ways to engage with the natural world for potential health improvements.

## The Case of Carole

Carole, a dedicated 34-year-old nurse, had always been passionate about her profession, tending to the well-being of others. However, her demanding job often left her feeling drained and stressed, both physically and emotionally. Seeking a way to improve her own health and vitality, Carole decided to explore the practice of grounding.

Six months prior, Carole had embarked on her grounding journey. Living in a suburban neighborhood, she found solace in the nearby park with lush greenery. Every day after her long shifts, Carole would kick off her shoes and walk barefoot on the soft grass, immersing herself in the soothing embrace of nature. In the beginning, Carole wasn't entirely sure what to expect from grounding, but she was open to the idea of connecting with the Earth's energy. She had read about the potential benefits, including reduced inflammation and stress relief, and she hoped that these benefits would materialize in her own life.

As the weeks turned into months, Carole started to notice subtle changes. The persistent aches in her joints seemed to diminish, and she found herself feeling more relaxed and grounded after each grounding session. She also realized that her sleep quality had improved; she woke up feeling refreshed and ready to face the day ahead. The most noticeable change for Carole, however, was her weight. Over the course of six months, she had shed a few pounds without even actively trying. Her clothes fit better, and she felt lighter on her feet. Carole attributed this positive change to a combination of factors—regular grounding sessions, increased physical activity from her walks, and a heightened awareness of her body's needs.

One evening, after another invigorating grounding session, Carole decided to reflect on her journey. She realized that grounding had not only brought physical benefits but also a renewed sense of balance and tranquility to her life. The park had become her sanctuary—a place where she could unwind, release the stress of her job, and connect with herself. Carole's friends and family had also noticed the positive changes in her. They remarked on her vibrant energy, her happier demeanor, and the subtle glow that seemed to emanate from her. Carole felt grateful for their support and couldn't help but encourage them to give the ground a try. With six months of consistent practice behind her, Carole had become a living testament to the potential benefits of grounding. The reduction in inflammation and weight had transformed her perspective on self-care. Carole continued her grounding routine, eager to see how this simple yet profound practice would continue to positively impact her life in the months and years to come.

## The Case of Bertha

At 83 years old, Bertha had lived a rich and fulfilling life, but her failing health had taken a toll on her overall well-being. The combination of physical discomfort and the worries that accompanied her health challenges had led to restless nights and a constant state of stress. Desperate to find relief, Bertha stumbled upon the concept of grounding and decided to give it a try. Having always enjoyed spending time outdoors, Bertha decided to embrace grounding through a beloved activity: gardening. With a renewed sense of determination, she embarked on her grounding journey with an adventurous spirit and a pair of gardening gloves for practicality. However, it was the decision to go barefoot that truly transformed her experience.

On a sunny morning, Bertha stepped out into her garden, feeling the cool earth beneath her feet. She let go of her worries and allowed herself to connect with the natural world around her. As she tended to her plants, she noticed the sensations of the soil, the texture of the leaves, and the gentle breeze on her skin. Weeks turned into months, and Bertha faithfully continued her barefoot gardening routine. It wasn't long before she began to notice changes in her health and well-being. Most notably, her sleep started to improve. Gone were the nights of tossing and turning; instead, she found herself drifting into restful slumber with ease. The stress that had once kept her awake seemed to melt away as she cultivated her garden and reconnected with the Earth.

Bertha's physical health began to show signs of improvement as well. Her aches and pains lessened, and her overall energy levels increased. The act of grounding, or immersing herself in the simple pleasures of nature, had become a source of solace and healing for her aging body. As Bertha continued her grounding practice, she marveled at the transformation she had undergone in just a few short months. She reveled in the beauty of her garden, each flower and plant a testament to her dedication and the power of the Earth to restore balance. The daily ritual of tending to her garden, barefoot and connected, had become a cherished part of her routine.

Friends and family began to notice the change in Bertha. Her smile was brighter, her laughter more frequent, and her stories filled with a newfound sense of vitality. When they asked about the secret to her newfound well-being, Bertha happily shared her grounding journey. With the support and encouragement of her loved ones, Bertha's grounding practice continued to thrive. Her garden flourished, and so did she. At 83 years old, she had discovered a source of comfort and healing that extended beyond the boundaries of her garden and into every aspect of her life. The act of going barefoot in the garden had brought her a renewed sense of peace, better sleep, and a level of stress reduction she had never thought possible. As she walked through her garden, feeling the Earth beneath her feet, Bertha knew that she had found a timeless remedy that had transformed her golden years into a season of joy and tranquility.

## The Burden of Shoes

Many women could greatly improve their lives by spending some time barefoot. Too many want to rival Imelda Marcos' collection. The former First Lady of the Philippines had an immense collection of shoes. The negative effects of wearing high heels are numerous. These effects include foot pain, altered posture, increased pressure on the front of the feet, and a higher risk of ankle sprains. The alignment of the spine is disrupted by high heels. It affects the natural curvature of the lower back and leads to poor posture. Additionally, high heels shift the body's weight forward, which can increase pressure on the knees and contribute to joint pain over time. The prolonged use of high heel shoes may even lead to the development of osteoarthritis in the knees and hips due to heightened joint stress.

Men are not exempt from shoe-related issues. Poorly fitting shoes or those with narrow toe boxes have led to foot deformities such as bunions, hammertoes, and corns. The rigidity of shoe soles limits the natural movement and flexibility of foot muscles, resulting in weakened muscles and a decreased ability to support the arches of the feet. Ill-fitting or unsupportive shoes can cause foot pain, including conditions like plantar fasciitis and arch pain. Shoes with thick soles or unstable designs can disrupt balance and increase the risk of falls and injuries. Additionally, tightly fitting or poorly ventilated shoes create a moist environment that heightens the risk of fungal infections, athlete's foot and blisters. The burden of wearing shoes, particularly ill-fitting or unsupportive ones, is considerable for both women and men. Addressing these concerns and occasionally going barefoot can help mitigate these negative effects and contribute to better foot health and overall well-being.

## Taking Action

Given the spiritual significance and potential health benefits of grounding, coupled with the drawbacks of shoes, it's time to consider a return to our natural roots. While we may not abandon shoes entirely, integrating more time spent barefoot, particularly in natural environments, could provide a holistic approach to health and well-being. In doing so, we embrace the practices of spiritual and physical grounding, and allow ourselves to reconnect with nature and restore balance to our lives. So, act now—take your shoes off your feet and experience the profound connection that comes from being grounded with the Earth. Detox from the overabundance of electricity in your body. Touch the ground and send the charge into the earth!

## References

Oschman, J. L., Chevalier, G., & Brown, R. (2015). The effects of grounding (earthing) on inflammation, the immune response, wound healing, and prevention and treatment of chronic inflammatory and autoimmune diseases. *Journal of Inflammation Research, 8*, 83–96. https://doi.org/10.2147/JIR.S69656

# CHAPTER 5

# Act Now: Life Is Short

*Human life is but a fleeting note. Our brevity serves as a reminder to seize every moment, to cherish our connections, and to safeguard that which is precious."*

Human life is but a fleeting thread. We find ourselves navigating through the corridors of time, driven by the ticking clock that echoes with the refrain: "Life is short." This mantra, derived from the pages of history and scriptures, resonates across the ages, reminding us that our time on Earth is limited and unpredictable. As we unravel the intricate layers of this truth, we uncover seven ways in which life's brevity colors our existence.

First, life is short comparatively. When we compare human life to the vastness of the universe and the immense timeline of existence, our lifespans appear incredibly brief. The universe is estimated to be around 13.8 billion years old, and in comparison, a typical human life that spans several decades seems minuscule. In the silent expanse of the night sky, a tapestry of stars unfurls, each one a distant beacon in the cosmic sea. In the midst of this celestial splendor, our world spins, carrying with it the stories of billions of lives. Yet, when we contemplate the grandeur of the universe, the whisper of mortality becomes undeniable. Life is short, a fleeting candle flame in the vast darkness of space. As we stand beneath the vaulted canopy of stars, it's easy to feel humbled by the sheer magnitude of existence. The universe, stretching across unfathomable distances and ages, invites us to step back and reconsider our place within it. Our lifespans, which we measure in decades, become mere heartbeats when juxtaposed against the epic saga of cosmic evolution.

Think, for a moment, of the countless galaxies, each containing billions of stars, each with the potential to nurture planets and life. Our own solar system, a speck within the Milky Way galaxy, is but a drop in the cosmic ocean. And yet, within the boundaries of this tiny blue orb called Earth, we carve out our existence. With every sunrise, with every twinkle of the stars, the universe unfurls its age-old narrative. Galaxies collide, and stars are born, a ballet of celestial forces that have danced for billions of years. In this cosmic spectacle, our lives flicker like fireflies, illuminating the night for an ephemeral moment before being swallowed by the shadows.

The journey of light itself underscores the brevity of our existence. As starlight travels across the universe to reach our eyes, it carries with it stories of galaxies that existed long before our planet was even formed. The light we see today might have begun its journey when the first human footprints were etched into the Earth's surface. As we stand at the crossroads of space and time, we realize that our lives are not just short; they are minuscule, a blink of an eye in the cosmic symphony. Yet, this awareness need not bring despair. Instead, it can ignite a fire within us, a fire that fuels our yearning to explore, to create, to love, and to make our mark on this grand tapestry. When we gaze at the stars, we see more than twinkling lights; we see a reminder that we are part of something greater, a part of the universe's story. The universe's vastness invites us to embrace the fleeting nature of our existence, to cherish every heartbeat, every breath, and every connection we make. In this realization, we find the impetus to live fully, strive for greatness, and contribute our unique thread to the cosmic fabric. Yes, longevity has its place.

Marvel at the stars and galaxies above, for they offer us a glimpse into the cosmic dance that has been unfolding for eons. Let us remember that life's brevity is not a reason for despair but a call to action. Every moment we have is a gift, an opportunity to create, to love, and to leave our mark on the universe's canvas. For even in our fleeting existence, we can shine as bright as the stars themselves.

Second, life is short chronologically. Our lives are relatively short compared to the overall duration of human existence. The recorded history of humanity spans only a few thousand years, and even the oldest civilizations are relatively recent. When considering the billions of years that have passed since the formation of the Earth, the timespan of human life becomes but a fleeting moment. Humanity's journey unfolds like a delicate thread, woven through the eons with the warp and weft of civilizations and cultures. Yet, as we step back to examine the vast canvas of existence, it becomes evident that the span of human life is but a fleeting note in the symphony of time. Our lives are short, measured against the backdrop of the billions of years that have shaped the story of our planet. When we look at the history of the Earth, we find that the recorded history of humanity is a mere whisper within the ancient echoes of geological time. The rocks and sediments beneath our feet hold tales of epochs and eras, of ancient seas and towering mountains, of the rise and fall of countless species long before the first humans walked the Earth.

The fossils that lie hidden in the layers of Earth's crust tell stories that stretch back hundreds of millions of years, while the age of the universe itself, a staggering 13.8 billion years, dwarfs even the most ancient civilizations. Against this vast expanse of time, the journey of humanity is a recent addition, a chapter that has only begun to be written in the last few thousand years. As we ponder the profound depths of time, the fleeting nature of individual lives becomes starkly evident. In the span of a single lifetime, generations rise and fall, empires crumble and give way to new regimes, and languages and customs evolve. The pyramids of Egypt, the ancient cities of Mesopotamia, and the forgotten tribes of the past all share their stories with the wind that carries their whispers through the ages.

Consider the countless generations that have come before us, whose triumphs and tragedies have paved the path to our present. The collective wisdom, the innovations, and the artistry that they contributed have shaped the mosaic of our shared human experience. Yet, as we marvel at their achievements, we must also acknowledge that our time here is transient. Human history, our lives are but a stroke in a masterpiece that spans millennia. The tales of emperors and explorers, philosophers and poets, builders and dreamers, are woven together in a fabric that stretches beyond our comprehension. As our lives play out against this backdrop, we are challenged to consider the legacy we leave behind. Our existence is a fleeting spark, a chapter that will be written and rewritten by the generations that follow. It is a reminder that, while we may not hold the pen to the entire story, we have the power to infuse our moments with meaning. The echoes of our deeds may fade into the mists of time, but the ripples we create will continue to touch lives in ways we cannot fathom. Let us embrace the humbling truth that life is short chronologically. Let it be the fuel that ignites our passions, the force that compels us to reach out and connect, to learn, to create, and to leave behind footprints that echo through the annals of history. In doing so, we can honor those who came before us and inspire those who will come after us, ensuring that the tapestry of humanity continues to flourish, one fleeting moment at a time.

Third, life is short collectively. Human life is also short from a collective standpoint; everyone is just a small part of the vast human population. With more than 7 billion people currently inhabiting the planet, our time on Earth seems brief compared to the collective experience of humanity. Imagine standing on the shore of an endless sea, gazing out at the waves that stretch to the horizon. Each wave represents a life, a unique story, a single thread woven into the intricate tapestry of humanity. Yet, as you observe this vast expanse of existence, you realize that each wave, each life, is but a fleeting moment in the boundless ocean of time. Life is short, not only in the span of an individual's journey but also in the grand context of the collective human experience.

In a world bustling with over 7 billion souls, the sense of individuality can be overpowering. We carry dreams, hopes, and fears. We journey through our own paths, pursue our passions and weather life's storms. But when we lift our gaze and consider the entirety of human existence, the boundaries of individual lives blur, giving way to the realization that we are part of a greater whole. Our lives, when viewed collectively, are mere ripples in the stream of time. The story of human journey has been written across countless generations, cultures, and civilizations, and our lives contribute to a chapter in the ever-evolving story. As we reflect on the scope of this shared journey, our individual experiences gain perspective, revealing the transient nature of our time on Earth.

Think of the ancient civilizations that once thrived, leaving behind relics and ruins that whisper of their triumphs and tribulations. The pharaohs of Egypt, the philosophers of Greece, and the dynasties of China – all have woven their threads into the rich fabric of history. Yet, as we ponder their legacies, we recognize that their time in the spotlight was brief compared to the rich heritage of mankind. The bridges they built, the stories they told, and the knowledge they amassed have echoed across time. Their stories are but fragments; they remind us that even the most enduring empires eventually fade into the annals of time.

We stand united by technology and communication that bridge vast distances, and now the collective human experience takes on a new dimension. The struggles and triumphs of one corner of the world are shared with others, forging connections that transcend borders. But even in this era of interconnectedness, the realization remains that our time together, our time as a collective, is fleeting. Humanity is woven by billions of hands, and each hand contributes a small part to the mosaic of life. Just as the tide ebbs and flows, civilizations rise and fall, leaving their mark on the sands of time. Our lives, our stories, our contributions – they are the brushstrokes that paint the canvas of human history. As we navigate our individual journeys, let us remember that life is short collectively. Let it be a reminder that our actions, however small they may seem, have the power to ripple through time, and shape the destinies of generations to come. Act Now, and let our voices join the chorus of human experience, and harmonize with the stories of those who came before us and resonating with those who will follow.

Fourth, life is short culturally. Cultures and societies have evolved over long periods, often spanning centuries or even millennia. Compared to the longevity of cultural traditions, customs, and knowledge accumulated over generations, an individual's lifetime is short. Cultural progress and change occur over extended periods, making the brevity of human life apparent. Cultures and societies emerge like vibrant threads, each one weaving its unique story through the annals of time. Yet, when we step back to survey the vast expanse of cultural evolution, we are confronted with the truth that the lifespans of individual cultures are fleeting in the grand continuum of human heritage. Life is short culturally, a poignant reminder that even the most enduring traditions and knowledge are subject to the currents of change. Change is constant.

Across the globe, civilizations have risen and flourished, imprinting their identities onto the pages of history. From the ancient pyramids of Egypt to the intricate temples of Angkor Wat, the wonders of architecture, art, and philosophy stand as testaments to the creativity and resilience of the human spirit. Yet, as we marvel at these achievements, we must also acknowledge that the cultures that gave birth to them are but chapters in the grand saga. Consider the tales and legends that have been passed down through generations, shared around campfires, whispered in sacred spaces, and etched onto parchment. These stories, woven into the cultural fabric, carry the essence of societies long gone. However, the sands of time do not discriminate; even the most cherished narratives may erode with the passage of centuries.

Languages, too, emerge as vessels of culture. They carry the nuances of human experience from one generation to the next. We have come to realize that each one is a unique lens through which we perceive reality. Yet, just as cultures evolve, languages transform and adapt, revealing the ever-changing nature of our collective existence. Even the most enduring customs and rituals, handed down through generations, are not immune to the winds of change. As societies shift and adapt to new paradigms, the traditions that once held communities together may fade into obscurity. The art forms that once danced in the spotlight may retreat to the shadows, replaced by new expressions of creativity. Yet, the brevity of cultural life need not be a source of sorrow. Instead, it can inspire us to engage with a sense of urgency to treasure and preserve the treasures of our heritage. Just as each generation contributes to the evolving narrative of humanity, we are entrusted with the task of carrying forward the legacy of our forebearers. Our time in this cultural experience is a torch that we pass from hand to hand, ensuring that the stories, the traditions, and the wisdom continue to illuminate the path for those who follow. As we immerse ourselves in the vibrant hues of culture, let us recognize that life is short culturally. It is a reminder to honor the past, to celebrate the present, and to contribute our strokes to the canvas of human expression. Dance to the rhythms of tradition and innovation. Let our steps be purposeful, our voices resonant, and our actions guided by the understanding that our contributions, however small, shape the course of cultural evolution. In the dance of existence, let us move with grace, knowing that we are part of a larger choreography that spans time, transcends boundaries, and celebrates the essence of what it means to be human.

Fifth, life is short biologically. From a biological standpoint, human life is relatively short compared to other organisms. Some species of trees can live for thousands of years, while certain tortoises can survive for over a century. In comparison, the average human lifespan of around 70-80 years appears limited. Life is short developmentally, and human life is short regarding our developmental stages. The journey from infancy to adulthood involves rapid physical and cognitive growth, which can seem fleeting when looking back. Childhood, adolescence, and early adulthood, during which significant developmental milestones occur, pass relatively quickly in the grand scheme of life. The stage is set for the grand performance of life. Each actor, each species, takes its place in the intricate choreography of existence. Yet, as the curtain rises and falls, as the seasons paint their vibrant hues upon the canvas of Earth, one truth remains resolute: life is short biologically. In the vast tapestry of the living world, our time is but a fleeting note in the symphony of nature.

Consider the ancient giants that grace the landscapes of our planet – the sequoias that touch the sky and the turtles that have roamed the oceans for ages. These guardians of time stand as living testaments to the slow, measured pace of life. And then, in contrast, there is the human journey, a brief flicker amidst the span of Earth's history. In the microcosms of nature, we encounter organisms that flit and flutter, their lifecycles mere blinks in the grand scheme. The mayfly emerges from the waters, dances in the air for a day, and departs as swiftly as it came. The lifespan of a butterfly, once it emerges from its cocoon, can often be measured in weeks. Against the backdrop of such brevity, our human existence, spanning a handful of decades, is a short chapter in the book of life.

From birth to death, we traverse the stages of life in rapid succession, akin to a musical crescendo that rises and fades with the passage of time. Childhood, with its sense of wonder and discovery, passes swiftly. Adolescence, marked by growth and transformation, is a whirlwind of change. Adulthood, with its responsibilities and ambitions, often feels like a sprint toward the horizon. Our biological clock, while ticking relentlessly, also serves as a poignant reminder of the beauty and fragility of life. Just as a rose blooms in its resplendent glory before withering away, our bodies, too, follow a rhythm of growth and decay. Our hearts beat countless times, our breaths number in the millions, and with each passing moment, we inch closer to the final act. And yet, it is this very brevity that lends life its preciousness. The urgency to savor every experience, to forge connections, to leave an indelible mark arises from the awareness that our time here is limited. Our biological transience gifts us with the capacity to appreciate the beauty of a sunset, to revel in the embrace of loved ones, and to seek meaning in the journey.

Our existence may be short biologically, but it is also a melody that joins the chorus of countless organisms that have graced the Earth before us. From the minuscule microbes to the towering trees, from the fleeting insects to the majestic mammals, all contribute their unique notes to the grand symphony of existence. Step onto the stage of life, and let us embrace our biological impermanence. Let our days be lived with intention, our moments savored like the sweetest melodies, and our actions resonate with the understanding that we are part of the ongoing rhythm of life. For even in the midst of our brevity, our contributions can echo across time, harmonizing with the heartbeat of nature itself.

Sixth, life is short personally. On a personal level, human life can feel short due to the limited time available to pursue personal goals, fulfill aspirations, and experience everything for which we are destined. With so many possibilities and experiences to explore, it is common for individuals to feel that life is passing by quickly. Every chapter in our personal stories is a collection of moments, each one a precious gem in the mosaic of our lives. Yet, as we journey through the labyrinth of experiences, we come to realize that life is short personally. Our days, while filled with potential and opportunity, are a limited currency. Thus, it urges us to seize the fleeting gift of moments and make them truly count.

From the first breath of infancy to the final sigh of old age, our lives unfold like pages in a book. And each chapter tells a different story. Yet, as we turn the pages, we sense the swift passage of time, the way memories blur into a mosaic of colors and emotions. Our childhood, with its innocence and wonder, slips through our fingers like sand. Adolescence, with its trials and triumphs, is a fleeting storm on the horizon. Adulthood, with its responsibilities and aspirations, is a marathon that seems to speed by in the blink of an eye. As we navigate our individual journeys, the clock's hands move relentlessly, urging us forward. The dreams we nurture, the friendships we forge, the milestones we achieve – they all unfold against the backdrop of a ticking clock that waits for no one. And yet, it is precisely this urgency that imparts life with its vibrancy and depth. Consider the experiences that resonate most deeply – the laughter that echoes through shared moments, the tears that mark profound encounters, the embraces that speak volumes without words. These fragments of time, rich in emotion and connection, remind us that our lives are woven from the fabric of fleeting experiences.

As the seasons change and the years unfold, we find ourselves caught in the currents of responsibility and routine. The pursuit of goals and ambitions often demands our attention, leading us to put off the things we yearn to do. But the truth remains that life's brevity is an unrelenting teacher, nudging us to take that journey, make that call, and chase that dream – today, not tomorrow. Our time here is a masterpiece waiting to be painted. It is a reminder that each day is a canvas, awaiting the brushstrokes of intention, creativity, and purpose. The moments that seem mundane may someday become the colors that define our life's portrait.

As we journey through our personal experiences, let us cherish the moments that bring us joy, the connections that make us feel alive, and the aspirations that fuel our dreams. Let us rise to the challenge that life is short personally, embracing the gift of today, knowing that each moment is an opportunity to infuse our existence with meaning. The memories we create, the laughter we share, the love we give – they are the brushstrokes that paint the canvas of our lives with vibrancy. In the face of life's transience, let us not merely exist but thrive. For in the trials of personal moments, we find the music of our soul, an echo that lingers even when the final note is played.

Seventh, life is short environmentally. Human life is affected by the changing environment and the impact of climate change. As ecosystems transform and species face extinction, our time on Earth coincides with significant environmental shifts. These changes can alter the availability of resources, the stability of habitats, and the overall balance of the planet, highlighting the transience of human life. In the embrace of the natural world, we find a symphony of ecosystems, a dance of species, and a canvas painted with the hues of Earth's beauty. Yet, as we traverse this intricate landscape, we realize that life is short environmentally. The planet we call home is in a state of constant transformation, and the impact of climate change serves as a stark reminder that even the most enduring aspects of our existence are subject to the ebb and flow of environmental shifts. Consider the majestic glaciers that have carved their mark on mountains for centuries, their frozen rivers of ice flowing with timeless grace. But as we bear witness to their retreat in the face of warming temperatures, we come to understand that the environmental equilibrium we once took for granted is shifting. The landscapes we've known, the habitats that nurtured life, are undergoing profound changes. As the seasons blur into one another and weather patterns become less predictable, we are reminded that nature is fragile. The delicate balance that supports the diversities of life on Earth is under threat. Species that once thrived are facing extinction, and ecosystems that once flourished are struggling to adapt to the pace of change.

And in the midst of this environmental flux, human lives are intricately woven. Our cities, economies, and societies are built upon the foundation of the environment we inhabit. The oceans that regulate our climate, the forests that filter our air, and the delicate intricacies of ecosystems all play a vital role in sustaining our existence. Yet, our actions, from industrialization to pollution, have sent ripples of disruption through the web of life. Climate change, driven by human activities, has altered the very fabric of our environment. Rising temperatures, melting ice, and shifting weather patterns have far-reaching consequences. Rising sea levels threaten coastal communities, while more frequent and intense weather events disrupt lives and livelihoods. The consequences of these changes are felt across borders and generations. In environmental life, we are both actors and audience. The choices we make today echo across time, shaping the world we leave for our descendants. The urgency to address climate change, embrace sustainable practices, and protect the delicate balance of our planet is not just a matter of convenience; it is a matter of survival. As we navigate the shifting sands of environmental change, let us remember that life is short environmentally. Our time on Earth coincides with a critical juncture in the planet's history, where our actions have the power to tip the scales toward a more harmonious coexistence with nature. Let us be stewards of the environment, advocates for change, and guardians of the delicate ecosystems that support us. In the face of environmental challenges, our lives are a testament to the interconnectedness of all living things. The choices we make reverberate through the ecosystems we inhabit, the species we share this world with, and the legacy we leave behind. Let us embrace the responsibility that life is short environmentally and work together to ensure that the symphony of life continues to resonate with harmony and balance. Yes, the world is moving towards its ultimate end, but we do not have a mandate to accelerate the process. That's the prerogative of God.

Comparatively, our individual lifespans appear minuscule compared to the universe's vastness and the timeline of existence.

Chronologically, human life is brief when considering the overall duration of human existence and the billions of years since Earth's formation. Collectively, as part of a vast human population, our time on Earth seems limited. Culturally, the brevity of life is evident when compared to the longevity of cultural traditions and knowledge. Biologically, our lifespans are relatively short compared to other organisms. Personally, the limited time available to pursue goals and experience the world can make life feel short. Environmentally, human life is affected by the changing world and the impact of climate change, emphasizing the transience of our existence. In life, every thread is woven with purpose and significance. From the chronicles of ancient biblical figures to the sounds of contemporary existence, the refrain echoes with unwavering clarity: "Act now, for life is short." With each sunrise and each heartbeat, we are gifted a chance to paint our strokes upon the canvas of time. Let us embrace the seven-fold wisdom that life's brevity imparts, and in doing so, infuse our days with purpose, passion, and gratitude.

## Urgent Things to do Now!

In the heart of New City, a man named Ethan had dedicated his life to ensuring the safety of the children attending New City School. With a warm smile and a watchful eye, he greeted students every morning and bid them farewell every afternoon, becoming a beloved figure in the community. However, fate had a different plan for Ethan. One fateful evening, as he was returning home from his shift, he suffered a sudden and unexpected heart attack. Despite the best efforts of paramedics, Ethan passed away, leaving behind a shocked and grieving community.

As news of Ethan's passing spread, his friends and colleagues were devastated not only by the loss of their dear friend but also by the financial turmoil that had emerged. It was discovered that Ethan had not taken the time to put his financial affairs in order. His mother's name was listed as the beneficiary on all his financial accounts, an oversight that went unnoticed until it was too late. Tragically, his mother had also passed away six months before him, leaving no legal beneficiary for his accounts. With no immediate family to claim his assets and no clear directives in place, Ethan's finances were frozen, and the funds that should have been available for his final expenses were inaccessible. His friends, who had known him as a kind and selfless man, now faced the grim reality of having to raise funds to give him a proper burial.

Ethan's closest friends rallied together in the midst of their grief, determined to honor his memory. They organized a community fundraiser, reaching out to the families and children whose safety he had cared for over the years. The response was overwhelming. Families, students, and fellow staff members united to show their gratitude for Ethan's years of dedication. Donations poured in, a testament to the impact he had made on so many lives. Through their collective efforts, Ethan's friends were able to raise the funds needed to give him a dignified farewell. The funeral was a bittersweet gathering, filled with tears and stories of his kindness. As his friends stood by his graveside, they reflected on the lesson that his passing had imparted – the importance of ensuring that one's financial affairs are in order, even in the face of life's uncertainties. Ethan's legacy lived on in the memories of those he had touched, and his story became a cautionary tale within the community. It served as a reminder to everyone that taking the time to update beneficiary designations, organize financial accounts, and communicate one's wishes can spare loved ones from unnecessary burdens during a time of mourning.

New City School erected a memorial in Ethan's honor, a place where students and staff could reflect on his kindness and dedication. His friends, though saddened by his untimely departure, found solace in the fact that his memory had inspired positive change within their lives, prompting them to ensure that their own financial houses were in order and to treasure the moments they shared with their loved ones while they still could.

## Update Life Insurance Policies

Life is dynamic, and your financial and family circumstances can change over time. If you've experienced significant life events such as getting married, having children, buying a home, or changing jobs, your current life insurance coverage might no longer be sufficient to meet the needs of your loved one. The purpose of life insurance is to provide financial protection for your dependents in case of your untimely death. If your policy hasn't been updated in a while, the coverage amount may not accurately reflect the financial needs of your family or beneficiaries. Reviewing the beneficiaries and the percentage of what they get if you were to pass. Life insurance policies typically allow you to designate beneficiaries who will receive the benefits in case of your death. It's important to review and update these beneficiary designations to ensure they align with your current wishes and family situation. Depending on the type of life insurance policy you have, the premiums you pay may be adjustable. By updating your policy, you can potentially adjust premium payments to better suit your current financial situation. Life insurance products and features evolve over time. By updating your policy, you might have the opportunity to take advantage of new benefits, options, or riders that were not available when you initially purchased the policy. Some policies, such as permanent or cash value policies, accumulate a cash value component over time. By updating your policy, you can make sure that this cash value is growing as intended and aligning with your financial goals. If you have an investment-linked life insurance policy, it's important to review the performance of the investments within the policy. Adjustments may be necessary to ensure that your policy is on track to meet your financial goals. Estate planning is critical. Life insurance is often used as a tool in estate planning to provide liquidity for estate taxes and other expenses. Updating your policy can help ensure that your estate plan remains effective and up to date. If your health has improved since you initially obtained your life insurance policy, you might be eligible for better rates or more favorable terms by updating the policy. Regularly updating your life insurance policy ensures that you have peace of mind, knowing that your loved ones will be financially protected in case of your passing. Act now. Life insurance is an essential component of financial planning, and keeping your policy up to date helps ensure that it continues to serve its intended purpose effectively. It's a responsible step to take in light of the uncertainties of life.

## Update Wills into Trusts

A trust is a legal arrangement in which one party (the trustee) holds and manages assets for the benefit of another party (the beneficiary). One of the primary advantages of using a trust is that it can help your beneficiaries avoid the probate process. Probate is the legal process through which a will is validated, and assets are distributed. It can be time-consuming and expensive, and the details become a public record. By placing assets in a trust, they can be distributed to beneficiaries more efficiently and privately. Depending on the value of your estate, it might be subject to estate taxes. Certain types of trusts, such as irrevocable life insurance trusts (ILITs) or generation-skipping trusts, can help reduce the impact of estate taxes on your beneficiaries. Trusts offer more control and flexibility compared to wills. You can specify conditions for distribution, staggered payouts, and even provide for beneficiaries over the long term, ensuring that assets are managed according to your wishes. If you have minor children or dependents with special needs, a trust can provide for their financial needs in a structured manner while allowing a trustee to manage the funds on their behalf. Certain trusts, like revocable living trusts, can provide asset protection benefits during your lifetime.

They can shield assets from creditors or legal claims. Unlike wills, trusts are generally private documents. This means that the details of your estate plan and beneficiaries remain confidential.

## Update All Financial Accounts

Updating financial accounts is crucial to ensure that your assets are properly managed and distributed according to your wishes. Many financial accounts, such as retirement accounts (e.g., IRAs, 401(k) s) and life insurance policies, allow you to designate beneficiaries. It's essential to regularly review and update these designations to ensure they reflect your current wishes. These designations typically override instructions in your will or trust. Consider how your financial accounts are owned. For example, jointly owned accounts may automatically pass to the surviving owner, bypassing your estate plan. You might need to adjust ownership to align with your overall estate strategy. Your financial accounts should work in harmony with your overall estate plan. Ensure that the distribution of assets through accounts matches the instructions in your will or trust. Changes in laws and regulations can impact the way financial accounts are treated upon your passing. Regularly reviewing and updating your accounts can help you take advantage of new opportunities or adapt to changes in the legal landscape. Over time, you might accumulate multiple accounts with different financial institutions. Consolidating accounts can make it easier for your loved ones to manage your affairs when the time comes.

Don't forget about your digital assets. Update your online account information, passwords, and instructions for accessing and managing digital accounts. Updating wills into trusts and financial accounts is an essential part of effective estate planning. It ensures that your assets are distributed as you intend, minimizes legal complexities, protects your beneficiaries, and provides you with greater control over your legacy. Consulting with legal and financial professionals can help you make informed decisions tailored to your specific circumstances.

## Spend Quality Time

Spending quality time is a sign of love. Rather than focusing solely on practical matters, prioritize spending quality time with loved ones. Make memories, strengthen relationships, and cherish moments that matter. Time seems to slip through our fingers like grains of sand. The true essence of our existence lies not solely in the practicalities that occupy our days but in the moments of connection and shared experience with our loved ones. It's in these moments that the tapestry gains its true colors and depth – the threads of love, laughter, and shared memories weaving together to create a masterpiece of human connection. Amid the demands of modern life, we often find ourselves entangled in a web of responsibilities and commitments. We're swept away by the constant hum of emails, deadlines, bills, and to-do lists. Yet, within this busy world, a fundamental truth beckons us to awaken: spending quality time is the purest expression of love.

Imagine a family gathered around a table, savoring a home-cooked meal. The clinking of cutlery, the shared stories, and the laughter that fills the room form an invisible bond that strengthens the ties of kinship. The touch of a parent's hand on a child's shoulder, the whispered conversations with a partner in the quiet hours of the evening – these are the brushstrokes that paint a canvas of intimacy and warmth. In the fast-paced rhythm of life, we're often tempted to postpone moments of togetherness, thinking that there will always be more time. But life's brevity teaches us a poignant lesson – time is a fleeting gift, and the present moment is the only one we truly possess. It's within this realization that the urgency to cherish and prioritize quality time with loved ones emerges. Gatherings need not be grand or extravagant; it's the authenticity of the experience that counts. A simple walk in the park, a heartfelt conversation over a cup of coffee, or even shared silence as the sun sets – these are the moments that etch themselves into the tapestry of memory, creating an indelible mark of love.

In the embrace of loved ones, time slows down. The laughter becomes a melody, the stories become chapters, and the shared experiences become the foundation upon which relationships thrive. In these moments, the weight of practical concerns temporarily fades, allowing us to truly see and appreciate the unique beauty of the souls we hold dear. The legacy of our lives is not found in bank accounts, possessions, or accomplishments alone. It's sculpted through the impressions we leave on the hearts of those we touch. The love we nurture, the time we invest, and the memories we create form the legacy that endures beyond our earthly existence.

Heed the wisdom that life imparts and embarked on a journey to prioritize what truly matters. Let us unfurl the sails of our hearts and navigate the waters of togetherness guided by the compass of love. As we weave the threads of shared experiences, we contribute to the masterpiece of our lives – a tapestry that reflects the immeasurable depth of our connections and the profound richness of the moments we've shared.

## Create a Legacy of Goodness

As you create a legacy, consider contributing to causes that matter to you or leaving behind a positive legacy. This could involve donating to charity, starting a scholarship, or getting involved in community service. Mend broken relationships by forgiving and seeking forgiveness. Let go of grudges and unresolved conflicts to find emotional closure. And find the time to document life stories. We should be willing to share our personal stories, experiences, and wisdom with future generations. This can be done through writing, video recordings, or other forms of media. It comes naturally as we spend time reflecting on the meaning and purpose of life. Engaging in meditation or mindfulness practices helps us to find inner peace and clarity. We did not enter this life quietly; we cried our way out of the womb, and we must continue to scream for life until the last minute. So, travel with purpose. Places that are seen in books are places to explore while you are here! While traveling to desired destinations is important, also consider engaging in meaningful travel experiences that connect you with local cultures and communities.

Declutter your physical and digital spaces. This not only helps organize your life but can also make things easier for your loved ones when the time comes. Say "I Love You." Don't underestimate the power of expressing your feelings. Tell your loved ones that you care about them, as these words hold tremendous significance. Joy in Small Moments: Embrace the present moment and find joy in everyday activities. Life's brevity reminds us to savor the little things. Be thankful. Health and Well-being: Prioritize your physical and mental well-being. Focus on a balanced diet, regular exercise, and stress management to enjoy a better quality of life. Never stop growing. Pursue personal growth and lifelong learning. Engage in activities that challenge you intellectually and creatively.

# CHAPTER 6

# Act Now: "Prevent is Better than Cure!"

⟨◇◇◇◇◇◇◇◇◇◇◇◇◇◇◇◇◇⟩

*"Anticipating and averting is wiser than mending."*

⟨◇◇◇◇◇◇◇◇◇◇◇◇◇◇◇◇◇⟩

The proverb "Prevention is better than cure" suggests that it is wiser and more advantageous to take preventive measures to avoid problems or illnesses rather than waiting for issues to occur and then trying to fix them. In various contexts, this principle is commonly applied and has significant implications in areas like healthcare, cybersecurity, finance, and social matters.

## Healthcare

In the area of health care, the age-old adage "Prevention is better than cure" rings truer than ever. As modern medicine advances, the emphasis on proactive measures to maintain well-being has gained prominence. Preventive health care covers a range of essential practices that can help individuals avoid illness, enhance vitality, and lead fulfilling lives.

Good dental hygiene is more than just a cosmetic concern; it's a critical aspect of overall health. It is essential to provide a smile for a lifetime. Proper brushing, flossing, and regular dental check-ups not only promote oral health but also contribute to the prevention of various systemic health issues, including heart disease and diabetes. The chapter delves into the importance of maintaining healthy teeth and gums, emphasizing their role in preserving a vibrant smile and overall well-being. In an increasingly digital age, eye health often takes a back seat. However, regular eye exams, appropriate screen usage, and protecting your eyes from UV radiation are crucial for maintaining optimal vision. There are strategies to prevent eye strain, computer vision syndrome, and age-related eye conditions, underlining the significance of clear and comfortable vision.

A well-balanced diet is the cornerstone of preventive health care. Nourishment through diet is the foundation of health. The chapter delves into the importance of consuming a variety of nutrient-rich foods, including whole grains, lean proteins, fruits, and vegetables. It explores how dietary choices influence energy levels, weight management, and the prevention of chronic diseases such as heart disease and type 2 diabetes because of their depletion in our modern foods. Vitamins and trace minerals supplementation are necessary. They play an essential role in maintaining bodily functions and bolstering the immune system. Micronutrients are key to good health and their deficiency impacts our bodies significantly. There are natural food sources and supplements that can help individuals meet their nutritional needs.

## Moving Towards Wellness

Physical activity isn't just about staying fit; it's a key component of disease prevention. The chapter discusses the benefits of regular exercise, including cardiovascular health, weight management, and stress reduction. From brisk walks to more intense workouts, it covers a range of options to suit individual preferences and lifestyles. Walk for your life; walk to experience longevity. Additionally, exercise enhances mental health. Mental health is an integral part of overall well-being. Stress management, mindfulness, and seeking support when needed are basic health management skills.

From indoor air quality to reducing exposure to harmful chemicals, it offers practical tips for promoting health within one's living space. Volatile organic compounds (VOCs) are emitted from household products such as paints, cleaning supplies, furniture, and carpets. They can contribute to poor indoor air quality and have been linked to various health issues. Smoking indoors releases a wide range of harmful chemicals and particulates into the air, posing serious health risks to both smokers and non-smokers. Biological contaminants such as mold, dust mites, pet dander, and pollen can lead to allergic reactions and exacerbate respiratory conditions. Fine particles suspended in the air can come from sources like cooking, burning candles, and outdoor pollution. They can negatively affect respiratory health. Radon, a naturally occurring radioactive gas, radon can seep into homes from the ground, potentially causing lung cancer. Carbon Monoxide is produced by combustion appliances like gas stoves and furnaces; carbon monoxide is a colorless, odorless gas that can be deadly in high concentrations. Formaldehyde is often found in building materials and furniture. Formaldehyde is a VOC that can irritate the eyes, nose, and throat. Pesticides such as residues from household pesticides can contribute to indoor air pollution, especially if not used and stored properly. Indoor aerosols such as aerosol sprays, including air fresheners, can release particles and chemicals into the air. Asbestos is found in some building materials, and asbestos fibers can become airborne when disturbed, posing a risk to respiratory health. To remove or limit indoor air pollution, it's important to properly ventilate your home by opening windows when weather permits, use air purifiers with HEPA filters to remove particulate matter, avoid smoking indoors, choose low-VOC or

VOC-free household products, maintain indoor plants that can help improve air quality, regularly clean and vacuum to reduce dust and allergens, and address any water leaks or moisture issues promptly to prevent mold growth.

Preventive health care also includes regular medical check-ups and screenings. Regular medical check-ups and screenings are integral components of preventive health care, offering a proactive approach to maintaining well-being. These routine evaluations, conducted by healthcare professionals, encompass thorough examinations and comprehensive assessments of an individual's health. By reviewing medical history, conducting physical examinations, and tailoring screenings to personal factors, these check-ups provide the means to detect potential health risks and underlying conditions at an early stage. This early detection enables timely intervention, enhancing the effectiveness of treatments and potentially reducing the burden on healthcare systems. Moreover, regular interactions with healthcare providers foster strong patient-provider relationships, empowering individuals to make informed decisions about their health and contribute to healthier communities.

Incorporating regular medical check-ups and screenings into one's preventive health care routine serves as a proactive measure to safeguard well-being. Through these evaluations, healthcare professionals can identify emerging health concerns, offering timely interventions and personalized guidance. These measures not only enable early detection but also establish patient-provider relationships built on trust and open communication. By embracing these practices, individuals take charge of their health, reduce the impact of potential health risks, and contribute to a healthier society at large. One of my pet peeves is to remind my doctor of my age and ask for what screenings or tests a man of my age should receive. It makes for interesting discussions, always!

## A Holistic Approach to Health

The holistic nature of preventive health care underscores the importance of integrating healthy eating, exercise, mental well-being, and medical care for lifelong wellness. In a world grappling with increasing health challenges, prioritizing preventive health care is an empowering decision. Seize control of your well-being. Make informed choices of prevention, foster a path towards a healthier and more fulfilling life. Regular exercise, a balanced diet, and conscious lifestyle choices serve as preventative measures against chronic illnesses like diabetes and heart disease. Additionally, vaccinations exemplify preventive medicine. They safeguard individuals and communities from infectious diseases before they can spread and cause harm. Good health is great wealth! Act Now!

# CHAPTER 7

# Act Now: Climate Change is Real

We are confronted with an undeniable and unprecedented crisis: climate change. The Earth, the cradle of all life as we know it, is groaning under the weight of humanity's actions, and its voice speaks to us through the dire consequences we now face. Rising temperatures, ferocious storms, melting glaciers, and the harrowing loss of precious biodiversity are no longer mere specters of the future; they are the stark realities of the present. Climate change is impacting various places around the world in a multitude of ways. The Arctic is warming at nearly twice the global average rate. This has led to the rapid melting of ice, endangering polar bear populations, disrupting traditional ways of life for indigenous peoples, and contributing to rising sea levels. Rising sea levels and more frequent extreme tides are causing increased flooding in Venice. The famous city is struggling to protect its historic architecture and cultural heritage. Warming waters and ocean acidification are causing widespread coral bleaching and die-off in the Great Barrier Reef. This threatens marine biodiversity and the livelihoods of those dependent on reef ecosystems. Persistent droughts and an increase in wildfires are becoming more common in California due to climate change. These events pose threats to water resources, air quality, and human safety. Climate change is contributing to more severe droughts and forest fires in the Amazon. This threatens the world's largest rainforest and its role in regulating global climate. Rising sea levels and increased cyclone intensity are causing coastal flooding and displacement of people in Bangladesh. Millions are at risk from these climate-related disasters. Extended periods of drought and desertification are affecting agricultural productivity and food security in the Sahel. This has led to conflicts over dwindling resources. As one of the world's lowest-lying countries, the Maldives is highly vulnerable to sea-level rise. The government is taking measures to protect the islands, but their future remains uncertain. Rapidly melting permafrost is causing infrastructure damage, coastal erosion, and threatening native Alaskan communities. This is forcing people to relocate and disrupting traditional ways of life. The Antarctic Peninsula is experiencing some of the fastest warming on the planet. This warming is contributing to the disintegration of ice shelves and glaciers, leading to rising sea levels worldwide.

The urgency of the situation cannot be overstated. Climate change is no longer a distant threat or an abstract concept. It is a force that is reshaping our world, affecting every corner of the globe, and leaving no one untouched. It transcends political ideologies, borders, and beliefs. It is a crisis that demands our immediate attention, concerted effort, and unwavering commitment to safeguard the Earth for ourselves, our children, and countless generations yet to come. Why is it crucial to safeguard our planet? The answer is embedded not only in the wisdom of science but also in the timeless guidance of the scriptures. The sacred texts of various traditions echo a common message of stewardship—a divine mandate to protect and preserve the Earth. In this sacred call, we find both moral and spiritual imperatives that compel us to act.

Climate change affects us in multifaceted ways. It disrupts our ecosystems, endangers our food and water security, and threatens our very way of life. It exacerbates poverty, inequality, and social unrest. It is a crisis that touches every aspect of human existence and calls into question our responsibilities to one another and to the Earth itself. While the impacts of climate change are felt globally, they are not evenly distributed. Vulnerable communities, often the least responsible for the emissions causing this crisis, bear the brunt of its consequences. The most profound impacts are felt in low-lying coastal regions, where sea levels rise relentlessly, and coastal cities face the specter of submersion. In arid regions, droughts intensify, leading to water scarcity and conflict. In densely populated urban areas, extreme heatwaves pose life-threatening risks.

Why is it that the most profound impacts of climate change are often visited upon those who have contributed the least to this crisis? Why do poor people suffer because of what rich people do? The answer is a stark reminder of the injustice embedded within the climate crisis. The vulnerable are left to grapple with its consequences. We must delve into the heart of the matter and explore the ethical, moral, and spiritual dimensions of climate change. We must examine the imperative for environmental stewardship as a divine call to action. We must inspire people from all walks of life to commit to a shared mission of protecting the Earth, not tomorrow, but today when the urgency is greatest, and the need is most profound.

## The Divine Creation

We must begin at the beginning—the Book of Genesis. Genesis paints a vivid picture of God's creative power and wisdom. It tells of the separation of light from darkness, the division of waters to form the sky and seas, the emergence of dry land, and the lush sprouting of vegetation. Each step in this divine process is punctuated by the refrain: "And God saw that it was good." However, it is in the culmination of this creative masterpiece that we find the heart of the message. In Genesis 1:31, we are presented with the profound declaration: "God saw everything that he had made, and behold, it was very good." This statement transcends mere approval; it serves as a testament to the inherent goodness and sanctity of the Earth and all life that inhabits it.

The Creator's pronouncement of "very good" reflects the harmony, balance, and beauty that permeated the Earth at its inception. It conveys the idea that every component of creation—the land, the seas, the plants, the animals, and humanity itself—holds intrinsic value and significance. This divine perspective underscores that the Earth is not a mere resource to be exploited or a backdrop to human existence. Instead, it is a sacred gift, a masterpiece worthy of reverence and care. From this perspective, the act of creation becomes a manifestation of God's love and benevolence towards His creation. It is an act of grace that invites humanity to participate in the ongoing story of creation, to become stewards of the Earth rather than dominators of it. In this role as stewards, we are entrusted with the responsibility to nurture, protect, and preserve the planet's intrinsic goodness.

In embracing this divine view of creation, we are compelled to recognize our profound interconnectedness with all living beings and the environment. We must acknowledge that our actions have consequences not only for ourselves but for the intricate web of life that God set into motion. Our biblical mandate is clear: to safeguard and cherish this precious gift, to honor the sanctity of life, and to tread lightly upon the Earth, leaving it as "very good" for generations to come. The divine creation narrative in Genesis calls upon us to approach our relationship with the Earth with humility, reverence, and a sense of moral duty. It reminds us that the Earth is not merely a physical entity but a testament to the Creator's wisdom, a reflection of His goodness, and an enduring testament to His love for all of creation.

## Stewardship of God's Creation

The Bible teaches us that God entrusted humanity with dominion over the Earth, as stated in Genesis 1:26: "Then God said, 'Let us make man in our image, after our likeness. And let them have dominion over the fish of the sea and over the birds of the heavens and over the livestock and over all the earth and over every creeping thing that creeps on the earth." However, this dominion should not be misconstrued as an excuse for exploitation and neglect. Instead, it carries with it a profound responsibility—to care for and protect God's creation. At first glance, this passage may seem to grant humanity unbridled authority and control over the Earth, a license to exploit its resources and creatures at will. However, a deeper examination reveals a far more nuanced and profound message—one of stewardship, not domination.

To grasp the essence of this divine teaching, we must first acknowledge that the term "dominion" has been historically misinterpreted as an endorsement of exploitation and neglect. In truth, it is an invitation to emulate the qualities and attributes of our Creator, who entrusted us with this privilege. When God created humankind in His image and likeness, He endowed us with qualities such as wisdom, creativity, compassion, and responsibility. It is within this context of divine reflection that our role as stewards of the Earth emerges. Dominion, in this biblical sense, entails responsible care and oversight—a sacred duty to safeguard, nurture, and protect the Earth and all its inhabitants.

We are not given dominion as a license to exploit but rather as a mandate to be caretakers of God's creation. Just as a wise and benevolent king rules with justice and compassion, so too are we called to exercise dominion with wisdom and care. Our dominion is a trust—a divine commission that carries with it a profound responsibility to act in harmony with God's intentions for the Earth. In the words of Psalm 24:1, "The earth is the Lord's and the fullness thereof, the world and those who dwell therein." This scripture underscores that, ultimately, the Earth belongs to God, and we are temporary custodians. Our role as stewards requires us to manage its resources sustainably, protect its biodiversity, and ensure its health for future generations. Stewardship is a sacred partnership between humanity and the Creator, where we are entrusted with the Earth's care. It is a call to action, an ethical obligation, and a moral imperative. It compels us to align our actions with the divine purpose of preserving and nurturing the Earth's inherent goodness, sanctity, and beauty.

## The Principle of Stewardship

The concept of stewardship is a recurring theme in the Bible. The principle of stewardship emerges as a recurring and powerful theme, guiding humanity in its relationship with the Creator and the world He has entrusted to us. This principle embodies the profound responsibility we bear as caretakers of God's creation, urging us to manage it wisely, responsibly, and with accountability.

In the parable of the talents, found in the Gospel of Matthew 25:14–30, Jesus imparts a lesson with the concept of stewardship. In this story, a wealthy master entrusts his servants with varying amounts of money or talents before embarking on a journey. Upon his return, he assesses their actions and investments. To the diligent and faithful servants who multiplied their talents, the master responds with commendation and reward. However, to the fearful and unproductive servant who buried his talent, the master's judgment is stern. This parable serves as a powerful allegory for stewardship. Each talent symbolizes a resource, gift, or responsibility bestowed upon us by the Creator. Just as the servants were entrusted with talents, we, too, are entrusted with the Earth and its vast array of resources, ecosystems, and life forms. The parable underscores that we are not passive beneficiaries but active participants in the ongoing narrative of creation. From this perspective, stewardship is more than a mere duty; it is a sacred calling. It is a recognition that all that we have, including the Earth itself, is a gift from God, and we are accountable for how we use and nurture these gifts. It emphasizes that our actions have consequences, not just for ourselves but for the entire web of life and future generations.

The principle of stewardship extends beyond the parable of talents. It permeates the Bible's teachings, from the Old Testament's call to "till and keep" the Garden of Eden (Genesis 2:15) to the New Testament's exhortations to care for widows, orphans, and the oppressed (James 1:27). In these teachings, we find a consistent thread of responsibility, compassion, and accountability. As stewards of God's creation, we are called to recognize the intrinsic value and sanctity of the Earth. We must adopt a mindset that seeks to protect and preserve rather than exploit and deplete. Stewardship challenges us to make choices that reflect our commitment to sustainable living, conservation, and the well-being of all living beings. We must embrace the principle of stewardship and acknowledge that the Earth is not a resource to be consumed but a treasure to be cherished. We honor the trust that God has placed in us and strive to leave a legacy of responsible care and nurturing for future generations. Ultimately, stewardship is an embodiment of our love and reverence for the Creator, His creation, and the interconnectedness of all life.

## The Golden Rule

In the heart of Jesus' teachings lies a timeless principle, one that transcends the boundaries of culture, religion, and time itself—the Golden Rule. This foundational teaching encapsulates the essence of compassion and empathy, urging us to treat others as we wish to be treated. In Matthew 7:12, Jesus imparts this profound wisdom, saying, "So whatever you wish that others would do to you, do also to them." The Golden Rule may seem like a simple ethical guideline for our interactions with fellow human beings, but its reach extends far beyond the realm of interpersonal relationships. It beckons us to consider the consequences of our actions, not only for ourselves but for others, including future generations and the entire web of life on Earth. When we apply the Golden Rule to environmental stewardship, its relevance becomes abundantly clear. We are called to contemplate how our choices and behaviors affect not only our immediate well-being but also the well-being of all living creatures, the health of the planet, and the prospects of future generations.

The Golden Rule challenges us to broaden our perspective and recognize the interconnectedness of all life. It asks us to reflect on the impact of our decisions on the natural world and the intricate balance of ecosystems. By doing so, we acknowledge that our actions have far-reaching consequences that extend beyond our own lifetimes. In the context of environmental stewardship, the Golden Rule inspires us to be mindful of our ecological footprint. It encourages us to live sustainably, reduce waste, and make choices that minimize harm to the environment. It compels us to consider the long-term implications of our consumption patterns, resource use, and pollution, as well as their effects on future generations who will inherit the Earth we leave behind. Moreover, the Golden Rule fosters a sense of responsibility for the well-being of all living beings. It prompts us to advocate for the protection of endangered species, the preservation of biodiversity, and the mitigation of climate change. It invites us to stand in solidarity with vulnerable communities who bear the brunt of environmental injustices, recognizing that their suffering is intertwined with our choices.

The Golden Rule becomes a guiding light for environmental stewardship—a moral compass that steers us toward a path of compassion, responsibility, and reverence for the Earth. It reminds us that our actions, no matter how seemingly insignificant, ripple through the fabric of creation, impacting the lives of countless beings. Therefore, let us heed the wisdom of this age-old teaching and strive to leave a legacy of love, care, and sustainability for the Earth and all who call it home.

## The Call to Justice

Throughout the Bible, there is a strong call for justice. Caring for the environment is not only an act of stewardship but also an act of environmental justice. Climate change disproportionately affects the most vulnerable populations around the world, thus poverty and inequality. From a biblical perspective, we are called to seek justice and protect the marginalized, which includes safeguarding their environments and livelihoods.

I strongly discourage and condemn any actions or intentions to hasten an apocalypse or cause harm to the Earth. Such beliefs or actions are destructive, unethical, and harmful to all life on our planet. Our responsibility as inhabitants of this world is to protect and preserve it for future generations, not to contribute to its destruction. Climate change, environmental degradation, and other global challenges are serious issues that require collective efforts to address in a responsible and sustainable manner. Instead of seeking harm, we should work together to find solutions, promote environmental conservation, and advocate for positive change. It is essential to engage in constructive dialogue, seek common ground, and support policies and initiatives that promote the well-being of our planet and all its inhabitants. If you encounter individuals who express such harmful intentions, it is important to encourage them to reconsider their actions and engage in more positive and constructive ways to address their concerns. Promoting awareness, education, and responsible environmental stewardship is a far more productive and ethical approach to addressing the challenges facing our world today.

## A Divine Imperative

From the divine act of creation to the principles of stewardship, empathy, and justice, the Bible provides a compelling framework for why we must protect the Earth from the perils of climate change. It is not just an environmental issue; it is a moral and spiritual imperative. We are called to act now, to preserve the sanctity of God's creation for future generations, and to fulfill our duty as responsible stewards of this precious gift. As we embark on this journey to combat climate change, let us remember the biblical wisdom that guides us and the sacred responsibility we bear to protect our planet—our home.

# CHAPTER 8

# Act Now: Block, Cancel, Delete

∞∞∞∞∞∞∞∞∞∞∞∞∞∞∞

*"Forgiveness is the key that unblocks, reconciles, and rewrites our relationships, and it illuminates the path to healing and unity."*

∞∞∞∞∞∞∞∞∞∞∞∞∞∞∞

Relationships play a pivotal role in shaping our well-being and happiness. However, not all connections are positive or conducive to our growth. Toxic relationships, characterized by negativity, manipulation, and emotional drain, can cast shadows on our journey toward fulfillment. We must either: "Block, Cancel, or Delete" people to prioritize our mental and emotional health by putting toxic individuals aside.

## Recognizing Toxic Relationships: A Vital Step

Before embarking on the journey of "Block, Cancel, Delete," it's essential to recognize the signs of a toxic relationship. These signs may include constant criticism, manipulation, excessive negativity, lack of support, and emotional or psychological abuse. Identifying these patterns empowers us to make informed decisions about who we allow into our lives. Blocking toxic individuals is a step toward safeguarding your mental and emotional well-being. Just as you would build a fence to protect your physical space, blocking allows you to establish emotional boundaries. This can include blocking or unfriending individuals on social media, muting notifications, or even changing your contact information if necessary.

Blocking toxic individuals is a crucial and empowering step in ensuring the preservation of your mental and emotional well-being. Similar to how one constructs a fence to defend their physical space, blocking serves as a tool to delineate emotional boundaries. By strategically utilizing methods like blocking or unfriending on social media platforms, muting notifications, or, in extreme cases, altering contact information, you actively control the access toxic individuals have to your life. This approach helps you curate a healthier environment, shielding yourself from negativity, drama, and emotional harm while fostering a space where positivity and genuine connections can flourish.

Imagine you have a family member who consistently belittles your achievements and undermines your self-confidence through hurtful comments. Despite numerous attempts to communicate your feelings, the negativity persists. Recognizing the toll it takes on your mental well-being, you decide to block this family member on social media and your phone. This decision allows you to create a protective barrier around your emotional state, fostering a sense of peace and self-worth. With this toxic influence removed from your online interactions and daily life, you find yourself better equipped to focus on positive relationships and personal growth. It is not hatred of someone; it's an act of self-care!

## Cancel: Disengaging from Negativity

The act of canceling a toxic relationship involves disengaging from negativity and reclaiming your emotional energy. This might mean ending frequent interactions, reducing communication, or even having a candid conversation about your decision. By canceling toxic connections, you create space for positivity and personal growth. End relationships that no longer serve you!

Canceling a toxic relationship is a liberating process that entails freeing yourself from the clutches of negativity and reclaiming the emotional energy that once drained you. This could encompass various actions, such as gradually decreasing the frequency of interactions, deliberately limiting communication, or even having an honest conversation with the individual about your decision to disengage. By making the choice to cancel such toxic connections, you intentionally carve out a space in your life that is no longer occupied by negativity, allowing room for positivity to flourish and paving the way for your personal growth and well-being.

Let's say you've had a long-standing friendship with someone who habitually criticizes you, diminishes your achievements, and thrives on drama. As time goes on, you realize that this relationship has been impacting your self-esteem and overall happiness in a detrimental way. Recognizing the need for change, you decide to cancel this toxic relationship. You have an open and honest conversation with your friend, expressing how their behavior has affected you and explaining that you need to prioritize your own well-being. This step not only serves as an act of self-care but also creates space for healthier friendships and a more positive mindset. As you gradually distance yourself from negativity, you rediscover your emotional energy and find yourself on a path of personal growth and empowerment. There are people to whom you are no longer assigned.

## Delete: Removing Their Influence

Deleting toxic individuals from our lives is a necessity. Deleting a toxic individual's influence from your life is a symbolic act of reclaiming your autonomy. This might involve removing reminders of the person, such as photos, messages, or gifts. By eliminating their presence, you allow yourself to heal and move forward without the weight of their negative impact. It comes down to the preservation of your mental health. Toxic relationships can have detrimental effects on your mental health, causing stress, anxiety, and even depression. Implementing "Block, Cancel, Delete" allows you to prioritize your mental well-being and create a space free from emotional turmoil. Nothing comes before your need to promote Personal Growth. By freeing yourself from toxic relationships, you create room for personal growth and self-discovery. The absence of negativity allows you to focus on your own goals, aspirations, and pursuits that bring you joy. We know the value of a good relationship. Nurturing such positive relationships is crucial to our wellbeing. Clearing our lives of toxic influences makes space for positive, supportive relationships to thrive. Surrounding yourself with people who uplift and inspire you can lead to greater happiness and a stronger sense of community. Reclaim your power by fostering emotional resilience. "Block, Cancel, Delete" empowers you to set boundaries and stand up for your emotional well-being. This resilience will serve you well in future relationships and challenges.

## Remember Your Worth

The decision to implement "Block, Cancel, Delete" is an affirmation of your worth. It's a declaration that you deserve relationships that bring positivity, respect, and mutual support. It's acknowledging that your mental and emotional well-being are non-negotiable priorities. When we make the deliberate choice to implement the "Block, Cancel, Delete" approach, we are essentially affirming our intrinsic worth and embracing our right to a life enriched by positive and nurturing relationships. This proactive decision serves as a powerful declaration that we deserve connections that exude optimism, exhibit mutual respect, and offer unwavering support. It's a conscious recognition that the sanctity of our mental and emotional well-being takes precedence above all else. This process doesn't stem from a lack of love or compassion for others; rather, it emanates from the realization that certain individuals do not contribute positively to our growth and advancement. By adopting this approach, we actively create an environment that fosters our personal evolution and aligns with the trajectory of our aspirations, ensuring that our journey is characterized by meaningful connections and the pursuit of our highest potential.

While the act of distancing oneself from toxic relationships may be challenging, it's a powerful step toward a healthier, more fulfilling life. By blocking negativity, canceling emotional drain, and deleting their influence, you take control of your narrative, choosing relationships that align with your values and contribute positively to your journey. Embrace this transformative act as a means to create space for the happiness, growth, and empowerment you deserve.

## Reconnecting Broken Bonds: Introducing Old Friends Back into Our Lives

The question arises: can we truly rekindle the flames of old friendships or even resurrect connections with those who once walked the thin line between friends and frenemies? The profound truth embedded within this query is that people possess an innate capacity for transformation; they can evolve, shift perspectives, and mature over time. With this realization comes the contemplation: if someone has genuinely changed, should they be granted the gift of forgiveness and acceptance? The digital realm provides a parallel—a keyboard shortcut, "Alt + Enter," allowing us to initiate a new line while keeping the current one intact—a metaphor mirroring the extraordinary power inherent in life itself. Just as we expertly craft a new line within a document, we can author a reimagined narrative for our lives by welcoming back those friends who were once erased from our social landscape. The intricate threads of human interaction intertwine, forming the tapestry of our existence. Breathing life into old friendships, rekindling the dormant embers, infuses vitality and depth into the ongoing tale we collectively and individually write. It's a testament to the resilient, evolving nature of human connections, illustrating that just as a document's composition is enriched by the new lines we craft, our life's journey gains richness from the relationships we nurture, both old and new.

When embarking on the journey to rekindle old relationships, it's essential to tread carefully and thoughtfully. While the prospect of reconnecting with someone from your past can be exciting, it's crucial to approach the process with mindfulness. First and foremost, assess your own intentions and motivations for reigniting the connection. Reflect on whether you genuinely want to reestablish a positive bond or if you're seeking validation, closure, or something else entirely. Additionally, acknowledge that both you and the other person may have evolved and changed over time. Avoid clinging to past grievances or expectations, and instead, approach the relationship with an open heart and a willingness to accept the present reality. Establish clear boundaries and take things gradually, allowing trust and rapport to naturally rebuild. Effective communication is key—have honest conversations about your respective experiences, emotions, and intentions. Remember that rekindling old relationships can be rewarding, but it requires sensitivity, patience, and an understanding of the potential challenges that come with revisiting the past. You can rekindle old friendship, but you cannot put old snakes into your bosom!

## The Importance of Nurturing Connections

Imagine scrolling through your social media feed, and suddenly, a familiar name appears – that friend from your past who was once an integral part of your life. Time and circumstances led to the fading of that connection, but the memory of shared laughter, tears, and experiences remains vivid. Reintroducing old friends into your life is like reopening a book you once cherished, discovering the story where you left off, and continuing the journey together. Just as Alt + Enter allows us to create a new line and continue our thoughts, revisiting past friendships lets us retrace the steps that led us away. Take a moment to reflect on the reasons why those connections were lost. Was it due to geographical separation, changing priorities, misunderstandings, or simply the passage of time? Understanding the factors that caused the detachment is essential before reaching out. Acknowledging the past paves the way for a sincere and meaningful reconnection. Reconnecting with an old friend is akin to crafting a heartfelt message. Approach the reunion with authenticity and respect. Acknowledge the passage of time and express your genuine interest in reigniting the friendship. Share the memories that still resonate and the impact that person had on your life. A simple message saying, "I've often thought about the great times we had and would love to catch up," can set the stage for a joyful reconnection.

## Embracing Change or the Re-Union

Just as we adapt our writing style when starting a new line, we must adapt to the changes that time has brought to our lives and the lives of our old friends. People evolve, experiences shape us, and circumstances shift. Embrace the changes that have taken place and show a willingness to explore the new chapters each of you has written. The keyboard shortcut Alt + Enter is initiated by your choice. Similarly, taking the first step to reintroduce an old friend is a decision only you can make. Overcoming hesitation and reaching out requires courage, but the potential rewards – rekindled laughter, shared memories, and the comfort of familiarity – outweigh the initial apprehension. Reconnecting doesn't guarantee an instant revival of the same dynamic you once shared. Some friendships may rekindle effortlessly, while others might require patience and understanding. Respect each other's boundaries and allow the relationship to evolve naturally. Avoid placing unrealistic expectations on the reunion, and be prepared for various outcomes.

As you hit the Enter key to start a new line, savor the experience of rekindling old friendships. Schedule a video call, plan a meetup, or simply engage in heartfelt conversations. Share your respective journeys, exchange stories, and rekindle the camaraderie that once defined your bond. Cherish the opportunity to continue writing your story together, enriching it with the shared experiences and newfound wisdom you've gained.

In the symphony of life, the introduction of old friends back into our lives is a beautiful melody that harmonizes with our past, present, and future. Just as the Alt + Enter keyboard shortcut empowers us to create a new line, we hold the power to rewrite our personal narrative by reviving the connections we once cherished. Reconnecting with old friends is a testament to the resilience of human relationships and the enduring impact they have on the fabric of our lives.

## Perspectives

The biblical story of Joseph in the Book of Genesis serves as a profound example of moving beyond the "Block, Cancel, Delete" mindset when dealing with wrongs committed against us. Joseph, as the eleventh son of Jacob, faced betrayal and was sold into slavery by his jealous brothers. He could have chosen to block them out of his life, cancel any connection, and delete the possibility of reconciliation. However, as his journey unfolded, Joseph recognized the transformative power of forgiveness and second chances. When his brothers later sought help during a famine, Joseph chose not to block them from his presence or cancel their chance at redemption.

Instead, he revealed his identity, forgave their betrayal, and reconnected with them, ultimately reuniting his fractured family. This story emphasizes the significance of choosing reconciliation over resentment, demonstrating that by opening the door to forgiveness and reconnection, we can create opportunities for healing, unity, and the restoration of relationships that seemed irreparably damaged.

In the story of the Prodigal Son, a younger son asks his father for his share of the inheritance and then squanders it on reckless living. When he finds himself destitute and starving, he decides to return to his father's house, hoping to be taken in as a servant. However, his father runs to embrace him and throws a joyful celebration to welcome him back. The elder son, who remained obedient and faithful, is initially resentful and refuses to join the celebration. Yet the father's response is one of understanding and compassion. He invites the elder son to join the festivities, explaining that the return of his lost brother is a cause for rejoicing. From the perspective of "Block, Cancel, Delete," the father's actions align with the idea of forgiveness and reconciliation. Instead of blocking his younger son's return, canceling their relationship due to past mistakes, or deleting him from his life, the father exemplifies open arms, mercy, and a desire for unity. He embraces the returning son without dwelling on his mistakes, providing a powerful lesson in forgiveness. The story highlights that even in the face of betrayal and mistakes, the decision to forgive and reconnect can lead to the restoration of relationships and the healing of wounds. Just as the father did not block his son's return or cancel their bond, he chose to extend love and reconciliation, demonstrating that the power of grace and second chances can mend broken ties and foster a sense of belonging and unity within a family.

The story of my father's presence and absence is complex. It is woven with threads of pain, forgiveness, and redemption. When I entered high school, a crucial juncture in my life where guidance and support were most needed, my father's departure left a void that felt insurmountable. Struggling with his own battles, he battled alcoholism and failed to provide for our family's needs. His decision to leave and marry another, leaving my mother to shoulder the responsibilities alone, marked a painful chapter in our lives. His absence was more than physical; it felt like he had blocked us from his presence, fortune, and even his love. However, life has a way of surprising us. When I earned my first degree, there he was a flicker of unexpected presence in my life. And it wasn't just this solitary occasion. Whenever any of his children excelled, especially in the realm of academics, he reappeared like a beacon of recognition. It was an enigma, a paradox of emotions – the same person who had been absent during our times of greatest need now sought to be part of our achievements.

As time marched on, he grew older, and we, his children, became self-sufficient and employed. Despite the past, we chose to embrace a new chapter of forgiveness and compassion. We cared for him as his health waned, a decision rooted in a sense of responsibility and the understanding that every individual is complex, carrying their own burdens. In the end, the story came full circle as he passed away. The chapters of pain and absence were juxtaposed with moments of connection and care. We had forgiven him, not for his past mistakes, but for our own peace of mind. We had moved beyond the years of bitterness, acknowledging the frailties that shaped his choices. In his twilight years, we took care of him, a symbolic gesture that transcended our history and demonstrated the triumph of empathy over resentment. My story reminds us that forgiveness is not an erasure of the past but a choice to reclaim our own emotional well-being. We allowed him back into our lives not because he had earned it but because we had chosen the path of healing. It is a testament to the resilience of the human spirit and the capacity to rise above pain, embracing the journey of forgiveness and ultimately finding solace in the complexity of relationships.

## The Stone the Builders Reject

We must balance the need for our mental health against the quick dismissal of perceived enemies. But an enemy is an enemy, and most people enter our lives for a time and purpose. So, when considering the notions of "blocking, canceling, and deleting" toxic friendships, a counterargument emerges, intertwined with the powerful metaphor of "The stone which the builders refused is become the head stone of the corner." This age-old phrase illuminates the concept that something initially discarded or underestimated can unexpectedly evolve into a pivotal force. The stone's journey from rejection to cornerstone symbolizes hidden potential and unforeseen value. In the realm of relationships, it invites contemplation about the transformative power of resilience and the capacity for the underestimated to rise beyond adversity. It challenges the impulse to hastily sever ties, reminding us that immediate judgments may disregard the concealed depths within a person or situation. Just as a discarded stone can find itself as a foundation of eminence, overlooked connections might, with time and understanding, evolve into pillars of growth and wisdom. This juxtaposition of arguments underscores the complexity of human interactions, urging us to balance the act of discernment with the possibility of growth, both for ourselves and those we engage with. In general, someone with trust issues might approach the ideas presented in these perspectives with caution. Their previous experiences could lead them to prioritize protecting themselves from potential harm, which could involve being wary of rekindling old friendships or giving second chances to those who have hurt them in the past. They might view these perspectives as somewhat idealistic and optimistic, potentially downplaying the real pain and damage that toxic relationships have caused them. The process of healing and rebuilding trust takes time. It often involves therapy, self-reflection, and gradual steps toward opening up to new connections. While these perspectives offer valuable insights, they might need to be adapted to acknowledge and address the unique challenges and hesitations that individuals with trust issues face.

# CHAPTER 9

# Act Now: Loneliness Kills

"Loneliness costs the US economy an estimated **$406 billion a year**, in addition to the estimated **$6.7 billion a year** in Medicare costs for socially isolated older adults (Flower, Shaw, & Farid, 2017) "Loneliness kills" is a statement that highlights the severe negative impact that prolonged feelings of isolation and social disconnectedness can have on an individual's physical and mental health. So profound is this problem that New York has just employed DR. Ruth as its first loneliness ambassador!

Loneliness is an emotional state characterized by a sense of solitude and disconnection from one's surroundings. It encompasses the perception of lacking significant or intimate relationships and a feeling of not belonging. This emotional state arises from the dissonance between an individual's existing level of interpersonal connection and their desired level of connection. Notably, even individuals with a substantial social circle can experience loneliness. The experience of loneliness and isolation can be influenced by a multitude of factors, including cultural norms, demographic factors, and the environments in which individuals engage in various activities, such as living, working, learning, and socializing.

While loneliness is a subjective emotional experience, research has shown that chronic loneliness can lead to a wide range of adverse health outcomes. First, studies have linked loneliness to various physical health issues. Chronic loneliness is associated with increased stress levels, which can lead to higher blood pressure and weakened immune system function. Loneliness has also been linked to inflammation, cardiovascular problems, and even an increased risk of mortality. Over time, the toll of loneliness on the body can contribute to various chronic health conditions. Second, loneliness can significantly impact an individual's mental well-being. Prolonged feelings of isolation can lead to depression, anxiety, and other mental health disorders. The lack of social interaction and support can exacerbate existing mental health conditions and hinder the recovery process. Moreover, loneliness can create a cycle where social withdrawal leads to more loneliness, deepening the emotional distress. Third, studies have found that loneliness and social isolation are risk factors for cognitive decline and dementia in older adults. Social engagement and interaction are essential for maintaining cognitive function and brain health. Fourth, loneliness can adversely affect an individual's overall quality of life. It can lead to a lack of motivation, decreased interest in activities, and a reduced sense of purpose and belonging. People who feel lonely may have lower life satisfaction and struggle to find meaning in their daily lives. Fifth, loneliness not only affects individuals but can also strain relationships with others. When someone feels lonely, they may have difficulty forming and maintaining meaningful connections, leading to further social isolation and perpetuating the cycle of loneliness. Sixth, in extreme cases, chronic loneliness can lead to suicidal ideation. The emotional pain and hopelessness experienced by those who feel isolated and disconnected can become overwhelming and sometimes lead to tragic outcomes.

Addressing loneliness requires a multi-faceted approach involving both individual efforts and societal support. Encouraging social connections, promoting community engagement, and providing mental health support can all play a vital role in combating loneliness and its negative effects. Recognizing and supporting those experiencing loneliness is crucial in fostering a healthier and more compassionate society. Remember, reaching out to someone who may be feeling lonely can make a significant difference in their life. Inflammation comes before disease. Loneliness is one of the greatest drivers of inflammation in the body and is associated with cardiovascular disease, dementia, anxiety, and premature death. It is the stress that comes from inadequate connection. Whoever is lonely and isolated needs community, or soon he will exit this life— mortality of the socially disconnected.

Loneliness is more deadly than cigarettes. How does smoking 15 cigarettes a day impact an individual? People who are lonely or socially disconnected experience a negative impact on their health; it is like having the effects of smoking 15 cigarettes a day! Act Now, we were meant to act together, collaborate, associate, not isolate.

## You can be Lonely in a Crowd

Loneliness in the church requires a holistic approach that combines genuine hospitality, intentional community building, support systems, and a focus on individual well-being. It must establish a culture of connection and care, the church can play a significant role in alleviating loneliness and building a strong, supportive community. Addressing this issue requires that the church is a welcoming space for everyone. Friendly greeters, warm atmospheres, and a sense of inclusivity can help newcomers and long-time members feel more connected.

Small groups with intimate settings provide opportunities for deeper connections, meaningful conversations, and shared experiences, which can help combat loneliness. Mentorship programs where experienced members guide and support newer or less involved members not only help with spiritual growth but also provide a sense of belonging.

Church leaders and members to be attentive to signs of loneliness. Encourage them to reach out to individuals who may be experiencing isolation, inviting them to events, and ensuring they are included in the church's activities. Regular social events, gatherings, and community service projects must be a part of the church of every local congregation because such activities can provide opportunities for members to connect on a personal level, fostering a sense of community. Support groups for specific needs such as grief, addiction recovery, or mental health are needed, they can create a safe space for individuals to share their struggles and find support from others facing similar challenges. How are people so lonely during technological advancements? Technology must be utilized, and social media platforms used to facilitate communication and connection among members. Online forums, groups, and messaging can be valuable tools for maintaining contact between physical gatherings.

Engagement in community breaks up loneliness. Members, especially those who are retired, should get involved in volunteerism within and outside the church. Working together for a common cause builds a sense of purpose and community, reducing feelings of loneliness.

Sometimes, members need counseling services or support groups led by qualified professionals, especially for individuals facing severe loneliness, depression, or other mental health challenges. Additionally, emphasis on the importance of prayer and spiritual guidance as a means of finding strength and support.

The problem is that there is a growing exodus from and an increasing aversion to the church. Signs of the time!

# References

Flower, L., Shaw, J., & Farid, M. (November 2017). Medicare Spends More on Socially Isolated Older Adults. AARP Public Policy Institute. Accessed March 21, 2023, from https://www.aarp.org/content/dam/aarp/ppi/2017/10/medicare-spends-more-on-socially-isolated-older-adults.pdf

# CHAPTER 10

# Act Now: Speak the Truth without Vitriol

*Truth itself is neutral and transparent; it's a reflection of reality without distortion or bias. It stands on its own, uncolored by personal feelings or agendas.*

The art of speaking the truth with grace and kindness stands as a beacon of wisdom and compassion. It is not merely the words we choose but the tone and intention behind them that determine whether truth becomes a soothing balm or a sharp blade. When we explore the intricate dance of truth and language, we uncover a remarkable truth itself—that truth, when wrapped in tenderness, becomes a potent catalyst for growth and understanding.

Some people contend that truth can be seen as a "weapon" because when used strategically or in certain contexts, it can have a significant impact, both positive and negative. They argue that where there is a power dynamic where one party holds more information or knowledge than another, they can use that truth to manipulate or control the other party, thus creating an imbalance of power and giving the person with the truth a significant advantage. It can be argued that truth can be used as a weapon to expose wrongdoing, corruption, or unethical behavior, and once revealed, individuals or institutions can be held accountable for their actions.

Truth can be used to counter misinformation and false narratives. By presenting facts and evidence, individuals can "fight back" against falsehoods and protect the integrity of accurate information. When armed with the truth, individuals can persuade and influence others to their point of view. This can be used in political, social, or business contexts to advance certain agendas. In legal contexts, the truth is essential for ensuring justice is served. Lawyers and legal professionals use evidence and facts as "weapons" to build strong cases and present their arguments effectively. In competitive environments, such as business or sports, possessing accurate information can provide a distinct advantage over opponents. This is particularly relevant when making strategic decisions or formulating tactics. The media can be used to propagate certain truths to influence public opinion or to serve specific interests. In this way, truth can be weaponized to shape narratives and perceptions. Truth can have a powerful emotional impact when it relates to personal experiences or sensitive topics. Sharing personal truths or stories can evoke empathy and understanding, but it can also be used to manipulate emotions for a particular purpose. Sometimes, truths can highlight divisions within societies or groups. When used tactically, truths can exacerbate conflicts or tensions, potentially causing harm. The concept of truth being a "weapon" is not inherently negative or positive. The ethical implications depend on how truth is wielded and the intentions behind its use. While truth can be powerful and influential, it's crucial to use it responsibly and with consideration for the potential consequences.

## A Healing Conversation

In a quiet corner of a cozy cafe, two friends, Mia and Alex, sat across from each other. Mia had noticed a change in Alex's behavior over the past few weeks—his usual vibrant energy had dulled, and his smiles seemed forced. Concerned about her friend's well-being, Mia had invited him to meet for a cup of coffee. As they sipped their drinks, Mia's heart raced. She knew that the truth she needed to share might be difficult for Alex to hear, but she believed it was necessary for his sake. Taking a deep breath, she began to speak, her words carefully chosen to convey her care and empathy.

"Mia, I've noticed that you've seemed a bit distant lately," she started gently. "I want you to know that I'm here for you, and if there's anything you'd like to talk about, I'm ready to listen." Alex looked into Mia's eyes, and for a moment, his guard seemed to waver. He had been grappling with personal challenges that he had kept hidden, unsure of how to voice them. Mia's sincere approach, however, struck a chord within him.

He hesitated for a moment before responding, "Mia, thank you for reaching out. You're right; I've been going through a tough time lately. I've been feeling overwhelmed with work and some personal issues. It's been hard to open up about it." Mia nodded, her gaze unwavering. "Alex, I appreciate your honesty. And I want you to know that you don't have to go through this alone. Sometimes, sharing our burdens with someone we trust can make a world of difference."

Alex let out a sigh of relief as if a weight had been lifted from his shoulders. Mia's understanding tone and nonjudgmental attitude made him feel safe and supported. He began to share more about the challenges he had been facing, the fears that had been haunting him, and the doubts that had taken root in his mind. As Alex spoke, Mia listened intently, nodding and occasionally offering words of reassurance. She didn't interrupt, didn't offer unsolicited advice, but simply allowed him to express himself. In that moment, truth became a soothing balm for both of them.

Mia and Alex forged a deeper bond of trust and understanding through their heartfelt conversation. The truth Mia shared and her empathetic approach allowed Alex to release pent-up emotions and confront his fears. He left the cafe that day feeling lighter, knowing that he had someone who genuinely cared about him. The healing power of truth lay not just in the words themselves but in the way they were delivered—with compassion, patience, and a genuine desire to help. Mia's ability to communicate her concerns without judgment and create a safe space for Alex to open up exemplified how truth when shared with kindness, can mend hearts and strengthen connections.

## Unveiling the Hidden Truth

The elegant ballroom was adorned with flowers and soft candlelight, a perfect setting for Maria and Michael's wedding reception. Guests mingled, laughter filled the air, and the atmosphere buzzed with joy. However, amidst the celebration, tension lingered, a secret known only to a few. Samantha, Maria's childhood friend, had discovered a truth that she believed needed to be revealed. She had come across evidence that suggested Michael might not be as honest as he appeared to be. Samantha felt conflicted, torn between her loyalty to Maria and her desire to spare her friend any pain.

As the night wore on and the music swelled, Samantha approached Maria, choosing a moment when they were alone. Her heart raced, knowing that what she was about to share could alter the course of the evening and potentially shatter Maria's happiness. "Maria, there's something I need to tell you," Samantha began hesitantly, her voice barely audible above the music. Maria turned toward Samantha, her eyes still sparkling with the excitement of her wedding day. "What is it, Samantha? Is something wrong?"

Samantha took a deep breath, the weight of her revelation pressing on her chest. "I recently came across some information about Michael. I didn't want to believe it at first, but I felt that you deserved to know the truth." Maria's expression shifted from curiosity to concern. She fixed her gaze on Samantha, her eyes narrowing. "What are you talking about, Samantha? What truth?"

Samantha swallowed hard, her heart heavy with the impending truth. "I found evidence that suggests Michael might not have been entirely honest about his past relationships. There's a chance he might be hiding something." Maria's face paled, and her fingers tightened around the edge of her dress. The festive atmosphere seemed to dim as the weight of Samantha's words settled in. The truth, which Samantha believed to be a sharp blade, had indeed pierced through the joyous occasion.

"Why didn't you tell me sooner?" Maria's voice wavered with a mixture of hurt and anger. Samantha's eyes glistened with remorse. "I didn't want to ruin your day, Maria. But I thought you deserved to know the truth before you make any life-changing decisions." Maria's mind raced, torn between her love for Michael and Samantha's revelation's uncertainty. The once-celebratory atmosphere now felt charged with tension, as if the truth had cast a shadow over the entire event. In this scenario, the truth became a sharp blade, cutting through the veil of celebration and revealing hidden doubts. Samantha's intention was to protect her friend, but the timing and context transformed the truth into a disruptive force. The wedding that was meant to be a joyous occasion was now tainted with uncertainty as Maria grappled with the newfound information.

An individual may discover an uncomfortable but necessary truth that must be shared. Picture them taking a deep breath, considering their words not just for their accuracy but also for their potential impact. This is the moment when truth transforms into something greater, a catalyst for positive change. As the words are spoken in a measured tone, their very essence becomes therapeutic. Even if momentarily taken aback, the listener senses the genuine concern and respect beneath the words. In that moment, the speaker evolves into a tutor, not in a condescending manner, but as a compassionate guide through a teachable moment.

The power of truth lies in its capacity to cut through the clutter and noise of misunderstanding. Imagine a dense forest filled with an array of tall trees, lush undergrowth, and tangled vines. In this forest, conversations buzz like a symphony of insects, each voice contributing to the chorus of noise. Amidst the cacophony, misunderstandings take root, like creeping vines that wind their way through the foliage, obscuring the path ahead. Now, picture a single ray of sunlight breaking through the canopy. This ray is the truth, a brilliant beam of clarity. As it touches the forest floor, its light severs through the tangle of vines and brushes aside the shadows. Where it shines, the clutter of misunderstanding retreats. People gather around the illuminated space, drawn to the light of truth. The clarity it brings allows them to see each other's faces and hear each other's words without distortion. Misconceptions that once twisted and turned like thorny branches dissolve under the gentle touch of the truth's light.

In this moment, the power of truth becomes evident. It acts as a sharp blade, cutting through the undergrowth of confusion, revealing the beauty of understanding beneath. Conversations that were once a cacophony transform into a harmonious dialogue where voices resonate without distortion. The truth stands as a beacon, guiding everyone out of the dense thicket of misunderstanding and into a clear space of shared understanding. Just as a ray of sunlight can illuminate a forest and dispel its shadows, truth has the ability to cut through the clutter and noise of misunderstanding, revealing the path to clarity and connection. When communicated with care, it holds the potential to unravel knots of confusion and forge connections of clarity. Consider the tranquility that settles after a heartfelt conversation, where truth is shared openly and gently. It's as if a weight has been lifted, replaced by a renewed sense of purpose and direction.

Acknowledge the delicate balance that must be maintained. Just as a healing potion loses its efficacy when mixed with bitterness, so does truth lose its impact when laced with vitriol. Speaking truth with harshness serves neither the speaker nor the listener. It does not transform but rather inflicts wounds that can take time to heal. Abusiveness, whether veiled in honesty or not, is not the path to progress. It creates walls where bridges could stand and festers resentment where understanding could grow.

## Speak the Truth in Love

Imagine a small, close-knit community with a vibrant church at its heart. This community values not only their faith but also the bonds they share with one another. John, a respected member of the community and an active churchgoer, has found himself entangled in an affair that goes against the values he and his community hold dear.

As whispers of John's infidelity spread, it became clear that the church board must address the situation. The elders gather, each with a heavy heart, knowing that they must navigate a delicate path—a path that exemplifies the biblical injunction to "speak the truth in love."

One evening, John is asked to meet with the church board in a private setting. The atmosphere is somber yet compassionate, as the elders recognize the importance of addressing the situation with both honesty and empathy. Their goal is not to condemn but to guide, not to shame, but to heal.

The meeting begins, and John stands before the board, his shoulders slumped with guilt and remorse. The board members look at him with a mixture of sternness and understanding, embodying the balance between truth and love. The board chairman speaks, his tone firm yet gentle. "John, we have become aware of the situation you're facing, and we're here because we care about you and this community. Our faith teaches us the value of honesty, repentance, and restoration. We believe that addressing this issue openly is essential for your spiritual growth and for the healing of those affected." John's eyes well up with tears as he nods, feeling the weight of his actions and the sincerity of the board's words. "We must speak the truth," continues the chairman, "not to condemn you, but to offer a path towards healing. Your actions have caused pain, but we also believe in forgiveness and redemption."

As the discussion unfolds, the board members share not only their concerns but also their support. They acknowledge that everyone makes mistakes and that facing the truth is the first step toward transformation. Their words convey that love does not mean turning a blind eye to wrongdoing but rather holding one another accountable for the sake of growth and community well-being. "Speaking the truth in love" is exemplified by the church board's approach to addressing John's adultery. They uphold the truth, acknowledging his actions and their impact while also extending love and understanding. This balance allows for an honest and compassionate conversation, fostering an environment of healing and growth rather than judgment and condemnation.

## How to Speak Truth with Skill

### Consider the Context and Prioritize Empathy

Before speaking your truth, take a moment to consider the context. Understand the situation, the emotions at play, and the potential impact of your words. Tailor your approach to fit the circumstances, whether it's a casual conversation or a serious matter.

Sarah noticed her colleague Alex's recent change in behavior. She approached him after a meeting, expressing concern about his well-being. Sarah listened attentively as Alex shared his challenges, offering support and suggesting resources. By considering the context and tailoring her approach to fit the situation, Sarah created a safe space for an open and understanding conversation—approach truth-sharing with empathy. Put yourself in the other person's shoes to grasp their perspective. This understanding helps you frame your words to acknowledge their feelings and foster open dialogue. In a quiet hospital room filled with soft daylight, Dr. Anderson stands beside the hospital bed where Emily, a weary and emotionally exhausted mother, lies. She had endured a long and arduous labor, her face etched with a mixture of pain and anticipation. Her husband sits nearby, holding her hand, his eyes a reflection of their shared hopes and fears.

Dr. Anderson, a compassionate and experienced obstetrician, takes a deep breath, knowing the heavy burden of truth he is about to share. He approaches the situation with utmost empathy, aware of the immense sorrow that awaits his words. Gently, he places a hand on Emily's shoulder, his touch a gesture of comfort amidst the impending storm. With a voice softened by compassion, he begins, "Emily, I want to express my deepest sympathy for the journey you've been on. You've shown remarkable strength throughout this difficult labor." Emily's gaze shifts from her husband to the doctor, a mixture of apprehension and a longing for answers in her eyes.

Dr. Anderson continues, "I'm so sorry to share that despite our best efforts, your newborn child did not survive. This is a heart-wrenching reality, and I understand that no words can truly ease the pain you're feeling right now. "Emily's eyes well up with tears, her hand clutching her husband's as if seeking solace and support. Her husband's grip tightens, a silent acknowledgment of the shared grief.

Dr. Anderson takes a pause, giving Emily and her husband a moment to process his words. He maintains a steady presence, aware of the importance of their emotional space. "As you navigate this incredibly challenging time, please know that you are not alone," he continues. "The hospital's support network is here for you, offering counseling and resources to help you cope with this loss." His words hang in the air, a fragile bridge connecting the unthinkable reality with the uncertain path ahead. "Please take all the time you need to process this," Dr. Anderson concludes gently. "Your emotions are valid, and we are here to provide any assistance you may require." The room is filled with a poignant silence, the weight of their shared sorrow palpable. In this somber moment, Dr. Anderson's approach to truth-sharing with empathy becomes a lifeline. He has recognized the depth of Emily's pain, put himself in her shoes, and framed his words with the utmost sensitivity, fostering an environment where her feelings are acknowledged, and her grief is respected.

Amidst the darkness of loss, Dr. Anderson's compassionate delivery offers a glimmer of humanity and support, a reminder that even in the most devastating moments, the power of empathy can provide solace.

## Choose the Right Timing

Timing is crucial. Choose a moment when the person is receptive and open to conversation. Avoid sharing difficult truths during highly emotional or stressful times.

In a quaint suburban home nestled on a tree-lined street, Jeremiah sat alone in his study, a swirl of emotions churning within him. The DNA test results before him unveiled a truth that had shaken the foundation of his world: none of his seven children were biologically his. The weight of this revelation hung heavy in the air, and he knew that he had to find a way to share this truth with his family. Gathering his thoughts, Jeremiah called for a family meeting that evening. His heart pounded as he watched his children gather in the living room, their faces a mix of curiosity and concern. His wife, Sarah, stood beside him, her hand gently resting on his shoulder. As everyone settled in, Jeremiah took a deep breath and began, his voice steady but tinged with vulnerability. "I want to talk to you all about something important. Recently, I discovered something that has taken me by surprise, and I believe it's only fair that I share it with you."

The room grew quiet, the anticipation palpable. Jeremiah continued, "Through DNA testing, I've learned that none of you are biologically my children. This revelation has been a shock to me, and I understand that it may be a shock to all of you as well." His words hung in the air, a heavy silence enveloping the room. He could see the range of emotions on his children's faces—confusion, disbelief, and even sadness. Jeremiah spoke again, this time with gentle reassurance. "I want you all to know that my love for each of you remains unwavering. While the biological connection may not be there, the bond we've built over the years is real and meaningful. You are my children in every way that matters."

His wife, Sarah, stepped forward, her eyes reflecting a mixture of empathy and compassion. "We understand that this news might be difficult to process," she said. "We are here to support you and answer any questions you might have." As the family absorbed the truth, a murmur of conversation gradually filled the room. Each child's reaction was unique, but a common thread emerged—the recognition that the love and connections they had shared were not defined solely by biology.

In the days that followed, Jeremiah and Sarah engaged in open conversations with each of their children, addressing their concerns, answering their questions, and offering emotional support. It wasn't an easy journey, but it was a journey they undertook together, a testament to the strength of their familial bonds. Over time, as the initial shock waned, the family began to find solace in their shared experiences, memories, and the love they had built as a unit. Jeremiah's courage in sharing the truth, framed with empathy and understanding, allowed their family to navigate an unexpected path with grace.

Through this shared journey, Jeremiah and his children learned that the definition of family is not confined to genetics alone. It is a tapestry woven with love, resilience, and the choice to stand together, even in the face of life's most profound revelations.

## Use Respectful Language

Craft your words carefully to ensure they are respectful and non-confrontational. Use "I" statements to express your thoughts and feelings, reducing the likelihood of the other person becoming defensive.

### Scenario 1: Marquis's Open Reprimand

At a bustling family gathering, the room echoed with laughter and conversation. Marquis, a high school student, quietly sipped his drink in a corner, his face downcast. The subject of his struggles in school had become a topic of discussion, and soon, the condescending remarks began.

His older sibling, Leo, known for their cutting remarks, seized the opportunity. "Marquis, I hear you're failing that subject. Can't believe you're not even smart enough to get a passing grade. Maybe you're just not cut out for it." Marquis's face flushed with embarrassment as the room fell silent. The reprimand was a public humiliation, leaving him feeling small and inadequate in front of relatives. The approach lacked empathy and compassion, chipping away at his self-esteem.

### Scenario 2: Keisha's Private Support

In the same household, Keisha, another high school student, faced similar struggles with the same subject. However, her experience was vastly different. Her older sibling, Maya, recognized the value of empathy and support.

One evening, after dinner, Maya pulled Keisha aside to chat privately. With a gentle smile, she said, "Hey, I heard you've been finding that subject challenging. It's okay, you know? We all have subjects we struggle with. If you want, I can help you find a tutor who can give you some extra support." Keisha's eyes welled up with gratitude. Maya's approach was a stark contrast to what Marquis had experienced. Maya's support was given in a way that acknowledged Keisha's feelings, offered a solution without judgment, and maintained her dignity.

## The Value of Empathy and Lack Thereof

In the first scenario, Marquis's open reprimand highlighted the lack of empathy and the harmful impact of condescension. Leo's words not only embarrassed Marquis but also eroded his confidence, making him feel inadequate and unsupported. The public humiliation did nothing to address the issue constructively but instead perpetuated negativity.

In the second scenario, Keisha's private support emphasized the value of empathy and understanding. Maya's approach acknowledged Keisha's struggles without belittling her. By offering a solution in a compassionate manner, Maya empowered Keisha to seek help without fear of judgment. This approach demonstrated the importance of creating an environment where individuals can openly discuss their challenges and receive the support they need to overcome them. Condescension and humiliation can damage relationships and self-esteem, while empathy and private support can foster growth, resilience, and a sense of belonging.

## Be Transparent and Honest

Share the truth transparently, using accurate and honest information. Sugarcoating or distorting the truth can lead to confusion and undermine trust. Paul and Mary had been married for several years, and their relationship was built on trust, love, and open communication. Despite their strong bond, there was one aspect of their marriage that weighed heavily on Mary's heart. Her history of sexual abuse had left deep emotional scars, making it difficult for her to fully enjoy intimacy with her husband.

One evening, as they sat together on the couch, Mary's heart raced with anxiety. She knew she needed to address the issue that had been affecting their relationship, but the fear of Paul's reaction held her back. Gathering her courage, she turned to him and said, "Paul, there's something I need to talk to you about."

Paul noticed the seriousness in her voice and gave her his full attention. "Of course, Mary. You know you can talk to me about anything. "Taking a deep breath, Mary began, "You've probably noticed that I've been struggling with intimacy. It's not because I don't love you or desire you, but I have a history of sexual abuse that has left me feeling scared and anxious."

Paul's expression softened as he listened, his heart aching for the pain Mary had endured. He reached out and took her hand, offering silent support. Mary continued, "I want to be transparent and honest with you about this. I want us to work through it together, but I need you to know that it's not your fault. It's something I've been carrying for a long time."

Paul's eyes filled with compassion as he gently squeezed her hand. "Thank you for opening up to me, Mary. I'm so sorry that you've had to go through this. You're incredibly strong for sharing your feelings with me." He paused for a moment before continuing, "I want you to know that I love you deeply, and our relationship means more to me than anything else. We'll navigate this together, and I'm here to support you in any way you need." Mary felt a wave of relief wash over her. Paul's understanding and unwavering support reassured her that their connection was strong enough to weather this challenge. She wiped away a tear and managed to smile.

Over the coming weeks and months, Paul and Mary worked together to find ways to make their intimate moments comfortable for both. They sought professional help, attended therapy sessions, and engaged in open conversations about their needs and boundaries. Through their dedication to honesty, understanding, and empathy, Paul and Mary strengthened their relationship and provided a safe space for healing. Their journey taught them that being transparent and honest about difficult topics can lead to deeper intimacy, trust, and a bond that transcends any obstacles they may face.

## Focus on Solutions

If the truth pertains to a problem or issue, propose potential solutions. This demonstrates your commitment to finding a positive resolution and can transform the conversation into a collaborative problem-solving effort.

"Focusing on solutions" is a principle that encourages individuals to shift their attention from dwelling on problems to actively seeking ways to address them. It involves acknowledging challenges, issues, or truths and then dedicating energy and thought toward finding effective ways to resolve or mitigate those challenges. This approach is especially relevant when dealing with difficult truths or issues that require thoughtful consideration to navigate.

When the truth pertains to a problem or issue, "focusing on solutions" involves proposing potential courses of action or strategies that can help alleviate the situation. Rather than getting stuck in the negativity of the problem itself, this principle encourages a proactive mindset that seeks to identify actionable steps forward.

For instance, if someone discovers a flaw in a project they're working on, "focusing on solutions" means not only acknowledging the flaw but also brainstorming and discussing ideas for how to rectify it. Instead of dwelling on blame or frustration, individuals prioritize finding ways to correct the mistake and ensure the project's success.

In relationships, "focusing on solutions" can be crucial when discussing challenging topics. If a couple is facing financial difficulties, for example, this principle encourages them to work together to explore various ways to manage their finances better, create a budget, or seek additional sources of income. Rather than letting the issue strain their relationship, they collaborate to find solutions that alleviate the stress and move them toward a more stable situation.

In essence, "focusing on solutions" is about channeling energy toward positive actions rather than getting bogged down by problems. It promotes a proactive and constructive approach to challenges, fostering a sense of empowerment and a belief that with effort and creativity, issues can be overcome. By proposing potential solutions when dealing with truths related to problems or issues, individuals can transform adversity into an opportunity for growth, learning, and positive change.

## Listen Actively and Acknowledge Emotions

Effective truth-sharing is a two-way street. Listen actively to the other person's response, validating their feelings and ensuring that they feel heard. Emotions often accompany the truth, especially when it's difficult to hear. Acknowledge the emotions that arise and create a safe space for the person to express their feelings.

In Christian teachings, Jesus is often regarded as a figure of great compassion, empathy, and active listening. His actions and teachings exemplify these principles. He consistently demonstrated compassion and empathy towards those he interacted with. He showed genuine concern for people's emotional well-being and took the time to understand their struggles and challenges. Throughout the Gospels, there are instances where Jesus engages in one-on-one conversations, truly listening to the concerns and emotions of individuals. For example, in the story of the woman caught in adultery (John 8:1-11), Jesus listens to her accusers and then addresses her with empathy and understanding. Jesus often used parables, which are stories that convey deep truths, to engage his listeners and evoke emotional responses. He used relatable scenarios to teach important lessons, showing an understanding of human emotions and using them to drive home his points. Jesus performed numerous miracles, including healing the sick and emotionally comforting those suffering. His acts of healing addressed physical ailments and demonstrated his awareness of people's emotional pain. He met people where they were. Jesus met people in their unique circumstances and emotions. For instance, the story of the prodigal son (Luke 15:11-32) shows Jesus' willingness to engage with different emotions like repentance, forgiveness, and reconciliation. Jesus acknowledged and validated the emotions of those around him. He wept with those who were grieving, such as when he mourned the death of his friend Lazarus (John 11:35). This act of weeping demonstrated his deep emotional connection with people.

Jesus often engaged in open dialogues with his disciples and followers. He encouraged questions and discussions, creating an environment where people felt comfortable expressing their thoughts and emotions. He displayed a non-judgmental attitude, welcoming people from all walks of life without condemnation. This attitude likely encouraged people to open up and share their feelings and concerns. His life and teachings provide numerous examples of active listening and acknowledging emotions. His compassion, empathy, willingness to engage with individuals personally, and ability to connect with people's emotions make him a powerful model for these principles.

## Offer Support

Some people will listen attentively to your plight, but they will walk away after that, offering no assistance at all. It was just a cathartic moment for them. After sharing the truth, offer your support. Let the person know you're there for them, whether they need guidance, assistance, or someone to listen. Offering support involves providing assistance, encouragement, and understanding to the person with whom you've shared the truth. The type of support you offer can vary based on the situation and the individual's needs. Here are some ways you can provide support. It could include emotional Support by showing empathy and understanding for their feelings, acknowledging their emotions and experiences, providing problem-solving assistance, offering words of encouragement and motivation, sharing relevant resources, articles, or information that could help them better understand the situation, or provide guidance on next steps; offering your time; providing physical assistance such as running errands, providing transportation, or assisting with tasks; provide reassurance and ongoing support through follow-up! Everyone's needs are different, so it's important to tailor your support to the individual and the specific situation. The key is to be attentive, compassionate, and willing to stand by their side as they navigate the challenges or emotions brought about by the truth you've shared.

## Practice Self-Reflection and Embrace Flexibility

Continuously examine your intentions for sharing the truth. Ensure your motives are rooted in a genuine desire to promote understanding and growth rather than hurt or control. Be open to the possibility that your perspective might not be the only valid one. Embrace flexibility and be willing to adjust your viewpoint based on new information. Speaking truth effectively is an art that combines authenticity, empathy, and skill. It's about fostering connections, enabling growth, and promoting positive change while respecting the dignity and emotions of all involved. You create a space where understanding and transformation can flourish by wielding truth with compassion.

## The Truths we Face

Several profound truths can serve as guiding principles for a meaningful and fulfilling life. First, impermanence and change. We must acknowledge that the only constant in life is change. Everything, including situations, emotions, and circumstances, is not permanent. Embracing change and learning to navigate it can lead to greater adaptability and resilience. Second, we must discover who we are. Self-discovery and understanding oneself—thoughts, emotions, strengths, and weaknesses—is a lifelong journey. Self-awareness enables personal growth and helps navigate relationships and life decisions more effectively. Third, people do not have to be heartless! Empathy and kindness go a long way! Treating others with empathy and kindness can have a profound impact on their lives and one's own well-being. The power of compassion can foster connection and understanding. Fourth, people need connections and relationships. Meaningful relationships are fundamental to human happiness. Investing time and effort in nurturing connections with family, friends, and community can lead to a richer life. In a world that has become increasingly interconnected due to technology and globalization, the idea that "no man is an island" holds great significance. It reminds us that our well-being and success are intertwined with the well-being and success of those around us. This principle encourages cooperation, empathy, and a sense of shared responsibility, ultimately contributing to a more harmonious and supportive society. Fifth, we must enjoy each day! Some people are present but not a part of their world. Being fully present in the current moment can help reduce stress, anxiety, and regrets. Practicing mindfulness fosters an appreciation for life's simple joys. Sixth, we must take personal responsibility for our actions! Taking responsibility for one's actions, choices, and their consequences empowers individuals to shape their lives. Blaming external factors hinders personal growth. Seventh, learning and growth are a part of life. Life is a continuous learning journey. Embracing new experiences, challenges, and opportunities for growth contributes to personal development. Seventh, don't be an ungrateful person. Cultivating gratitude for what one has can shift focus from what's lacking to what's abundant, leading to greater contentment and happiness. Some of the most ungrateful are those that you helped the most! They include your close friends and members of your family! Some are never satisfied with the plethora of sacrifices that you have made on their behalf. Eight, the world is diverse. The estimated global population of white individuals is around 10-12% of the total world population. Approximately 88% are people of color, pied beauty. Recognizing and respecting the diverse perspectives, cultures, and beliefs of others can lead to greater understanding and harmony in a global society. Ninth, make a mark, find your purpose, and contribute to life. Finding a sense of purpose and contributing positively to society can provide a sense of fulfillment. Making a meaningful impact on others' lives brings a deep sense of satisfaction.

Finally, we must recognize that we are imperfect beings in an imperfect world. Hence, we need balance to maintain our well-being. Prioritizing physical, mental, and emotional well-being ensures a balanced and sustainable lifestyle. Neglecting any aspect can impact the overall quality of life. No one is perfect. Embracing imperfections and learning from mistakes is crucial to personal growth and self-compassion.

In a bustling city known for its prestigious university and renowned hospital, there lived an astute professor named Dr. Liston Bent and a dedicated charge nurse named Esther Vassell. Both were respected in their fields and were known for their unwavering commitment to their work.

Dr. Bent was a brilliant professor of psychology at the university. He had spent years researching and teaching about the human mind, delving into the complexities of emotions and behaviors. His lectures were engaging, and his insights were often sought by students and colleagues alike. Dr. Bent's passion for understanding the intricacies of the mind was boundless, and he devoted long hours to his research and teaching.

On the other hand, Esther Vassell was the charge nurse of a busy and demanding hospital ward. She was responsible for managing the nursing staff, overseeing patient care, and ensuring that the ward ran smoothly. Esther was known for her exceptional organizational skills, kindness toward patients, and ability to keep calm in the face of challenging situations. Her dedication to providing quality healthcare was unparalleled, and she often went above and beyond to ensure the well-being of her patients and staff.

However, as the years went by, Dr. Bent and Esther became increasingly overwhelmed by their responsibilities. The demands of their professions began to take a toll on their mental and emotional well-being. Dr. Bent's exhaustive research and teaching schedule left him with little time for self-care. He started experiencing bouts of anxiety and sleeplessness, his once-lively enthusiasm replaced by a sense of exhaustion. Similarly, Esther's days at the hospital grew longer and more grueling. She faced staffing shortages, administrative pressures, and emotionally taxing situations on a daily basis. The weight of her responsibilities became too much to bear, and she found herself becoming emotionally distant from her patients and colleagues. The empathy that had once defined her interactions started to wane, replaced by a sense of detachment.

Fate brought Dr. Bent and Esther together at a local cafe one day. They struck up a conversation, sharing their experiences and challenges. As they talked, they realized that despite their different fields, they were both facing burnout—a state of emotional, mental, and physical exhaustion caused by prolonged stress. Recognizing the severity of their situations, Dr. Bent and Esther decided to seek help. They each reached out to mental health professionals, started practicing self-care routines, and gradually reduced their workloads. It was a difficult journey, but they regained their equilibrium over time.

Dr. Bent and Esther emerged from their burnout stronger and more resilient through therapy, support from friends and family, and a newfound dedication to prioritizing their well-being. Dr. Bent adjusted his work schedule and started pursuing hobbies he loved, while Esther implemented changes in her ward that promoted a healthier work environment for herself and her staff. Their experiences transformed them both. Dr. Bent began integrating mindfulness practices into his research and teaching, advocating for mental health awareness among his students. Esther became an advocate for nurse well-being, championing initiatives that focused on preventing burnout and promoting self-care within the hospital.

Their paths intersected once more at a mental health and well-being conference in healthcare and academia. They shared their stories with the audience, emphasizing the importance of recognizing burnout early and seeking help. Their joint presentation touched the hearts of many, inspiring them to prioritize their own well-being and support others facing similar challenges.

## The Application of Truth

Truth, at its essence, is not meant to be wielded as a weapon but as a tool for building bridges and fostering connections. When wrapped in the gentle cloak of compassion and conveyed with the warmth of love, truth becomes a force for good. It elevates conversations, encourages introspection, and facilitates growth. It resonates in the hearts of both speaker and listener, leaving behind a legacy of understanding and unity.

In a world where communication often feels transactional, a commitment to speaking truth without harshness is a declaration of one's dedication to genuine connections. It is a testament to the belief that, even in the face of uncomfortable realities, humanity's shared journey is best navigated with empathy and respect. The next time we are faced with a truth that must be shared, we can choose the path of kindness. In that choice, we step into the shoes of a tutor, a healer, and a guide—illuminating the path toward growth and understanding.

The essence of truth isn't about using it as a weapon to harm or hurt others. Instead, it's a tool for clarity, understanding, and growth. Truth can illuminate the path to resolution and reconciliation when wielded responsibly and with integrity. It can guide us toward better decisions and help us navigate the complexities of life with honesty and authenticity. When truth is used as a weapon, it loses its power to inspire positive change. Instead of promoting understanding and resolution, it fosters conflict and division. Using truth responsibly is recognizing its potential to heal and build rather than tear down. It's a reminder that our intentions and how we convey the truth are just as important as the truth itself.

# CHAPTER 11

# Act Now: Stress Kills!

"Stress kills" is a statement that emphasizes the harmful impact of chronic or extreme stress on a person's physical and mental health. While stress is a natural response to challenging situations and can sometimes be beneficial in the short term, long-term or overwhelming stress can lead to a range of adverse health outcomes. Not all stress is negative. Positive stress, known as "eustress," can be beneficial and motivating, driving individuals to achieve goals and meet challenges. However, when stress becomes chronic or overwhelming, it can have negative implications for mental and physical well-being.

Prolonged stress can take a toll on the body and lead to various physical health problems. It can suppress the immune system, making individuals more susceptible to infections and illnesses. When stress becomes chronic, the body's stress response system stays activated, leading to increased levels of stress hormones like cortisol. Stress can result in elevated blood pressure, weakened immune system function, and inflammation, which are risk factors for numerous health conditions. Chronic stress has been linked to heart disease, diabetes, digestive issues, and a higher susceptibility to infections.

Stress can have a significant impact on mental well-being. Chronic stress increases the risk of developing mental health disorders such as anxiety and depression. It can also exacerbate existing mental health conditions, making them more difficult to manage. Also, constant stress can lead to cognitive difficulties, memory problems, and difficulty concentrating. Stress can disrupt sleep patterns, leading to insomnia or poor sleep quality. Sleep is essential for physical and mental restoration, and chronic sleep disturbances can further exacerbate stress levels, creating a vicious cycle. People experiencing high-stress levels may resort to unhealthy coping mechanisms, such as overeating, excessive alcohol consumption, or substance abuse, to temporarily alleviate their stress. These behaviors can contribute to health issues and negatively impact overall well-being. Chronic stress can strain relationships with family, friends, and colleagues. Irritability, withdrawal, and decreased communication are common consequences of stress, which can further isolate individuals and create additional stressors. Stress is a significant risk factor for cardiovascular diseases. The constant release of stress hormones and increased blood pressure can damage blood vessels, leading to atherosclerosis (narrowing of arteries) and an increased risk of heart attacks and strokes.

Managing stress effectively is crucial for maintaining overall health and well-being. Engaging in stress-reducing activities like exercise, meditation, deep breathing, spending time in nature, and seeking support from friends, family, or mental health professionals can help alleviate stress and its negative consequences. Recognizing the signs of chronic stress and taking proactive steps to address it is essential in preventing its harmful effects on physical and mental health.

## Managing Stress, Biblically

What do you do when you are overwhelmed and you feel like you might have a heart attack? Elijah was so distraught by Jezebel's constant antagonism that he ran from home, hid in a cave, and wished for death! On the other hand, King David said, "From the end of the earth will I cry unto thee, when my heart is overwhelmed: lead me to the rock that is higher than I" (Psa. 61:2). In the face of stress, David acknowledges his own limitations and the overwhelming nature of his circumstances. By calling on God and asking to be led to the rock higher than him, he is seeking refuge and security in God's unchanging and steadfast nature. The metaphor of the rock conveys stability, strength, and a foundation that can withstand life's challenges.

The ubiquity of stress forces us to find a rock, river, reprieve, or respite. The demands of modern society seem too much! Demanding work schedules, long hours, tight deadlines, and job insecurity contribute to work-related stress. Capitalistic emphasis on productivity and career success leads to high levels of job-related pressure and even suicide. Economic challenges, debt, and financial instability are significant stressors. The cost of living, housing expenses, and concerns about retirement can contribute to financial stress for many individuals and families. Constant connectivity and information overload, often facilitated by smartphones and social media, can lead to a sense of being overwhelmed. The pressure to stay constantly connected and the fear of missing out (FOMO) contribute to stress. Social media platforms can contribute to stress by fostering a culture of comparison. People often compare their lives, achievements, and appearances with others, leading to feelings of inadequacy or dissatisfaction.

Balancing work and family responsibilities, parenting challenges, and issues within family dynamics contribute to stress. Modern family structures and changing societal expectations can add complexity to familial relationships. Concerns about personal health, access to healthcare, and the health of loved ones can be significant stressors. Lifestyle-related health issues like sedentary behavior and poor nutrition also contribute to stress. Environmental factors, including climate change, natural disasters, and pollution, contribute to stress. Concerns about the environment and the future of the planet can be sources of anxiety. Global events, such as political unrest, terrorism, and pandemics, contribute to a sense of uncertainty and insecurity. Constant exposure to distressing news through media channels can heighten stress levels.

Urban living and long commutes can lead to increased stress levels. The fast-paced nature of city life, congestion, and commuting time contribute to the overall stress burden. Societal expectations of success, achievement, beauty standards, and gender roles can contribute to stress. The pressure to conform to societal norms and expectations can be overwhelming. Difficulty in balancing work, personal life, and leisure activities can lead to chronic stress. The blurred boundaries between work and personal life, especially with remote work, can contribute to a sense of being constantly on call.

Stress is thus an inherent part of the human experience in a fallen world; life has always challenges and tribulations. Considering God's sovereignty, we are urged to trust in the Lord with all our hearts and submit to His plan. It is the first step in fostering relief from stress and anxiety. Second, we must not discount the potency of prayer as a powerful tool. We can draw on biblical examples of Jesus in the Garden of Gethsemane and Philippians 4:6-7 to find strength, guidance, and solace in God through prayer.

Third, we must follow the biblical foundation of rest or the Sabbath. People need both physical and spiritual rest as a means of managing stress. We should seek support from fellow believers and foster a sense of community and shared burdens. We cast our anxieties on God and embrace practical ways to release our worries. Jesus invited the weary and burdened to find rest in Him. (Matt. 11:28-30).

The writer to the Philippians was didactic: "Do not be anxious about anything, but in every situation, by prayer and petition, with thanksgiving, present your requests to God. And the peace of God, which transcends all understanding, will guard your hearts and your minds in Christ Jesus" (Phil. 4:6-7, NIV).

# CHAPTER 12

# Act Now: Unforgiveness is Dangerous!

*"Unforgiveness is the anchor that holds us in the stormy seas of bitterness, but forgiveness is the compass that guides us to calmer waters, allowing our souls to sail freely towards the shores of healing and compassion."*

Unforgiveness is a heavy burden that weighs down the soul, keeping us shackled to the pain of the past. In this chapter, we explore the dangers of holding onto grudges and the transformative power of forgiveness. By understanding the consequences of unforgiveness, we can learn to let go and experience the profound liberation that forgiveness brings.

Unforgiveness is a perilous trap that robs us of our happiness, peace, and potential for growth. By recognizing its dangers and choosing to forgive, we free ourselves from the chains of the past and open our hearts to healing and compassion. Embracing forgiveness may not be easy, but it is a transformative journey that liberates the soul and allows us to step into a future filled with hope, joy and renewed vitality. The path to healing begins with a choice: the choice to let go of unforgiveness and embrace the life-changing power of forgiveness.

Mr. James Hodge and his wife Marie lived in a small suburban town. They were once deeply in love, their hearts intertwined like solid vines, and their laughter filled their home. For many years, they cherished each other's company and relished the simple joys of life. Yet, as time passed, a storm began to brew in their marital haven. A successful businessman, James found himself entrapped in a whirlwind of work and temptation. He succumbed to the allure of another woman, and an affair ensued. Marie, with a heartbroken spirit, discovered her husband's betrayal.

Marie, a woman of unwavering principles, could not fathom forgiving her husband for his infidelity. Her pain was deep and insurmountable, and a relentless unforgiveness consumed her. Arguments and bitterness clouded their home, and the love they once shared seemed like a distant memory. Heavy with anger and resentment, Marie's heart began to wither away like a delicate flower left untended. Her unforgiveness grew like cancer, eroding her spirit and physical health. She could not escape the web of bitterness that had ensnared her.

One fateful day, as the weight of her anger grew too much to bear, Marie's heart gave in to the relentless burden of unforgiveness. She passed away, leaving behind a grieving husband and a shattered love that could never be made whole. After Marie's death, James was left with a heavy heart and profound regret for the choices that had torn their love asunder. He couldn't help but wonder if he could have done things differently, if he could have avoided the affair and preserved the love they once shared.

Years passed, and James found himself living in sunny Florida, where he met a woman who captured his heart again. They fell in love and built a life together, one grounded in trust, understanding, and a commitment to never repeat the mistakes of the past. With this new love, James discovered the power of forgiveness and redemption. He realized that forgiveness wasn't just an act of mercy for others but a path to healing and personal growth. Together, James and his second wife created a life filled with joy, respect, and appreciation for the love they shared. In their new journey, they found that love, strengthened by forgiveness, could mend even the deepest of wounds.

The story of Mr. James Hodge and his second chance at love in the warm embrace of Florida serves as a poignant reminder that unforgiveness kills. And the offender can find happiness after your demise.

## The Toxicity of Unforgiveness

Unforgiveness, like an invasive vine, winds its way into the depths of our souls, trapping us in a relentless cycle of resentment, anger, and bitterness. It is an evil force that clings to the chambers of our hearts, refusing to release its grip. When we hold onto past hurts, we unwittingly invite a venomous presence into our lives, one that festers silently and thrives on our pain. The roots of this toxicity run deep, penetrating our very core and poisoning our thoughts, attitudes, and perceptions. Like a corrosive agent, unforgiveness corrupts the spirit and corrodes the harmony of our existence. It disrupts the natural flow of our emotions and blights our capacity for joy and serenity. In the clutches of unforgiveness, we become prisoners of our own making, unable to break free from the chains of our past grievances. The pain and bitterness we harbor serve as a self-inflicted wound, constantly reopening and never being allowed to heal. Our minds replay the injustices and betrayals, each retelling fueling the fire of anger, further feeding the harmful cycle.

This corrosive grip on our hearts and minds has far-reaching consequences, rippling through the tapestry of our lives. It poisons our relationships, turning them into battlefields of unresolved conflicts and unspoken pain. Those we hold grudges against are unknowingly consigned to the role of the villain in our ongoing internal drama.

Perhaps most tragically, unforgiveness keeps us bound in the past, unable to move forward and embrace the fullness of life's potential. It becomes a heavy anchor that weighs us down, preventing us from navigating the currents of change and growth. Our vision is clouded by the bitterness we hold, obscuring the beauty of the present moment and the possibilities that await on the horizon.

In truth, unforgiveness is a trap that erodes our peace of mind and constrains our spirit. It is a poison that seeps into the very fabric of our existence, rendering us less than we are meant to be. To break free from this noxious grip, we must summon the courage to release the past, embrace forgiveness, and allow our hearts to heal, once more capable of experiencing life's true beauty and potential. It removes our moral capacity to receive our forgiveness, as it is written, "For if you forgive other people when they sin against you, your heavenly Father will also forgive you. But if you do not forgive others their sins, your Father will not forgive your sins" (Matt. 6:14-15, NIV).

## Unforgiveness hurts the body, Soul and Spirit

Unforgiveness is a breeding ground for chronic anger and hostility. If left unaddressed, this emotional turbulence can become a catalyst for a cascade of physical afflictions. Numerous studies have illuminated the detrimental effects of prolonged anger and hatred on our bodies. This enduring emotional burden raises stress levels to an alarming degree, which, in turn, becomes a silent saboteur to our cardiovascular health. Unforgiveness can drive a wedge between us and tranquility, fostering an environment where heart problems, such as hypertension and heart disease, can take root and flourish. Our body's immunity is another realm where unforgiveness exerts a palpable toll. The unrelenting burden of harboring grudges and resentment appears to cast a shadow on our immune systems. When we fail to forgive, we are, in essence, undermining our body's ability to protect itself. It's as if our emotional baggage serves as an insidious invitation for illnesses to infiltrate our lives more readily.

In addition to its physical consequences, unforgiveness casts a long shadow over our mental health. The persistent bitterness and resentment can usher in a gloomy cloud of anxiety and depression. The mind, too, is an intricate ecosystem, deeply affected by our choices, including the choice to forgive or withhold it. The refusal to forgive leaves the door ajar for anxiety to infiltrate our thoughts and depression to shroud our perception of the world. On the flip side, forgiveness is like a soothing balm that can mend the wounds unforgiveness inflicts on our well-being. Studies have consistently shown that embracing forgiveness is associated with profound mental and physical health improvements. Forgiveness is a powerful elixir that reduces stress, uplifts our mood, and, by extension, benefits our cardiovascular system. It strengthens our immune defenses, thus equipping us to withstand the trials of life more effectively. The link between unforgiveness and its impact on both mental and physical health is a clear reminder of the interconnectedness of our emotional, mental, and physical states. Though challenging, The choice to forgive holds the potential to liberate us from the shackles of emotional distress and foster a state of well-being that transcends the boundaries of the heart and extends to the body and mind.

## The Erosion of Connection

Unforgiveness is a strong force that silently infiltrates the bonds we share with our loved ones, friends, and colleagues, leaving a trail of irreparable damage in its wake. Trust, open communication, and an unspoken pact of mutual support are at the heart of every healthy relationship. Unforgiveness, however, becomes a powerful barrier that obstructs these vital elements. When unforgiveness takes root, it erects emotional walls that stand as formidable barriers to effective communication. The words we speak may be laden with resentment and hurt, while our ears become deafened to the concerns and perspectives of the other party. Trust, that fragile yet essential cornerstone of any relationship, is eroded by unforgiveness. Trust allows us to be vulnerable, confide in each other, and lean on one another in times of need. With its lingering bitterness, unforgiveness casts a long shadow over trust, making it difficult to restore the sense of security and reliability that should underpin any meaningful connection.

As long as grudges persist, the relationship's potential for reconciliation and growth remains stunted. The walls of unforgiveness obscure the path forward, preventing the nurture of a relationship. The art of growing together and learning from the past becomes a distant dream, perpetuating a cycle of conflict and stagnation.

## Unforgiveness causes Stagnation and Lack of Personal Growth

Unforgiveness does not just poison our relationships; it shackles our souls. It prevents us from charting our course toward personal growth and a brighter future. On the other hand, forgiveness is a beacon, illuminating the path forward. We remain trapped in a time capsule of pain and resentment when we hold onto unforgiveness. With all its wounds, the past dictates our present and, in doing so, stifles our ability to embrace the potential of the future. We are bound to a static existence, unable to break free from the chains of grievances that restrict our personal development.

Forgiveness is the key to unlocking this capsule of stagnation. It allows us to break free from the past and its burdens, enabling us to move forward with greater self-awareness and resilience. By forgiving, we release the grip that the past has on our lives and empower ourselves to explore new horizons, embrace fresh opportunities, and nurture our personal growth. Forgiveness opens the door to personal growth, self-awareness, and an enriched life experience. It empowers us to shed the baggage of the past, learn from our experiences, and embrace the possibilities of the future. Rather than remaining trapped in the shadows of yesterday, forgiveness invites us to step into the sunlight of tomorrow, where the promise of personal growth and fulfillment beckons.

## The Hardening of Hearts

Unforgiveness, like a slow-acting poison, can gradually harden our hearts, rendering us less capable of empathizing with the trials and tribulations of others. This emotional hardening has a ripple effect, extending its icy grip on our relationships and our connection with our inner emotional landscape. We unknowingly lock ourselves within an emotional fortress when we clutch onto unforgiveness. Unforgiveness makes it increasingly challenging to reach out and truly understand the struggles and suffering of others. Our hearts, weighed down by resentment, struggle to extend a hand of empathy, which is an essential element of genuine human connection.

Paradoxically, unforgiveness also distances us from our own emotions. We become so consumed by the negative emotions of holding grudges that we neglect our inner world. It creates a cycle where we cannot extend compassion to others and practice self-compassion, thereby undermining our emotional well-being.

## Let Go of Unforgiveness

It isn't easy, but we must, for our own survival, let go of unforgiveness. Choosing forgiveness is not a sign of condoning or forgetting the hurtful actions of others. It is, in fact, a profound act of courage and self-liberation. By forgiving, we emancipate ourselves from the heavy chains of pain and resentment. It is a gift, not to the wrongdoer, but to us, offering release from the suffocating burden of carrying grudges.

Forgiveness is not synonymous with absolution. Rather, it signifies a decision to let go of the emotional baggage we carry. It doesn't mean excusing or forgetting the wrongdoing but relinquishing our attachment to the suffering it has caused. When we forgive, we shed the weight of our grievances. It is akin to casting off a heavy backpack filled with rocks we've been carrying for far too long. This process allows us to stand taller, breathe easier, and walk with newfound lightness, free from the shackles of the past.

## Restoration and Growth

Forgiveness, a transformative force, holds the key to healing, not only for us but also for those whom we choose to forgive. Its effects are far-reaching, touching upon our emotional well-being, our inner tranquility, and our capacity for compassion. Forgiveness paves the way for emotional healing. We find solace and relief if we release the grip of resentment and pain. The scars of past wounds begin to fade, and we regain a sense of emotional equilibrium. This process allows us to experience life with greater peace and serenity. Forgiveness possesses the unique power to mend broken relationships. It creates space for reconciliation and growth, breathing new life into connections that were once strained. By extending forgiveness, we offer a chance for the restoration of trust and mutual understanding. Forgiveness is not just an act of compassion towards others but also an act of self-compassion. It rejuvenates our capacity for empathy, not only towards those we choose to forgive but towards ourselves as well. In essence, forgiveness is a transformative force that nourishes the soul, allowing us to move forward with grace, resilience, and a heart that is open to the beauty of human connection.

# CHAPTER 13

# Act Now: Embrace Parenthood

Dear Expectant Parents,

Congratulations on this incredible moment in your lives! As you stand on the threshold of parenthood, a remarkable journey awaits you—a journey that begins with the powerful words "Right Now!" These two words hold more significance than you might imagine. They are a call to embrace the transformative experience you are about to embark upon and a reminder of the profound love and responsibility that will shape your days ahead.

Right now, you find yourselves on the verge of a profound transition. This is your time to nurture, to learn, and to lay the foundation for the beautiful bond you will share with your child. The choices you make, the patience you exhibit, and the love you pour forth will have a lasting impact on the life you're bringing into this world.

Right now, you may be experiencing a blend of excitement and trepidation. Embrace these emotions! The journey into parenthood is marked by a range of feelings, and every uncertainty you face is an opportunity for growth. Step into this new chapter with an open heart, ready to learn and adapt as you navigate the uncharted waters of raising a child.

Right now, remember that mistakes are part of the journey. No one has all the answers, and parenthood is a continuous learning experience. Allow yourselves to learn from the challenges and celebrate the successes, both big and small. Your child will thrive not only in moments of perfection but also in your willingness to learn and grow together.

Right now, foster a connection that will shape your child's world. Parenthood isn't just about taking care of physical needs; it's about nurturing a deep, emotional connection. Create an environment of love, trust, and open communication. As you welcome your child into the world, you are also welcoming them into a lifelong journey of unconditional love.

Right now, set intentions for the kind of parents you aspire to be. Parenthood is a privilege and a responsibility. Take time to reflect on the values you want to instill, the memories you want to create, and the support you want to offer. These intentions will guide you as you make decisions and face challenges along the way.

Right now, prioritize self-care and your relationship. Parenthood can be all-encompassing, but it's important to take moments for yourselves and maintain the bond you share as partners. A strong partnership provides a stable foundation upon which you can build a loving and nurturing environment for your child.

This moment is fleeting, yet its impact is profound. Parenthood will be a journey of wonder, growth, and immense love. So, as you anticipate the arrival of your little one, grasp the significance of "Right Now!" Embrace each stage, each milestone, and each tender moment with a heart full of love and readiness. I wish you a breathtaking journey into parenthood—a journey marked by joy, unity, and the extraordinary power of "Right Now!"

## Subject: Embrace the Journey - Your Time is "Right Now!"

High School Freshmen

Dear High School Freshmen,

Congratulations on embarking upon a new chapter of your academic journey! As you step into the vibrant halls of high school, I want you to understand the power that lies in the words "Right Now!" These two words are not just a phrase; they are a call to action, a reminder of the potential that lies within each of you, waiting to be unleashed upon the world.

Right now, you stand at the crossroads of endless possibilities. This is your time to shine, to explore, and to grow. The choices you make, the friendships you forge, and the dedication you show will shape the trajectory of your high school experience and beyond.

**Right now**, you might be feeling a mix of excitement and nervousness. Embrace those feelings! Every new beginning comes with a bit of uncertainty, but it's in those moments of discomfort that you truly discover your strengths. Allow yourself to step out of your comfort zone and engage in new experiences, whether it's joining a club, trying out for a sports team, or participating in a debate. The more you challenge yourself, the more you'll learn and develop.

**Right now**, remember that mistakes are stepping stones to success. Don't fear failure; rather, embrace it as a valuable teacher. Every misstep is an opportunity to learn, adapt, and improve. Your journey through high school will be marked by both triumphs and setbacks, but it's the resilience you show in the face of adversity that will define your character.

**Right now**, make connections that matter. High school isn't just about academics; it's also about building relationships that will shape your future. Forge connections with teachers, mentors, and peers who inspire and support you. Surround yourself with individuals who challenge you to be better, who believe in your potential, and who uplift you in times of doubt.

**Right now**, set goals that propel you forward. Whether it's acing a challenging course, pursuing a passion project, or contributing to your community, having goals will give you direction and purpose. Break these goals into smaller, manageable steps, and celebrate each accomplishment along the way. Remember, the journey matters as much as the destination.

**Right now**, prioritize self-care. High school can be demanding, both mentally and emotionally. Make sure to find moments of rest and rejuvenation. Cultivate hobbies that bring you joy, engage in physical activity, practice mindfulness, and maintain a healthy balance between your studies and personal life.

In the grand tapestry of life, this moment is fleeting, but its impact can be everlasting. The high school will be a whirlwind of memories, lessons, and growth. So, as you step into your first class, remember the significance of "Right Now!" Embrace every opportunity, learn from every experience, and seize the reins of your journey with confidence and determination. Wishing you a remarkable high school experience filled with laughter, learning, and personal growth. You have the power to shape your own destiny—starting "Right Now!"

## Subject: Embrace the Adventure - Your Time is "Right Now!"

Dear College Freshmen,

Congratulations on successfully navigating the transition from high school to this exciting new chapter of your academic journey! As you step onto the campus and into the lecture halls of your college, I want you to grasp the immense power encapsulated within the words "Right Now!" These two words are not mere expressions; they are a rallying cry, a reminder of the boundless potential that resides within each of you, waiting to be unleashed upon the world.

Right now, you find yourselves at the threshold of limitless opportunities. This is your moment to shine, to explore, and to evolve. The decisions you make, the relationships you foster, and the commitment you exhibit will shape not just your college experience but also your path beyond these hallowed halls.

**Right now**, you might be feeling a mixture of anticipation and uncertainty. Embrace these emotions! Every new beginning comes with its share of challenges, but it is in these moments of discomfort that you truly come to understand your capabilities. Dare to step beyond your comfort zone, whether by engaging in thought-provoking discussions, joining a diverse range of student organizations, or diving into research projects. The more you stretch your boundaries, the more you will learn and grow.

**Right now**, acknowledge that setbacks are stepping stones to success. Do not shy away from failure; instead, see it as a valuable teacher. Every stumble is an opportunity to learn, adapt, and advance. Your journey through college will be marked by both triumphs and disappointments, but it is your resilience in the face of adversity that will define your character.

**Right now**, cultivate connections that hold significance. College is not just about academics; it is also about forming relationships that will sculpt your future. Forge bonds with professors, mentors, and peers who ignite your passion and encourage your growth. Surround yourselves with those who challenge your thinking, who see your potential, and who offer guidance during moments of uncertainty.

**Right now**, set objectives that drive you forward. Whether it's excelling in a complex subject, participating in a community outreach initiative, or launching a creative endeavor, having clear goals will provide you with direction and purpose. Break down these goals into manageable steps and celebrate every milestone along the way. Remember, the journey is as meaningful as the destination.

**Right now**, prioritize self-care. College life can be demanding, both mentally and emotionally. Ensure that you find moments to recharge and rejuvenate. Pursue hobbies that spark joy, engage in physical activities, practice mindfulness, and maintain a healthy equilibrium between academics and personal well-being.

Amidst the grand tapestry of life, this moment is fleeting, yet its impact can reverberate for years to come. College will be a whirlwind of experiences, lessons, and growth. So, as you enter your first class, grasp the significance of "Right Now!" Embrace every opportunity, glean wisdom from every challenge, and seize control of your journey with conviction and purpose. Wishing you an extraordinary college experience brimming with knowledge, camaraderie, and self-discovery. You possess the authority to mold your own destiny—commencing "Right Now!"

# CHAPTER 14

# Act Now: The Imperative of the Present

∞∞∞∞∞∞∞∞∞∞∞∞∞∞

*"That's the whole story. Here now is my final conclusion: Fear God and obey his commands, for this is everyone's duty" (NLT)*

∞∞∞∞∞∞∞∞∞∞∞∞∞∞

In our fast-paced world, we often find ourselves caught up in the whirlwind of ambition, driven by the pursuit of success, wealth, and power. We chase after fleeting pleasures, worldly desires, and momentary triumphs, all the while losing sight of the eternal purpose that beckons us. We become ensnared by the illusion that our actions are solely our own, disconnected from a higher calling. Yet, when we pause to reflect upon the timeless wisdom of Ecclesiastes, we are reminded that our duty is not a mere suggestion; it is an essential roadmap to a life of meaning, purpose, and fulfillment.

"Fear God"—a phrase that transcends religious boundaries and speaks to the core of our existence. It beckons us to recognize the divine presence that permeates the universe, to bow before the majesty of creation, and to humbly acknowledge that we are but small fragments in the grand tapestry of existence. To fear God is to stand in awe of the infinite, to find solace in the face of uncertainty, and to embrace a higher power that guides our steps.

"Fear God"—these two words have profound significance that reaches far beyond the confines of any specific religious doctrine. They encapsulate a universal concept that transcends cultural, geographical, and theological boundaries. To truly understand the depth of this phrase is to embark on a journey into the very essence of our human experience. At its core, "Fear God" beckons us to embark on a quest for spiritual awareness, one that transcends the limitations of religious dogma. It invites us to embark on a deeply personal exploration of the mysteries that surround us, the questions that haunt our minds, and the wonder that fills our hearts. It challenges us to look beyond the material realm to venture into the metaphysical and the transcendent.

To "Fear God" is to embark on a voyage of discovery, cast aside the veil of complacency, and delve into the infinite depths of existence. It prompts us to recognize the divine presence that saturates the cosmos, an omnipresent force that defies our attempts to confine it within the narrow bounds of our understanding. It is the acknowledgment that there is more to this universe than meets the eye, more than the tangible and the quantifiable. In the face of such vastness, we are humbled. We come to terms with our own limitations, our fleeting nature, and our inherent insignificance in the grand scheme of things. "Fear God" compels us to bow before the majesty of creation, to kneel in reverence before the unfathomable intricacies of the cosmos, and to admit our own vulnerability in the face of the unknown.

It is in this humility that we find strength. To "Fear God" is not a call to cower in fear but a summons to stand in awe of the infinite. It invites us to embrace the awe-inspiring beauty of existence, to marvel at the symphony of life, and to find solace in the face of uncertainty. In the embrace of the divine, we discover a wellspring of courage that enables us to face life's trials and tribulations with grace and fortitude. "Fear God" is an invitation to embrace a higher power that transcends our individuality. It is a recognition that we are not isolated entities but interconnected threads in the tapestry of existence. It urges us to look beyond ourselves and our immediate concerns, to acknowledge our interconnectedness with all living beings, and to take responsibility for the world we share. In this higher power, we find guidance—a moral compass that points us toward justice, compassion, and love. It is a force that calls us to be stewards of the Earth, caretakers of our fellow human beings, and champions of the downtrodden. It is the recognition that our actions ripple through the fabric of reality, affecting not only ourselves but the entire universe. So, "Fear God" is not a call to fear in the conventional sense but an invitation to embrace the profound mystery of existence. It is an acknowledgment of the divine presence surrounding us, an awe-inspired humility in the face of the unknown, and a guiding light directing our steps toward a life of purpose, compassion, and transcendence.

## Edwin

Edwin was a man of deep faith and unwavering reverence for God. He lived in a small, modest village nestled between rolling hills and lush meadows. Despite the simplicity of his life, he had always carried in his heart a profound fear of God—a reverence that guided his every action and decision.

One summer, a devastating drought descended upon the village. The once-green fields turned brown, and the streams that once flowed with crystal-clear water ran dry. The villagers, their livelihoods dependent on the land, faced the grim prospect of crop failure and famine. Edwin, as always, turned to his unwavering faith. He gathered the villagers in a humble prayer meeting beneath the shade of an ancient oak tree. With his eyes closed and hands clasped, he beseeched God for mercy and guidance. His prayer was not one of desperation but of deep trust that God would provide. Days turned into weeks, and the drought showed no signs of relenting. The villagers grew anxious, their faces etched with worry. But Edwin remained steadfast in his faith, and his fear of God did not waver.

One morning, as he set out to the parched fields to inspect the crops, Edwin noticed something remarkable. Amidst the dry and barren land, a single patch of soil remained moist and dark. Astonished, he knelt down and dug his hands into the earth, finding it teeming with worms and life. Word of this miraculous patch of fertile soil spread quickly throughout the village. Edwin gathered the villagers once more, and they all marveled at the inexplicable oasis amidst the drought. The community decided to plant their seeds in this blessed spot, trusting that God had provided a way. In the weeks that followed, a transformation unfolded. The crops planted in the blessed patch of soil grew with astonishing vigor. They thrived despite the unrelenting drought, and soon, the once-barren fields surrounding that miraculous patch also began to show signs of life. The villagers came to recognize this as a divine blessing, a testament to Edwin's unwavering faith and fear of God.

As the harvest season arrived, the village was spared from famine. They had enough food to sustain themselves through the harsh winter, and their gratitude to God knew no bounds. Edwin's fear of God had not only saved the village from disaster but had also brought them a bountiful blessing. The villagers saw in Edwin a living example of the power of faith and reverence for God. His unwavering trust had not only sustained him but had become a beacon of hope for the entire community. Edwin's fear of God had brought about a miraculous turn of events, demonstrating that faith and reverence could lead to unexpected blessings and abundance even in the face of adversity.

"To obey His commands" is not merely a passive act of compliance but rather an active and deliberate choice to align our lives with a higher purpose. It beckons us to embark on a profound moral journey, transcending our selfish desires and embracing principles that are greater than ourselves. In doing so, we become custodians of a sacred trust entrusted with the well-being of our souls and the entire human family.

The command to embrace compassion is a call to open our hearts to the suffering of others. It challenges us to look beyond our own needs and desires to see the pain and struggles of our fellow human beings. When we choose compassion, we extend a hand to the downtrodden, offer a shoulder to the weary, and show kindness to those who need it most. In this act of selflessness, we forge connections that bridge the gaps of indifference and bring warmth to the coldest corners of our world. Justice is a pillar upon which society stands, and obeying God's command to uphold justice is a beacon that guides us through the labyrinth of human interactions. It requires us to stand against oppression, advocate for the voiceless, and ensure fairness prevails. When we champion justice, we mend the tears in the fabric of our society, stitching together a tapestry where every individual, regardless of their station in life, can find dignity and equality. Righteousness is the moral compass that directs our actions toward what is good and virtuous. It challenges us to resist the temptations of dishonesty, greed, and immorality and, instead, to pursue the path of honesty, integrity, and virtue. When we strive for righteousness, we become beacons of integrity in a world often marred by corruption. Our actions inspire others to choose the higher road, and together, we contribute to a more noble and honorable society. Obedience to God's commands reminds us that we are not solitary beings but interconnected human family members. It underscores the idea that our destinies are intertwined and that the well-being of one affects the well-being of all. In this recognition, we find the strength to put aside divisions, prejudices, and animosities and, instead, to embrace the common thread of morality and virtue that binds us. Our unity becomes a powerful force for positive change in a world often torn by strife and discord. When we heed the call to obey God's commands, we become instruments of transformation. We bring harmony to a fractured world by fostering understanding and reconciliation. We offer healing to wounded hearts through acts of kindness, empathy, and forgiveness. We ignite the flame of hope in the hearts of the hopeless by showing them that love and compassion can overcome even the darkest of circumstances.

Obeying God's commands is a choice to be a beacon of light in a world that sometimes seems shrouded in darkness. It is a conscious decision to be a source of goodness, love, and righteousness. Through our actions guided by these principles, we fulfill our duty to God and become agents of positive change in the lives of those around us and the world. The duty to fear God and obey His commands is not an exclusive privilege bestowed upon a select few or reserved solely for those who wear the badge of devoutness. It is, instead, a birthright intrinsic to every soul that walks upon this Earth. It is the universal blueprint, a timeless guidepost that illuminates the path to a well-lived life that extends far beyond the transient boundaries of the here and now and touches the realms of the eternal. This sacred calling is a testament to all humanity's fundamental equality. It recognizes that the spark of divinity resides within every human heart, regardless of race, religion, nationality, or social status. It does not discriminate between the rich and the poor, the educated and the unlettered, the powerful and the marginalized. Instead, it embraces each individual as a bearer of moral responsibility, a steward of their own destiny, and a potential force for good in the world.

This birthright is not tethered to any specific place, time, or culture. It transcends the boundaries of geography and history. Whether one is born in the heart of a bustling metropolis or amid the serenity of a remote village, the duty to fear God and obey His commands remains an ever-present and unwavering truth. It is a universal code of conduct that speaks to the core of our shared humanity, reminding us of our interconnectedness and the moral compass that guides us on our collective journey.

The beauty of this birthright lies in its accessibility to all. It is not hidden behind esoteric rituals, obscure doctrines, or insurmountable barriers. Rather, it stands as an open invitation to every seeker, a beckoning call to those who are willing to listen and heed the wisdom of the ages. It is a treasure that awaits discovery, a wellspring of purpose and meaning that anyone can tap into with a willing heart and a sincere desire to align their life with higher principles. In embracing this sacred calling, individuals are empowered to transcend the ephemeral and touch the eternal. It is a profound recognition that the pursuits of this world, while important, are but fleeting moments in the grand tapestry of existence. By aligning our actions with the divine commands, we embark on a journey that transcends the confines of time and space. We leave a legacy that endures, a ripple effect that extends far beyond our individual lives, and a spiritual footprint upon the sands of eternity. The duty to fear God and obey His commands is not a privilege reserved for a select few but a birthright bestowed upon every human soul. It is a universal roadmap that guides us toward a life well-lived and connects us to the eternal. In embracing this calling, we recognize our shared humanity and the potential for positive transformation that resides within us all.

But why act now? Because the present moment is the only moment we truly possess. The past is a fading memory, and the future is a canvas yet to be painted. In the realm of eternity, the present is the gateway to transformation, redemption, and the fulfillment of our purpose. It is the chisel with which we shape our destiny. The urgency of now lies in the awareness that every breath, every heartbeat, and every choice carry the weight of eternity. To delay is to deny the beauty of this precious gift of life. To procrastinate is to squander the opportunities for growth, service, and love. As you turn the pages of your life's story, remember this chapter: Act Now. Fear God and obey His commands, for this is everyone's duty. The tapestry of your existence is woven with the threads of today's decisions. Embrace the present, for within it lies the power to transform your life, touch the lives of others, and leave a legacy that will echo through the ages.

The time is now, the choice is yours, and the duty is clear.

# CHAPTER 15

# How to Act

First, act spiritually. What is right is not determined by our feelings, politics, or culture. There must be a greater dimension or reason for what we do.

Acting with spiritual insight involves aligning our actions with a higher purpose and transcending personal biases and worldly influences. Here's an example to illustrate this idea:

## Making Ethical Business Decisions

Imagine you're a business leader faced with a challenging decision that could significantly impact your company's bottom line. The choice involves potentially cutting corners in production to increase profits, but you're aware that this might lead to subpar and unsafe products reaching consumers.

To act spiritually in this situation, you would:

1. **Seek Guidance.** Instead of relying solely on financial considerations, you would take a moment to reflect and seek guidance from a higher power. This could involve prayer, meditation, or seeking wisdom from your spiritual beliefs.

2.  **Prioritize Values.** You would remind yourself of the values that matter most to you and your company – integrity, quality, and the well-being of customers. These values become your compass, guiding your decision-making.

3.  **Transcend Immediate Gain.** While the immediate financial gain might be tempting, you would recognize that your actions have consequences beyond profits. You understand that the well-being and trust of your customers are paramount.

4.  **Consider the Greater Good. Acting spiritually means considering your company's success and the well-being of the community and society at** Will your decision contribute positively to the world?

5.  **Stay Accountable.** By acting spiritually, you're accountable to a higher moral standard. This accountability encourages you to make the right choice, even if it's more challenging in the short term.

In this scenario, acting spiritually leads you to prioritize product quality and consumer safety over immediate financial gains. This choice aligns with a deeper sense of purpose and contributes to the well-being of both your customers and the broader community. This example demonstrates how acting spiritually goes beyond conventional decision-making. It involves recognizing a greater dimension to your actions and letting your higher values guide you, even when external pressures might push you in a different direction. By acting spiritually, you make choices that reflect your commitment to something beyond mere personal interest or immediate gain.

Second, act expeditiously – We must act like we are on an expedition to accomplish something significant in the world. We must recognize the urgency of a situation and respond with a sense of purpose and determination. Here's an example to illustrate this concept:

## Example: Environmental Conservation Efforts

Imagine you're part of a local community concerned about the degradation of a nearby natural habitat due to pollution and deforestation. To act expeditiously in this scenario, you would:

1. **Assess the Situation.** You would quickly gather information about the extent of the environmental damage. This might involve studying data, conducting field assessments, and consulting experts to understand the urgency of the situation.

2. **Mobilize Resources.** Recognizing the need for swift action, you would rally community members, volunteers, and relevant organizations. You'd create a coalition of individuals who share your concern and passion for environmental conservation.

3. **Set Clear Goals.** Acting expeditiously requires a well-defined plan. You'd establish clear goals and a timeline for activities such as organizing cleanup drives, planting trees, and raising awareness about sustainable practices.

4. **Leverage Technology.** In the digital age, acting expeditiously often involves using technology to amplify efforts. You might set up a social media campaign to spread awareness, coordinate activities through online platforms, and even use satellite imagery to monitor progress.

5. **Collaborate Strategically.** Recognizing that time is of the essence, you'd collaborate with local authorities, environmental agencies, and businesses that can contribute resources and expertise. Collaboration enhances the impact of your efforts.

6. **Sustain Momentum.** Acting expeditiously isn't a one-time endeavor. You'd maintain the momentum by regularly assessing progress, adapting strategies as needed, and inspiring ongoing community involvement.

In this example, acting expeditiously drives you and your community to address the environmental crisis promptly and effectively. The urgency of the situation compels you to bypass procrastination and take immediate action. Treating the situation as an expedition infuses your efforts with a sense of adventure, determination, and purpose, akin to explorers embarking on a mission to achieve something significant. This approach emphasizes that some challenges demand swift and resolute action. By acting expeditiously, you acknowledge the finite nature of time and the need to seize the moment to create meaningful change. It's about channeling your energy and resources into a focused and determined effort to achieve your goals within a limited timeframe.

Third, act sagaciously. We must act with wisdom. To "act sagaciously" means to act with wisdom, prudence, and good judgment. It involves making thoughtful decisions based on careful consideration of the situation, potential outcomes, and the broader context. When someone acts sagaciously, they demonstrate the ability to navigate complex situations, anticipate consequences, and make choices that align with their values and goals. Acting sagaciously means applying spiritual insights and teachings to make wise decisions that contribute positively to the community, adhere to moral principles, and lead to harmonious outcomes. It involves seeking guidance from spiritual sources, considering the long-term effects of actions, and prioritizing values such as compassion, justice, and understanding. Acting sagaciously entails using wisdom and discernment to make beneficial, well-informed choices aligned with one's spiritual beliefs and ethical principles.

Fourth, act deliberately. Act with intention and purpose. Don't just wait for circumstances to align; take deliberate steps towards your goals. Plan your actions, set achievable milestones, and follow through with determination. Just as Jesus was deliberate in His teachings and actions, we should act with a clear sense of purpose. How can this principle be applied in various aspects of life? Consider the pursuit of educational goals. If you're a student with a strong desire to excel in your studies and pursue higher education. To act deliberately in this context, you would:

1. **Define Clear Goals.** You'd start by setting specific and achievable educational goals. These might include earning certain grades, participating in extracurricular activities, or gaining specific skills related to your desired field of study.

2. **Develop a Plan.** Acting deliberately involves creating a well-thought-out plan. You'd outline the courses you need to take, the projects you want to complete, and the study schedules that align with your goals.

3. **Break Down Tasks.** You'd break down your goals into smaller, manageable tasks to prevent feeling overwhelmed. This could involve weekly study goals, research assignments, and project deadlines.

4. **Allocate Resources.** Recognizing that achieving your educational aspirations requires resources, you'd allocate time, energy, and possibly financial resources for books, materials, and additional learning opportunities.

5. **Seek Guidance.** Just as Jesus sought guidance from his spiritual convictions, you might seek guidance from mentors, teachers, or advisors. Their insights can provide valuable perspectives and help you stay on track.

6. **Monitor Progress.** Regularly assess your progress against your plan. Celebrate achievements and make adjustments if needed. Deliberate action involves staying engaged with your goals and adapting as circumstances evolve.

7. **Stay Committed.** Acting deliberately requires commitment. Even when facing challenges or distractions, you remain dedicated to your goals, reminding yourself of the bigger picture and the value of your educational pursuits.

By acting deliberately in this scenario, you align your actions with a clear purpose: achieving educational excellence. Just as Jesus was intentional in His teachings and activities, you embody intentionality in your educational journey. This approach isn't about waiting for success to happen; it's about taking proactive steps to create the success you envision. Acting deliberately emphasizes your role as an active participant in shaping your future. It's a reminder that success often comes from deliberate, well-planned efforts rather than relying solely on chance. This principle encourages self-discipline, focus, and determination, which are essential qualities for achieving your goals in various aspects of life.

Fifth, act compassionately: Act with empathy and love for others. Jesus' teachings were centered around compassion and caring for those in need. When you act compassionately, you can impact people's lives meaningfully. Consider the needs of others, lend a helping hand, and show kindness wherever you go. How can this principle guide our behavior in different situations? Imagine you decide to volunteer at a local homeless shelter. To act compassionately in this context, you would:

1. **Understand Others' Stories.** Compassionate action begins with understanding the experiences and challenges faced by homeless individuals. You'd take the time to listen to their stories, fostering empathy and breaking down stereotypes.

2. **Provide Basic Needs.** Recognizing immediate needs, you'd contribute to providing essentials like food, clothing, and shelter. Your actions show that you care about their well-being and want to alleviate their suffering.

3. **Offer a Listening Ear.** Sometimes, compassionate action involves simply being there to listen. Homeless individuals might not have many opportunities to share their thoughts and feelings. By offering a nonjudgmental ear, you demonstrate empathy and respect.

4. **Show Respect and Dignity.** Acting compassionately means treating every individual with respect and preserving their

dignity. You'd interact with kindness, valuing each person's worth regardless of circumstances.

5. **Initiate Conversations.** Engage in conversations to learn more about the needs and aspirations of homeless individuals. You can offer assistance that aligns with their goals by showing genuine interest.

6. **Advocate for Change.** Compassionate action extends beyond immediate assistance. You might advocate for policies that address homelessness and work toward systemic change that can have a lasting impact.

7. **Encourage Others.** Your compassionate actions can inspire others to join the cause. By sharing your experiences and the positive impact of your actions, you contribute to a ripple effect of compassion in the community.

Acting compassionately reflects the teachings of Jesus and many other spiritual traditions, emphasizing the importance of caring for those who are marginalized or in need. It's a reminder that our actions can uplift and empower others, contributing to a more compassionate and understanding world. By infusing compassion into your interactions, you contribute to a positive cycle of kindness and promote the well-being of individuals and communities.

Sixth, act collaboratively. Act in unity with others. Jesus gathered disciples to spread his message and mission. Similarly, by collaborating with like-minded individuals or groups, you can amplify your efforts and bring about positive change more effectively. Teamwork and cooperation can lead to greater impact and lasting results. Imagine you're passionate about environmental conservation and want to make a meaningful impact in your community. To act collaboratively in this context, you would:

1. **Identify Allies.** Contact individuals, organizations, and groups that share your passion for environmental conservation.

By forming connections, you create a network of like-minded individuals who can work together toward a common goal.

2. **Share Resources.** Collaboration often involves pooling resources– time, expertise, or finances. You might partner with local businesses, educational institutions, and community centers to access the necessary resources for your campaign.

3. **Leverage Diverse Skills.** Collaborative efforts allow you to tap into diverse skills and talents. Individuals with different backgrounds can contribute unique perspectives, enhancing the overall effectiveness of your campaign.

4. **Set Common Objectives.** Clearly define and align your environmental conservation campaign's objectives with your collaborators' values. Having a shared purpose fosters unity and a sense of collective responsibility.

5. **Plan Joint Activities.** Organize events, workshops, clean-up drives, and awareness campaigns that involve multiple collaborators. Joint activities increase your reach and create a sense of camaraderie among participants.

6. **Maintain Open Communication.** Effective collaboration relies on open and transparent communication. Regularly update your collaborators on progress, challenges, and opportunities to ensure everyone remains informed and engaged.

7. **Celebrate Achievements.** When you achieve milestones or make progress, celebrate as a team. Recognize and appreciate the contributions of each collaborator, reinforcing the sense of unity and accomplishment.

In this example, acting collaboratively allows you to harness the power of collective efforts. Just as Jesus gathered disciples to spread his message, your collaboration with others magnifies your impact and influence. By working together, you can tackle larger-scale projects, reach a broader audience, and create lasting change in your community. Collaboration emphasizes the interconnectedness of individuals and their ability to achieve more when united by a common purpose. It also teaches valuable skills such as teamwork, negotiation, and adaptability, essential in achieving successful outcomes in various endeavors. Through collaborative action, you contribute to a stronger sense of community and a shared commitment to creating a better world.

Seventh, act consistently. Act with persistence and consistency. Following Jesus' example of unwavering commitment, stay dedicated to your cause over time. Often, change takes time and repeated effort. Maintain your focus, even when challenges arise, and keep taking steps forward. Consistency can lead to transformation. You have been asked to lead a community health and fitness initiative aimed at promoting healthier lifestyles.

To act consistently in this context, you would:

1. **Set a Clear Vision.** Define a clear vision for the initiative's impact on the community's health and well-being. A well-defined goal constantly reminds you of the purpose behind your actions.
2. **Establish Routine Activities.** Develop a regular schedule of activities such as fitness classes, workshops, and nutritional education sessions. Consistency in providing opportunities for engagement encourages community members to participate regularly.
3. **Foster Accountability.** Encourage participants to set personal health goals and track their progress. Regular check-ins and updates create a sense of accountability, motivating individuals to stay consistent in their efforts.
4. **Overcome Challenges.** Challenges are inevitable, but acting consistently means finding ways to overcome them. Adapt your approach rather than giving up when faced with obstacles like low participation or external factors.
5. **Celebrate Small Wins.** Acknowledge and celebrate even small achievements along the way. Consistent progress,

no matter how incremental, contributes to the overall transformation you're striving for.

6. **Provide Continuous Support.** Offer ongoing support and resources to participants. Whether through online platforms, newsletters, or community gatherings, maintaining a connection keeps individuals engaged and committed.

7. **Embrace Long-Term Commitment.** Just as Jesus' teachings required long-term commitment, recognize that transformative change takes time. Continue to act consistently even when results might not be immediately evident.

In this example, acting consistently means persistently pursuing the betterment of the community's health over time. The parallel to Jesus' unwavering commitment emphasizes that lasting change rarely happens overnight. By consistently showing up, providing resources, and maintaining a supportive environment, you create an environment conducive to transformation.

Consistency in actions breeds trust and reliability. People are more likely to engage when they see that your commitment is unwavering. Through repeated efforts, you contribute to creating lasting habits and positive change in individuals' lives, ultimately leading to the transformation you envisioned. Acting consistently reflects your dedication to a cause and your understanding that real progress requires ongoing effort. This principle encourages a steadfast approach that can weather challenges, inspire others, and ultimately lead to meaningful and sustainable transformation. Impetuous, unthoughtful, and capricious acts can indeed have serious consequences that lead to harm or destruction. These actions are characterized by their lack of careful consideration, hasty decision-making, and disregard for potential outcomes. Let's explore how each of these traits can contribute to negative consequences:

1. **Impetuous Acts.** Impetuous actions are driven by a sudden surge of emotion or a desire for immediate gratification.

They often lack thoughtful analysis and consideration of potential risks. When someone acts impulsively, they might not fully understand the implications of their actions, leading to unintended harm. For instance, making impulsive financial decisions without considering long-term consequences could result in financial instability.

2. **Unthoughtful Acts.** Unthoughtful actions stem from a lack of careful planning and reflection. Acting without assessing the situation, gathering information, or considering alternatives can result in poor choices. Unthoughtful actions can be seen in situations where individuals jump to conclusions without considering all available facts, leading to misunderstandings and conflict.

3. **Capricious Acts.** Capricious actions are driven by whims and fancies rather than rational thought. People who act capriciously may change their minds frequently or act on a whim without regard for consistency or the impact on others. Such behavior can create confusion, instability, and harm, especially when reliable and consistent decision-making is necessary.

Consequences of these behaviors can include:

- **Physical Harm.** Impetuous actions might lead to accidents or injuries due to recklessness or lack of foresight. For instance, driving recklessly without considering road conditions can result in accidents.
- **Damaged Relationships.** Unthoughtful actions, exemplified by hurtful comments, can strain relationships and lead to misunderstandings or conflicts.
- **Financial Loss.** Capricious decisions in economic matters can result in wasteful spending, loss of investments, or debt accumulation.

- **Missed Opportunities.** Hasty decision-making can lead to missed opportunities, as impulsive choices might not align with long-term goals.
- **Negative Reputation.** Repeated impetuous, unthoughtful, or erratic behavior can damage one's reputation, portraying a lack of responsibility and maturity.

To avoid negative outcomes, people should cultivate a mindset of thoughtful consideration, emotional regulation, and responsible decision-making. Taking the time to assess situations, gather information, and consider the potential impact of actions can greatly reduce the likelihood of harm or destruction resulting from impulsive, unthoughtful, or inconsistent behavior.

# CHAPTER 16

# Act Now: Move Forward

$\infty\infty\infty\infty\infty\infty\infty\infty\infty\infty$

*"We must seize the present and empower forward momentum!"*

$\infty\infty\infty\infty\infty\infty\infty\infty\infty\infty$

"Move Forward" is a call to action, a reminder of the boundless opportunities that await when we embrace the present and take decisive steps toward our dreams. By acting now and embracing the journey ahead, we can unleash our full potential and create a life of fulfillment and growth.

## Embracing the Power of Now

Embracing the power of now is a practice that can change the way you experience life. It's about releasing the burdens of the past, relinquishing future anxieties, and immersing yourself in the present. By doing so, you can make more informed decisions, live with purpose, cultivate gratitude, and nurture better relationships. Ultimately, it's a path to living a more fulfilling and enriched life. The present moment is the only time we truly possess. Embracing the power of now means letting go of past regrets and future anxieties. By fully immersing ourselves in the present, we can make informed decisions and take deliberate actions that propel us towards our desired future.

Living in the present moment, or "embracing the power of no," is a transformative mindset and practice that offers a profound sense of liberation, clarity, and fulfillment. Here, we delve into the concept more deeply, understanding how it can empower us to lead a richer, more purposeful life. The present moment is unlike any other. It is a fleeting, irreplaceable instant where our entire existence unfolds. Realizing the impermanence and uniqueness of this moment is a fundamental step in embracing the power of now. The past is a collection of memories, and the future is an abstract concept, but the present is where you experience life in its raw, unfiltered form. Letting go of past regrets is one of the most liberating aspects of embracing the present. The past, with its mistakes, missed opportunities, and regrets, can weigh heavily on our minds. By shifting our focus from dwelling on past wrongs to learning from them, we free ourselves from the emotional baggage that might be holding us back.

Anxiety about the future is another burden we often carry. Worrying about what's to come can cloud our thinking and create stress. Embracing the power of now means accepting that the future is uncertain and beyond our control. Being fully present in the moment can reduce anxiety and allow you to approach the future with a clearer mind. One of the central practices in embracing the present moment is mindfulness. It involves paying deliberate attention to your experiences, thoughts, and emotions as they occur. Mindfulness allows you to observe without judgment, thus helping you detach from your thoughts and become a conscious witness to your life.

Being fully present enhances your ability to make informed decisions. You can assess it more accurately and respond thoughtfully by giving your full attention to the current situation. The noise of past regrets and future worries fades, allowing you to think more clearly. Embracing the power of now helps you align your actions with your values and goals. When you're present, you can set meaningful intentions for each moment and engage with life more purposefully. Your actions become more deliberate and, as a result, contribute to a more meaningful and fulfilling future.

Gratitude and contentment are natural byproducts of being present. When you're fully engaged in the moment, you can appreciate the beauty and wonder of life as it unfolds. Gratitude for the little things and contentment with what you have are powerful emotional states that emanate from present-moment awareness. Present-moment awareness also improves relationships. When you're fully engaged in conversations and interactions, you can listen more attentively, understand others deeply, and respond with empathy. It fosters stronger connections and healthier interactions with loved ones and colleagues.

## Setting Clear Intentions

Setting clear intentions is not a mere exercise in wishful thinking; it is the bedrock upon which dreams are transformed into reality. It's a practice that fosters clarity, ignites passion, and aligns your actions with your values. With well-defined intentions, you move through life purposefully, ensuring that each step you take is a meaningful stride toward the future you envision. It empowers you to navigate the complexities of life with confidence, direction, and a profound sense of purpose. It is defining, with precision and clarity, the path we wish to tread, the goals we aspire to achieve, and the values we hold dear. Setting clear intentions is akin to carving out a road in the wilderness of our desires and aspirations. It highlights the 'why' behind our actions, helping us articulate our purpose. This clarity of purpose, in turn, provides a strong foundation upon which we can build our dreams and ambitions.

Intentions serve as a bridge between our current state and our envisioned future. They help us identify specific, measurable, and achievable goals. By articulating what we want to accomplish, we set the stage for planning and execution. We move from vague, abstract desires to concrete, actionable objectives. Our intentions are often intertwined with our passions. When we define our intentions, we tap into the wellsprings of what truly excites and motivates us. Fueled by passion, these intentions become the driving force behind our actions. They keep us moving forward even in the face of challenges.

Your intentions reflect your core values. When you set clear intentions, you declare your allegiance to the principles and beliefs that define who you are. This alignment between intentions and values offers your journey a sense of authenticity and integrity. An intention is like a roadmap that lays out the route you wish to take in your journey through life. It provides a structured and organized approach to attaining your goals. This roadmap prevents you from wandering aimlessly and ensures that every step you take is in harmony with your ultimate destination.

Setting clear intentions bestows a profound sense of meaning and purpose to your actions. It infuses even the simplest of tasks with a deeper significance. Each step becomes a part of the grander narrative you've scripted for your life, creating a tapestry of fulfillment and satisfaction. Intentions offer you a lens through which to view your choices and decisions. They act as filters, allowing you to assess whether a particular option or action aligns with your vision for the future. This clarity facilitates more deliberate and informed decision-making.

## Comeback from the Setback

Life's journey is a dynamic interplay of joys and hardships. Cultivating resilience is a transformative practice that equips us to confront adversity with courage, learn from setbacks, and view obstacles as opportunities for growth. With a resilient mindset, we not only endure the challenges of life but also emerge from them stronger, wiser, and more capable of thriving amidst the complexity of our journey. Resilience is a beacon that guides us through the storm, reminding us that our potential for growth and success is boundless, even in the face of adversity.

Challenges are integral to the human experience, and no one is immune to them. Cultivating resilience is about acknowledging the existence of these challenges and accepting them as a natural aspect of life. Rather than fearing or avoiding them, we learn to confront them with courage. Resilience embodies the ability to rebound, to rise after falling. It is not the absence of failure or disappointment but the capacity to face them head-on and emerge stronger. The resilient mindset teaches us that adversity is not a roadblock but a steppingstone on our journey.

A resilient perspective transforms obstacles into opportunities. Instead of viewing challenges as insurmountable barriers, we see them as chances for growth and learning. Every hurdle becomes a path to self-improvement and personal development. Resilience encourages a growth-oriented approach to life. It reminds us that we possess the ability to adapt and evolve. When we encounter adversity, we learn from it, adjusting our strategies and acquiring new skills that make us more capable and versatile in the future. A resilient mindset is underpinned by optimism and a positive outlook. It teaches us to focus on the possibilities and solutions rather than dwelling on the problems. This constructive approach helps us navigate adversity and spreads positive energy to those around us. Resilience manifests as unwavering determination. When setbacks occur, they encourage us to persist and keep progressing despite obstacles. It reminds us that the journey is a marathon, not a sprint, and that success often requires patience and persistence.

Resilience doesn't exist in isolation; it thrives in the support of community and relationships. Cultivating resilience also means building a network of friends and allies who can encourage and assist during trying times. The cultivation of resilience is an ongoing process. It involves self-awareness, self-compassion, and a commitment to personal growth. It's a continuous journey of honing our ability to adapt, learn, and thrive in the face of adversity.

## Types of Actions To Take Now

Moving forward requires action. It's not enough to dream or plan; we must take inspired action to turn our aspirations into reality. Taking that first step, no matter how small, ignites the momentum that fuels our progress.

Initial actions are actions that involve taking the very first step toward a goal or aspiration. This can be a small, manageable action, but its significance lies in breaking inertia and getting the momentum started. It's the spark that ignites the journey. Sustaining actions are the ongoing efforts required to maintain progress and keep moving forward. They involve consistency, dedication, and commitment to the task at hand. These actions ensure that the momentum continues and doesn't fizzle out. Course-Correcting Actions: As we move forward, we may encounter unexpected challenges or changes in circumstances. Course-correcting actions involve making necessary adjustments to stay on the right path. These actions are flexible and adaptable, ensuring that we continue making progress even when faced with obstacles. Innovative actions involve creative problem-solving and thinking outside the box. When we encounter roadblocks or need to optimize our approach, innovative actions can lead to breakthroughs and new solutions. Collaborative Actions: Often, we can achieve more by working with others. Collaborative actions involve partnering with individuals or teams who can contribute their expertise, resources, or support to help us reach our goals more effectively and efficiently. Reflective actions involve taking time to assess progress, learn from experiences, and make informed decisions. These actions ensure that our forward movement is purposeful and aligned with our evolving understanding of the situation. Sometimes, bold actions are needed to overcome significant obstacles or seize major opportunities. These actions require courage and a willingness to step out of our comfort zones to achieve significant progress.

Progress is often the result of many small, incremental actions. These actions are manageable steps that, when consistently pursued, lead to significant change over time. Seeking guidance and mentorship from those with more experience can be an action. Learning from the wisdom and advice of others can significantly impact the quality and speed of our progress. Inspired actions are those that emerge from a deep sense of purpose, passion, or inner drive. They are driven by a sense of meaning and align with our core values, making them particularly powerful in propelling us toward our aspirations. Taking action is the bridge that connects our dreams and plans to our desired reality. The types of actions we choose depend on the specific circumstances, goals, and challenges we encounter. By consciously selecting and implementing the right types of actions, we can navigate the journey of turning aspirations into tangible achievements with clarity, determination, and a sense of purpose.

## Scenario: Surviving a Natural Disaster

In the aftermath of a powerful earthquake that struck their coastal town, a group of residents found themselves in a dire situation. Their homes were destroyed, essential resources were scarce, and they faced a multitude of challenges. They had to take a series of actions to survive and rebuild their lives. The initial shock of the earthquake had left them stunned and immobilized. But as reality set in, they realized they had to take the first step. A small group of individuals gathered in a central location, taking a headcount and assessing their immediate needs. This initial action was vital in breaking the inertia and instilling a sense of collective purpose. It marked the beginning of their journey to recovery.

The survivors had to sustain their efforts in the following days and weeks. They organized shifts for collecting and distributing available supplies, set up makeshift shelters, and established a rudimentary communication system. Consistency, dedication, and commitment to these tasks were essential to maintain progress and ensure that the community didn't lose hope or direction. During their recovery process, they faced numerous unforeseen challenges. Food supplies ran low, medical issues arose, and they had to adapt to a rapidly changing environment. In response, they continually made course corrections. For example, when their initial water source was contaminated, they adjusted their approach to purify the available water, preventing a potential health crisis. These course-correcting actions allowed them to adapt to new circumstances and stay on the right path toward recovery.

As they encountered roadblocks and limitations, the survivors needed to think innovatively. They found creative solutions to challenges. For instance, lacking construction materials, they repurposed debris from the earthquake to build temporary shelters and fortify damaged buildings. Innovative actions allowed them to optimize their resources and overcome constraints. Recognizing the strength in numbers, they decided to pool their knowledge and skills. They formed teams for specific tasks, such as medical aid, shelter construction, and food distribution. Neighbors who were doctors or engineers collaborated with others to provide critical expertise. Additionally, they reached out to nearby towns for support, forming collaborative networks to share resources and knowledge, which enabled them to rebuild more effectively.

Here, a group of people was forced to take a variety of actions following a natural disaster. By initiating, sustaining, course-correcting, innovating, and collaborating, they not only survived but also built a resilient community that was better equipped to handle future challenges. These actions served as the foundation for their recovery, illustrating the importance of adaptability, collective effort, and creative problem-solving in the face of adversity.

## Scenario: Launching a Community Sustainability Project

In a small town with a strong commitment to environmental sustainability, a group of dedicated residents decided to take on the ambitious goal of launching a community sustainability project. Their journey required them to embrace a series of actions, each of which played a crucial role in their progress. A group of enthusiastic individuals with a passion for sustainability came together to initiate the project. They convened a community meeting to gauge interest and involvement. This first step broke the inertia and laid the foundation for their journey toward sustainability. After the initial excitement waned, they took time to reflect on their progress. They assessed the challenges they faced, the resources available, and their evolving understanding of the situation. Reflective actions led them to adjust their strategy, set realistic goals, and ensure that their forward movement was purposeful. Launching a community sustainability project requires bold actions. They realized they needed to secure funding for renewable energy infrastructure. This involved reaching out to investors, local businesses, and government agencies and securing loans. It took courage to present their case and step out of their comfort zones to pursue these opportunities.

With the funding secured, they embarked on a series of incremental actions to implement their sustainability initiatives. They started with small-scale projects like community gardens, recycling programs, and energy-efficient lighting. When consistently pursued, these manageable steps led to significant change over time. Recognizing the value of expertise and guidance, they sought out mentors who had experience in sustainability initiatives. They connected with seasoned environmentalists who provided insights, advice, and strategies for success. These mentoring actions significantly impacted the quality and speed of their progress. A deep sense of purpose and passion for environmental conservation drove their commitment to sustainability. Inspired actions included organizing educational events, leading community clean-up initiatives, and promoting sustainable practices. These actions aligned with their core values and resonated with the entire community, making them particularly powerful in propelling their sustainability aspirations. As time passed, the community's commitment to sustainability grew stronger. Reflective actions allowed them to continually assess and improve their projects, and inspired actions-maintained passion and drive. Through a combination of bold, incremental, mentoring, and inspired actions, they transformed their town into a thriving hub of sustainability, demonstrating the power of collective effort, determination, and a shared sense of purpose in achieving significant progress toward their goal.

Moving forward often involves embracing change, leaving behind the comfort of the familiar to venture into the unknown. Change can be intimidating but also a gateway to growth and self-discovery. Embracing change with an open heart allows us to evolve and adapt to new opportunities. While moving forward requires us to focus on the present, we can also draw valuable lessons from the past. Reflecting on past experiences helps us identify patterns, learn from mistakes, and use that wisdom to inform our future decisions. Amidst the pursuit of our goals, it's essential to celebrate our progress. Acknowledging and appreciating each milestone, no matter how small, bolsters our motivation and reinforces our belief in our abilities.

"Move Forward" encapsulates the essence of living life with intention, purpose, and courage. By seizing the present moment and taking decisive action, we empower ourselves to overcome challenges and embrace change gracefully. Each step forward brings us closer to our dreams, propelling us toward a future of limitless possibilities. Remember, the journey of moving forward is not linear, and there will be moments of doubt and uncertainty. However, with unwavering determination, resilience, and a commitment to acting now, we have the power to create a life filled with growth, fulfillment, and boundless joy. The time is now; the opportunity is yours. Move forward and embrace the adventure that awaits!

# CHAPTER 17

# Act Now: Write and Publish a Book

## The Endless Odyssey of Knowledge: From Ecclesiastes to the Digital Age

"Ecclesiastes 12:12, King James Version states, 'And further, by these, my son, be admonished: of making many books there is no end, and much study is a weariness of the flesh.' These words, attributed to the wise King Solomon, reflect a timeless sentiment about the ceaseless pursuit of knowledge and the weariness it can bring. As we stand on the precipice of the digital age, where information is at our fingertips, one may wonder: Would Solomon be surprised at the exponential increase in knowledge and the relentless creation of books in our modern world?" Why is it important to write our own stories?

## The Ancient Scribe

In the time of Solomon, the creation of books was a laborious and meticulous process. Scrolls were painstakingly crafted by scribes, preserving the wisdom of the ages—the limited availability of written knowledge made each book a precious repository of information. The scribes of his time would have had access to Papyrus Scrolls. Papyri were common materials for scrolls in ancient Egypt and other parts of the Near East. It is made from the pith of the papyrus plant, which was abundant along the Nile River. The plant's stalk was cut into strips, laid out in a grid pattern, and then pressed to form sheets. These sheets were joined together to create long rolls that could be used for writing. Papyrus scrolls were widely used in the ancient Mediterranean and the Near East. Animal skins, particularly those of sheep or goats, were another material used for scrolls. The skin would be cleaned, treated, and stretched, providing a durable surface for writing. These leather scrolls were often more robust and could withstand various environmental conditions, making them suitable for long-term use.

In certain regions, especially Mesopotamia, clay tablets were a common medium for writing. Instead of scrolls, scribes would inscribe information on flat, rectangular pieces of wet clay using a stylus. The clay would then be baked or left to dry, preserving the inscriptions. While clay tablets were not flexible like scrolls, they were widely used for various administrative, legal, and literary purposes. In some cases, particularly for important or ceremonial inscriptions, metal (such as gold or bronze) might be used as a writing surface. Metal scrolls were less common due to the cost and difficulty of working with metals, but they did exist for specific purposes. Linen, a textile made from the fibers of the flax plant, could also be used for writing. Linen scrolls were not as prevalent as papyrus, but they were known to be used in certain regions.

## The Printing Press Revolution

In the 15th century, the invention of the printing press by Johannes Gutenberg marked a transformative moment in the history of book creation. With the advent of this groundbreaking technology, the written word could be mass-produced on a scale previously unimaginable. This innovation democratized access to knowledge by making printed books more affordable and widely available. The proliferation of printed books during the Renaissance marked a pivotal turning point, shattering the exclusivity of book creation held by the elite. Now, information could be disseminated to a broader audience, fostering a more widespread intellectual culture and paving the way for the democratization of education and ideas.

## The Information Explosion

In the 21st century, we are witnessing an unprecedented information explosion propelled by the digital revolution. The traditional confines of books, tethered to paper and ink, have expanded into a multitude of electronic formats. The advent of the internet has fundamentally transformed how knowledge is created and disseminated, transcending geographical boundaries. This digital landscape has empowered individuals globally to contribute actively to the constantly expanding reservoir of information. The accessibility and immediacy of digital platforms have revolutionized the way we engage with and share knowledge, fostering a dynamic and interconnected global intellectual community.

Blogs, articles, e-books, and multimedia content now coexist harmoniously with traditional printed books in the contemporary landscape of information dissemination. The evolution of technology has ushered in a diverse array of platforms, allowing for a rich tapestry of written, visual, and interactive content. Blogs and articles provide dynamic, real-time perspectives, while e-books offer a portable and convenient alternative to traditional print. The integration of multimedia elements, such as videos and interactive graphics, enhances the depth and engagement of content. This coexistence reflects a dynamic shift in how information is consumed, offering individuals a spectrum of choices to cater to their preferences and the evolving nature of modern communication.

## If Solomon Could See

Would Solomon be surprised by this explosion of knowledge? The biblical wisdom attributed to him suggests an understanding of the burdens of seeking knowledge. In an era where information is abundant but discerning truth can be challenging, Solomon might caution against the weariness of navigating the vast sea of data. On the one hand, Solomon could appreciate the accessibility of knowledge and the democratization of information. The idea that anyone with an internet connection can contribute to the collective wisdom of humanity might align with the spirit of sharing knowledge for the betterment of society.

The overwhelming volume of information available today might resonate with Solomon's warning about the weariness of the flesh. The constant influx of data and the challenge of distinguishing between valuable insights and noise could be seen as a modern manifestation of the age-old struggle for wisdom. As we reflect on the journey from Ecclesiastes 12:12 to the present day, it becomes clear that the creation of books and the pursuit of knowledge have evolved dramatically. Solomon's timeless wisdom encourages us to approach the vast sea of information with discernment, recognizing that, despite the endless creation of books, the essence of true wisdom remains a timeless pursuit—one that requires not only the accumulation of knowledge but also the ability to navigate its complexities with a discerning mind and a steadfast spirit.

Furthermore, there is a quest to erase the history of black people and supplant it with misinformation. "Erasure" refers to a deliberate effort to eliminate or obscure the history, experiences, achievements, and contributions of black people. It involves attempting to wipe out, marginalize, or dismiss the rich and diverse narrative of black individuals and communities from the collective memory of society. This erasure can manifest in various forms, including the omission of important events and figures from historical records, the distortion of facts, the underrepresentation of black voices in educational curricula, and the propagation of stereotypes and misinformation. The act of erasure seeks to create a distorted and often biased narrative that downplays the significance of black history and diminishes the impact of black individuals on society. This intentional distortion can perpetuate systemic inequalities and contribute to a skewed understanding of historical events and cultural contributions.

Black people must write to counter erasure. They must be involved in acknowledging, preserving, and promoting the authentic history of their race. It requires challenging and rectifying misrepresentations, ensuring diverse voices are heard, and promoting inclusivity in educational materials, media, and public discourse. Acknowledging the erasure of black history is a crucial step toward fostering a more accurate and comprehensive understanding of our shared human experience.

Writing and documenting black history empowers individuals and communities by providing a platform for their voices and experiences. It allows black people to tell their own stories, showcasing diverse perspectives that challenge stereotypes and counteract historical misrepresentations. By taking control of the narrative, black individuals contribute to a more accurate and nuanced understanding of their experiences, achievements, and struggles.

Black history is rich and diverse, encompassing a wealth of cultural traditions, languages, art, music, and more. Documenting this history ensures that cultural heritage is preserved for future generations. By recording and sharing stories, traditions, and achievements, black people can maintain a strong connection to their roots and pass down a sense of identity and pride to subsequent generations. This preservation is essential for fostering a deep appreciation of cultural contributions and promoting a strong sense of belonging.

Historically, the narratives surrounding black communities have often been shaped by external perspectives, perpetuating stereotypes and marginalization. Writing one's history allows one to challenge and correct these narratives. By offering alternative perspectives and highlighting the complexities of black history, individuals can contribute to a more inclusive and accurate portrayal of the past. Our history from our perspective, in turn, promotes a better understanding of the struggles and triumphs that have shaped black communities.

Writing and documenting black history contributes to developing a strong sense of identity and pride within the community. Recognizing and celebrating the achievements and contributions of black individuals throughout history fosters a positive self-image and reinforces a collective sense of pride. This empowerment is crucial for overcoming historical injustices, fostering resilience, and inspiring future generations to achieve their full potential.

Writing and documenting black history are essential for empowerment, cultural preservation, challenging stereotypes, and fostering a strong sense of identity and pride. By taking control of their narrative, black individuals contribute to a more accurate, inclusive, and empowering understanding of their history and heritage.

Esteemed prospective writers,

I'm truly delighted to stand before you today to share a narrative, a comprehensive blueprint for a remarkable journey that many of you may have dreamt of: the journey of writing and publishing your own book. I know you have a story to tell, and the world would be bereft of your insights if you did not put on paper what was in the deep recesses of your heart. You have a story to tell or a message burning within you. It is a message you believe the world needs to hear. Are you ready to weave your ideas into a compelling narrative that captivates readers and makes a difference in their lives? Here is a guide. You may outline your book the way I've outlined this speech.

## The Chapters of Your Book

## Chapter 1
## Define Your Purpose and Audience

First, imagine standing at the crossroads of creativity. Ask yourself, "Why do I want to write a book?" Is it to inspire, educate, entertain, or provoke thought? Identify your purpose, your guiding star. Then, think of the readers—the audience you aim to touch. Who are they? What do they seek? Understanding your purpose and audience will shape your writing.

Take a moment to explore your deepest motivations. Writing a book is a significant commitment, so understanding your purpose is essential. Your purpose is the fuel that will drive you through the long hours of writing, editing, and revision. Are you driven by a burning desire to inspire others with your experiences and wisdom? Is it your goal to educate, share knowledge, and enlighten your readers? Do you aspire to entertain and whisk your audience away to far-off lands and adventures? Or perhaps you aim to provoke thought, challenging conventional beliefs and stimulating critical thinking.

Your purpose may be a combination of these elements or something entirely unique. Whatever it may be, hold it close to your heart as it becomes the cornerstone upon which your book will be built. As you've unearthed your purpose, it's time to consider the other half of the equation: your audience. Your words are not just ink on paper; they are a bridge connecting your thoughts with the hearts and minds of your readers. Who are these readers you aim to touch? What are their desires, needs, and aspirations? Understanding your audience is like tuning your radio to the right frequency—only then can you effectively transmit your message. Take a moment to envision your ideal reader:

- What age group do they belong to?
- Are they seeking escapism in fiction or seeking solutions in non-fiction?
- What are their interests and passions?
- What challenges do they face, and how can your book address them?
- What emotions do you want your writing to evoke in them?

The more vividly you paint this picture of your target audience, the more effectively you can craft a narrative that resonates with them. Keep in mind that your readers are real people with real experiences, and your words have the power to impact their lives. The magic of storytelling happens at the intersection of your purpose and your audience's needs. Your purpose provides the direction and guiding star while understanding your audience's desires ensures that your message reaches its intended destination. Imagine your purpose as the lighthouse, casting its light across the dark sea of uncertainty. Your audience is the ship, seeking guidance and illumination. When these elements align, the journey becomes clear, and your writing takes on a profound sense of purpose.

## Chapter 2
## Choose a Genre and Topic

Next, embark on a quest to select your genre and topic. Your choices should align with your passions and your readers' preferences. Picture your book's genre as the canvas and your topic as the vibrant colors that will bring your story to life.

The choice of genre and topic is akin to selecting the colors and canvas for a masterpiece. Just as an artist carefully selects their tools, you, as a writer, must choose the literary elements that will best bring your story to life. Remember, a genre is a category or type of literature characterized by specific themes, styles, and conventions. It's the unique flavor that defines your narrative. Think of it as the brush you'll use to paint your literary canvas. Genres are as diverse as the colors on an artist's palette. There's fiction and non-fiction, and within these broad categories, there's a spectrum of sub-genres. Fiction can encompass romance, mystery, science fiction, fantasy, historical fiction, and many more. Non-fiction can range from biography, self-help, and memoir to science, history, and travel writing. The key to selecting the right genre is to consider your passions and interests. What excites you? What kind of stories or subjects do you enjoy exploring? Your enthusiasm for your chosen genre will infuse your writing with authenticity and energy.

Once you've chosen your literary palette (genre), it's time to focus on the subject matter (topic). Genre guides where you decide what story you want to tell, and what message you want to convey, or what knowledge you want to share. Your topic is the vibrant color that will define your narrative. Think of your topic as the heart of your story. It's what makes your book unique, what sets it apart from others in the same genre. When selecting a topic, consider the following:

- Personal Passion: What subject matter ignites your passion? Writing about something you love will make the creative process more enjoyable and authentic.
- Audience Relevance: Reflect on your audience. What topics are they interested in? How can your chosen topic resonate with them?
- Uniqueness: What fresh perspective or unique angle can you bring to your chosen genre? How can you differentiate your story or content from others in the same category?

- Research and Knowledge: Does your chosen topic require research or expertise? Are you willing to invest the time and effort needed to become an authority in that subject?
- Emotional Connection: Consider how your chosen topic can evoke emotions in your readers. Will it inspire, intrigue, or challenge them?

Remember that your choice of topic can significantly influence the success and impact of your book. The subject matter will engage your readers and keep them turning the pages. The true magic of storytelling happens when your chosen genre and topic align seamlessly. It's when your passion for a particular genre intersects with your enthusiasm for a specific subject matter, creating a powerful synergy.

# Chapter 3
# Research and Planning

You must prepare to write. Research extensively gathers knowledge and ideas. Craft an outline, your treasure map, to navigate the intricate terrain of your story. Set goals and deadlines to guide your way. Think of this chapter as your essential survival guide, providing you with the tools to navigate the intricate terrain of your story. To unveil the hidden treasures of your story and translate them into your writing, you must begin with extensive research. Knowledge is your compass in this forest, guiding you toward authenticity and depth in your narrative.

Dive into the heart of your chosen topic. Immerse yourself in books, articles, documentaries, and expert interviews. The more you know, the richer your story will become. Research is paramount if your story is set in a specific time or place. Understand the nuances of that setting, its history, culture, and geography. Your readers should feel transported to this world. Characters are the lifeblood of your story. Get to know them intimately through research. Their backgrounds, motivations, and experiences should be well-drawn and believable. If your story involves technical or specialized knowledge (e.g., medical procedures, legal processes, scientific concepts), ensure your facts are accurate. Mistakes can break the reader's immersion.

Once you've gathered the knowledge and ideas from your research, it's time to craft your literary treasure map—an outline. Just as explorers plot their course before embarking on an adventure, you'll create a roadmap for your narrative. This outline will serve as your guiding star through the twists and turns of your story. Divide your story into chapters and scenes. Outline the key events, character developments, and emotional arcs that will occur in each. Decide on the overall structure of your book. Will it follow a linear timeline or employ non-linear storytelling techniques? Understanding the structure will help you maintain a cohesive narrative. Map out the growth and transformation of your characters. Where do they start, and where will they end up? How will their experiences shape them? Identify the overarching theme or message of your story. What do you want readers to take away from your book? Ensure that each element in your outline aligns with this theme.

Consider setting goals and deadlines as your compass. Goals provide you with direction, and deadlines instill discipline and urgency. Determine how many words you aim to write each day or week. Consistency is key to making progress—set milestones for completing sections of your outline. Develop a timeline for your entire project, including research, writing, editing, and publishing. Having a clear schedule will help you stay organized and on track. Share your goals and deadlines with a writing group, friend, or mentor who can hold you accountable and offer support.

# Chapter 4
## Develop Your Writing Routine

Creating a regular writing routine is your compass. Establish a schedule that fits your life's ebb and flow. Set word count targets for your daily or weekly writing sessions. Commitment to this routine is the key to progress. Just as a dedicated gardener tends to their plants with care, nurturing them with attention and consistency, so must you cultivate your writing practice. This chapter will explore the essential steps to develop a writing routine that will guide you through the vast landscape of your literary journey.

A writing routine is not a set of restrictive rules; it is a powerful ally that provides structure and direction to your creative process. Your compass is always pointing you toward your destination—your completed manuscript. Consider your daily life, responsibilities, and commitments. Your routine should seamlessly integrate with your lifestyle. Find a time and space where you can write consistently. Set clear, achievable goals for your writing sessions. The routine could be a daily word count target or a weekly writing time commitment. Goals provide motivation and a sense of accomplishment. Create a dedicated writing space where you feel comfortable and inspired. Whether it's a cozy nook in your home, a cafe with the perfect ambiance, or a peaceful park bench, your writing environment should encourage focus and creativity.

Writing is not just a skill; it's practice. Cultivate a daily ritual that signals to your brain that it's time to create. Designate a specific time of day for your writing. Consistency is key, whether it's early in the morning, during lunch breaks, or late at night. Identify common distractions and minimize them during your writing time. Turn off notifications, silence your phone, and create a dedicated writing playlist or ambient sounds if they help you concentrate. Consider starting your writing sessions with warm-up exercises. These can include journaling, free writing, or even revisiting and editing the previous day's work. This eases you into the creative flow. Share your goals and progress with a writing buddy or join a writing group. Accountability can help you stay committed to your routine.

Commitment to your writing routine is the key to progress. Just as consistent drops of water can carve a path through solid rock, your daily or weekly writing sessions will accumulate into a substantial body of work, even if they seem small. Acknowledge and celebrate your achievements, no matter how modest. Completing your daily word count or sticking to your schedule are victories worth commemorating.

There will be days when life gets in the way or writer's block strikes. Forgive yourself for missed sessions, and remember that setbacks are a natural part of the journey. Periodically reassess your routine. If you find that it's not working, be flexible enough to make the necessary adjustments. Developing a writing routine is not a rigid endeavor but a dynamic and evolving process. It's a practice that, over time, will nurture and cultivate your creative spirit. By aligning your routine with your life, setting achievable goals, and maintaining consistency, you'll harness the power to bring your literary vision to life. Just as a well-tended garden flourishes over time, so too will your writing blossom and thrive with dedication to your routine.

# Chapter 5
# Start Writing

As you begin to write, remember that the first draft is your rough sketch—a canvas filled with bold strokes of ideas. Don't be disheartened by its imperfections; embrace the process. It's crucial to recognize that the initial draft is like a rough sketch on a canvas, where ideas flow freely and unencumbered. In this phase, perfection is not the goal; rather, it's the raw expression of your creativity, a foundation upon which your literary masterpiece will be built. Embrace the process with open arms, understanding that imperfections are not failures but stepping stones towards excellence. Each word you write is a brushstroke, each sentence a layer of color, slowly bringing your vision to life. As you pour your thoughts onto the page, allow yourself the freedom to explore, to make mistakes, and to uncover the hidden gems that often lurk beneath the surface. Remember, the most important thing is to capture your story's essence, breathe life into your characters, and create a world that draws readers in. So, as you embark on this creative voyage, relinquish the fear of imperfection and trust in the power of your words to evolve and transform, for it is in this journey of discovery that your literary masterpiece will truly take shape.

## Chapter 6
## Editing and Revision

Grant your manuscript the gift of time to breathe, letting it age like a fine wine before you step into the role of the discerning editor. As you pore over your creation, seek out errors with a discerning eye, hunt down the haze that obscures clarity, and trace the threads of inconsistency to weave a seamless tapestry. But the journey doesn't stop there; sharing your work with readers or critique partners whose discerning eyes will provide fresh perspectives, offering insights and guidance that illuminate your path, is essential. And, when the time is right, consider enlisting the services of a professional editor, your literary mentor, whose seasoned hands will chisel and refine your narrative, addressing structural issues and ensuring your opus adheres to the conventions of your chosen genre. Editing and revision are not mere polishing; the sculptor's tools shape your literary gem, revealing its true brilliance for all to admire.

# Chapter 7
# Proofreading

In the grand scheme of crafting a book, proofreading is the crescendo, the moment when every note must harmonize flawlessly. It is the stage where your manuscript undergoes meticulous scrutiny, each word meticulously examined to ensure its immaculate presentation. The final polish is a formality and a pivotal act in your creative journey. As you embark on this endeavor, embrace the role of the vigilant guardian, poised to uncover any lurking errors that threaten the clarity of your narrative. Here, grammar, that steadfast sentinel of precision, must be upheld, where punctuation, the conductor of cadence, must be orchestrated with finesse, and where formatting, the frame of your masterpiece, must be flawless. Leave no stone unturned, for even the tiniest oversight can disrupt the reader's immersion and cast shadows upon your storytelling prowess. Proofreading, in essence, is the crowning jewel of your craftsmanship, the last act of devotion to your literary creation, and the assurance that your words will shine brightly, undiminished by the veil of errors. It is the culmination of perfection, the final touch that transforms your manuscript into a work of art, ready to captivate and inspire its audience. The final polish is crucial. Scrutinize every word for grammar, punctuation, and formatting errors. Leave no stone unturned.

# Chapter 8
# Cover Design

Your book's cover is its first impression. Invest in a captivating and professional design that reflects your story's essence. The design is the initial point of connection between the author's literary world and potential readers. The cover can be described as the first ambassador, offering readers a glimpse of the treasures hidden within the book's pages. There is a powerful need to invest in a captivating and professional cover that aligns with the essence of the story. It underscores the significance of first impressions, highlighting that readers do judge books by their covers. So, select imagery, fonts, colors, and layout that harmonize with the book's themes and mood, and invest in professionalism by working with a skilled cover designer who can create a marketable and visually appealing product.

## Chapter 9
## Formatting

Formatting is the bridge between your creative vision and the reader's experience. Consider seeking assistance from professionals or specialized software tailored to your publishing platform's requirements. Formatting can be a complex and technical process involving elements such as page layout, fonts, margins, and spacing, and it's vital that your manuscript meets the exact specifications of your chosen publishing platform. Many authors find it beneficial to enlist the expertise of a professional formatter or utilize formatting software, both of which can ensure that your book is presented to the world in a polished and visually pleasing manner. Don't underestimate the significance of this step; a well-formatted book not only enhances readability but also conveys professionalism and dedication to your craft, leaving a lasting impression on your readers. Format your manuscript according to the requirements of your chosen publishing platform. Ensure it's ready to be presented to the world.

## Chapter 10
## ISBN and Copyright and Publishing

It is important to safeguard your literary work. Obtaining an ISBN (International Standard Book Number) is like bestowing a unique identity upon your book, facilitating its discovery and access to the vast world of literature. Moreover, consider that copyright protection is akin to erecting a fortress around your creative endeavor, ensuring that your intellectual property remains exclusively yours. With these measures in place, you can make the crucial decision presented in the subsequent section: choosing your publishing path. Here, you stand at the crossroads, contemplating whether to seek validation from traditional publishers, chart your own course through self-publishing, or navigate a hybrid path combining both worlds' strengths. This choice will shape your masterpiece and impact how your literary work reaches the world. Obtain an ISBN for your book to mark its identity. Consider copyrighting your work to protect your creative endeavor.

## Chapter 11
## Distribution, Marketing, and Promotion

Now, you must bring your literary creation to readers' eager hands and hearts. The first decision at hand is how and where to distribute your book, considering the versatile formats of eBook, print, or audiobook. This choice is influenced by your goals and target audience, ensuring that your work reaches them in the most accessible and appealing way possible. But distribution is only the beginning. It would help if you also crafted a comprehensive marketing plan to illuminate your literary star. Building a robust online presence is your beacon, a virtual lighthouse guiding readers to your work. Engaging with book reviewers and influencers serves as the wind in your sails, propelling your book into the public eye. And finally, planning a memorable book launch event is the grand stage where your literary star takes its center. Let your book shine! Showcasing it to the world through strategic distribution, creative marketing, and the unwavering belief that your words are meant to be shared and celebrated is paramount. Determine where and how you want to distribute your book—eBook, print, or audiobook. Select distribution channels that suit your goals. Craft a marketing plan to engage your readers. Build your online presence, leverage book reviewers, and plan a memorable book launch event. Your book is your star; let the world see it shine.

## Chapter 12
## Launch Your Book, Gather Feedback, Reflect, and Plan

Set a grand launch date, a day when your creation will spread its wings. Execute your marketing plan, watch your book take flight, and adapt your strategy based on sales and reviews. The journey doesn't end with the book launch; it continues as you engage with readers, attend book signings, and participate in author events.

Listen to your readers. Collect their feedback and reviews to improve your future work. Consider their preferences for your next literary adventure. Lastly, reflect on this incredible journey. Take stock of what worked and what didn't. Consider your next story, your next adventure in the world of words. Embrace this narrative as your own. The path may be winding, filled with challenges and triumphs, but every step is a revelation, every word a victory. Writing and publishing a book is not just about penning words; it's about sharing your soul with the world, leaving a mark that endures through time.

## The Charge

Now, go forth and embark on your own literary odyssey, for within you lies a story waiting to be told—a story that could change lives and inspire generations to come. With every word you write, you breathe life into worlds unknown, characters unimagined, and ideas that can shape the future. This is your moment, your opportunity to craft stories that resonate, captivate, and endure. As you sail the seas of creativity, let passion be your compass and perseverance your anchor. May your writing journey be filled with endless creativity and boundless success, for the world eagerly awaits the magic that only you can conjure with your words. So, my fellow storytellers, let your stories soar, and may your literary legacy shine as a beacon for all who dare to dream and write. The world is yours for the taking—go and make it unforgettable!

## Summary of Pitfalls and Challenges

Aspiring authors should seek support from writing communities, attend writing workshops, and thoroughly research the publishing process to avoid the pitfalls of writing and publishing a book. They must be persistent, adaptable, and realistic about the challenges of writing and publishing a book. One of the biggest pitfalls is not having a clear plan for your book. Without a well-defined outline and goals, you may end up with a disorganized manuscript or lose motivation. Lack of planning is a fundamental pitfall that can derail the entire process of writing and publishing a book. It is akin to a cross-country journey without a map or destination. Without a clear roadmap in the form of a well-defined outline and writing goals, authors risk stumbling through an arduous and meandering creative process, potentially culminating in a disorganized manuscript, wavering motivation, and even abandoning their literary aspirations. Such a lack of foresight not only hampers the efficient progress of the project but also undermines the author's ability to craft a cohesive narrative, effectively convey their message, and navigate the intricate pathways of the publishing industry, ultimately jeopardizing the realization of their literary ambitions.

Many writers struggle with procrastination. It's important to set regular writing goals and stick to a schedule to avoid long periods of inactivity. Many writers grapple with the formidable adversary of procrastination, a persistent obstacle that can disrupt the creative process and impede progress. To combat this formidable foe, writers must adhere to a disciplined regimen, with regular writing goals and a steadfast commitment to a schedule. By setting these objectives and diligently sticking to them, authors can sidestep the pitfalls of prolonged inactivity, ensuring that their creative energies remain consistently engaged and that the inertia of procrastination does not compromise their writing aspirations. A writer's block can be frustrating and can stall your progress. Finding strategies to overcome it is essential, such as writing prompts or taking short breaks. Many writers grapple with the formidable adversary of procrastination, a persistent obstacle that can disrupt the creative process and impede progress. To combat this formidable foe, writers must adhere to a disciplined regimen, with regular writing goals and a steadfast commitment to a schedule. By setting these objectives and diligently sticking to them, authors can sidestep the pitfalls of prolonged inactivity, ensuring that their creative energies remain consistently engaged and that the inertia of procrastination does not compromise their writing aspirations. Authors often face self-doubt and imposter syndrome. Overcoming these feelings and gaining confidence in your work is crucial. Authors frequently grapple with self-doubt and imposter syndrome, a nagging sense that their writing lacks merit or doesn't belong in the literary world. This internal struggle can be paralyzing, hindering their creative process and preventing them from sharing their unique voices.

Nevertheless, surmounting these daunting emotions is paramount. Building confidence in one's work involves acknowledging that self-doubt is a standard part of the creative journey, seeking constructive feedback, honing writing skills through practice, and reminding oneself that even celebrated authors once wrestled with similar doubts. Ultimately, through perseverance and self-belief, authors can conquer imposter syndrome and continue to craft meaningful stories that resonate with readers.

Editing is a critical part of the writing process, and reviewing and revising your work objectively can be challenging. Consider hiring a professional editor to help with this stage. There are many unscrupulous individuals and companies in the publishing industry. Authors should be cautious when choosing publishing services and research thoroughly to avoid scams. Even if you've written a great book, it won't sell without effective marketing and promotion. Many authors struggle with this aspect and may need to invest time and resources into building an audience. Self-publishing can be expensive, and traditional publishing may not always be financially rewarding, especially for new authors. It's essential to have realistic expectations about the financial aspects of publishing.

Traditional publishing often involves rejection from agents and publishers. It can be disheartening, but persistence is vital. Many famous authors faced numerous rejections before finding success. Not everyone will love your book; negative reviews are part of the process. Learning to handle criticism and not take it personally is vital for an author's mental well-being. Many authors have other responsibilities, such as full-time jobs or family obligations. Finding a balance between writing and these responsibilities can be challenging. Authors must be aware of copyright laws and potential legal issues related to their work, mainly if they include copyrighted material or write about sensitive topics. Finally, writing a book can be emotionally and mentally draining. It's essential to recognize the signs of burnout and take breaks when needed to avoid exhaustion.

# CHAPTER 18

# Act Now: You Belong at the Table

## The Case of Mephibosheth

Some stories resonate across generations, tales of profound redemption and unwavering kindness that remind us of the eternal truth: that every soul, regardless of circumstance, deserves a place of honor. In the book of 2 Samuel, we encounter such a narrative—the story of Mephibosheth, a man whose life was irrevocably altered by accident but whose destiny was forever changed by the benevolence of a king.

A fateful accident occurred. Mephibosheth's journey begins in the shadow of adversity. As a child, he faced a crippling accident, a fall that left him physically impaired. The innocence of youth should have shielded him from such misfortune, but the world can be cruel, and accidents can happen. Mephibosheth's story teaches us that sometimes, life gives us unexpected blows, leaving us in a place of silence—Lo-debar—where our voices seem stifled, and our dreams appear distant. But amidst the turmoil of Mephibosheth's life, there arose a king who would become the embodiment of God's boundless grace. King David, driven not by obligation but by a heart of compassion, sought to show kindness to the house of Saul for the sake of his beloved friend, Jonathan. David's inquiry— "Is there still anyone left of the house of Saul, that I may show him kindness for

Jonathan's sake?"—serves as a beacon of hope for all who have felt marginalized, forgotten, or abandoned.

In Lo-debar, a place of silence, Mephibosheth's existence was marked by obscurity, fear, and a sense of unworthiness. But King David's pursuit of him heralded a transformation that echoes through the ages. Mephibosheth, residing in the house of Machir, had been estranged from his rightful inheritance. Yet, in the act of divine restoration, David declared, "I will restore to you all the land of Saul your father, and you shall eat at my table always." Mephibosheth's response was a humbling acknowledgment of his newfound destiny: "What is your servant that you should show regard for a dead dog such as I?" He recognized the sheer grace and mercy of his inclusion in the king's household, a place where he would dine at the royal table, side by side with the king's sons.

Your place is at the table. Mephibosheth's story is a parable for us all—a testament to the transformative power of divine love and compassion. Regardless of the accidents, injustices, or circumstances that have silenced our voices or kept us in the shadows, God's message is clear: You belong at the table. In Mephibosheth's redemption, we find our own. Like him, we are royalty in the eyes of our heavenly Father, deserving of a place of honor, grace, and abundance. Our accidents, pasts, and struggles do not define us; they are why we are welcomed with open arms. We are not dead dogs; we are cherished children of the King.

So, let it be known: "I am royalty, and I belong at the table." With this declaration, we embrace the legacy of Mephibosheth, living out our destinies as heirs to the boundless love and generosity of our King.

## Aeneas

In the book of Acts, we encounter a narrative pointing to divine promise and redemption—a story of Aeneas, who found himself bound by the chains of paralysis. Aeneas's journey from affliction to miraculous healing is a powerful testimony to God's unwavering love and His capacity to breathe new life into the most desperate circumstances. Aeneas' life was deactivated. Once vibrant and full of life, Aeneas found himself in a state of deactivation and decommission due to a debilitating illness. For eight long years, he lay bedridden, his condition rendering him powerless and immobile. The world had witnessed his fall, heard the judgments and criticisms of those around him, and witnessed the ugly spectacle of his predicament. His paralysis had become a symbol of despair and hopelessness.

A glimmer of divine hope emerged amid Aeneas's affliction. Peter, a disciple of Jesus, arrived in Lydda, and in an act of faith, he approached Aeneas. With words that carried the authority of heaven, Peter declared, "Jesus Christ heals you. Get up and roll up your mat." In that moment, the power of God surged through Aeneas's body, and he rose to his feet—an embodiment of faith, healing, and restoration. Aeneas's miraculous healing was a personal triumph and a catalyst for community transformation. All those who witnessed this incredible miracle, from Lydda to Sharon, turned to the Lord. His testimony became a beacon of hope, drawing others to the saving grace of Jesus Christ.

In Aeneas's story, we discover God's definitive word for all of us: God sees, and he knows. God sees the ugliness of our conditions, whether physical, emotional, or spiritual. He knows when we have fallen and hears the voices of criticism and judgment. He is acutely aware of our plight, struggles, and paralysis. However, in the depth of our affliction, God has ordained a date for our deliverance. He sees the loss but is the God of restoration and new beginnings. Just as God called Aeneas by name, He knows each one of us intimately. He sees us in our most vulnerable moments and understands the depth of our suffering. The number eight often symbolizes new beginnings in the Bible, and God declares that our eight days of new beginnings have arrived. It's a proclamation of renewal, transformation, and the dawn of a fresh chapter in our lives. So, let it be known: Your paralysis, your affliction, and your brokenness do not define you. God has seen your condition, knows your name, and has set a date for your deliverance. Your eight days of new beginnings are here, ushering in a season of healing, restoration, and transformation, not only for you but for all who witness His miraculous work in your life.

# CHAPTER 19

# Act Now: Get Deliverance from the Paralysis of Life

People often find themselves entangled in the web of paralysis—a state of limitation, restriction, and immobility that can manifest in various aspects of our lives. Whether physical, emotional, financial, or spiritual, paralysis can be debilitating, keeping us from realizing our true potential. But the story of Aeneas, as told in Acts 9:32–35, reveals that with faith and action, we can break free from the grip of paralysis and step into a life of purpose, abundance, and healing.

Aeneas moved from paralysis to liberation. Aeneas, a man whose name means "the praised one," was trapped in a paralyzing condition. He had been bedridden for eight years, unable to fully engage in life due to physical paralysis. His story mirrors the different forms of paralysis that afflict many today. However, Aeneas's encounter with Peter illustrates that there is a way out of the darkness of immobilization, inertia, and complacency.

People should liberate themselves from self-paralysis. Many people inadvertently paralyze themselves with their own words. They speak words of self-doubt, self-criticism, and negativity. When asked to describe himself, Aeneas referred to himself as a "dead dog." But, as his name suggests, he was meant to "exterminate the shame." In our lives, we must choose to speak words of blessing, affirmation, and faith. Don't let your words be a weapon of self-paralysis; use them to propel yourself forward. Words have immense power. Just as Peter used his words to lift Aeneas out of his state of limitation, we must use our words to bless, encourage, and empower others. Bless and do not curse; commend and do not offend; compliment and do not criticize. Be a source of liberation, not paralysis, for those around you.

We must liberate ourselves from financial paralysis. In Aeneas's case, physical paralysis often comes with financial paralysis. His inability to work due to his condition left him financially crippled. We, too, must take proactive steps to manage our finances wisely, including giving to the kingdom, creating budgets, and investing wisely. Financial liberation is an essential aspect of breaking free from paralysis.

We must liberate ourselves from hidden paralysis. Hidden paralysis can lurk beneath the surface, manifesting as self-doubt, secrets, unresolved trauma, regrets, or unfulfilled desires. It's crucial to address these hidden issues, seek therapy if needed, and confront the past to move forward in freedom. We must liberate ourselves from spiritual paralysis. Spiritual paralysis can manifest through demonic influence, oppressing individuals in various ways. We must discern the difference between the works of the flesh and the influence of demons. Seeking deliverance from spiritual oppression can be a vital step toward spiritual liberation. The story of Aeneas teaches us that we can choose to act now, to speak words of faith and blessing, and to confront the various forms of paralysis that may afflict us. Just as Aeneas rose from his mat at the command of Peter, we, too, can break free from our limitations and walk into a life filled with purpose, abundance, and healing. Act now, for your days of new beginnings have arrived.

We often find ourselves ensnared by emotional and social paralysis, two distinct but interconnected webs that can stifle our potential and hinder our well-being. Just as Aeneas faced physical paralysis, we, too, may confront emotional and social paralysis that restricts our growth and stifles our joy. This chapter explores the importance of acting now to liberate ourselves from these burdensome chains. Much like a male lion, whose life expectancy is shortened by the relentless grip of anger, we often find ourselves ensnared by negative emotions that gnaw at our well-being. The lion roars in anger, manufacturing its own diseases and hastening its own demise. Similarly, unresolved anger, sadness, fear, anxiety, guilt, shame, jealousy, envy, and bitterness can manifest as emotional paralysis, slowly corroding our inner vitality. It is imperative that we act now to protect ourselves from the ravages of these emotions. In some instances, physical ailments may be rooted in emotional turmoil. Doctors may struggle to diagnose illnesses, not realizing that the root cause lies in suppressed emotions. We must recognize that emotional well-being is intrinsically connected to physical health. To be liberated from emotional paralysis, we must confront and release these emotions, allowing ourselves to heal from within. Emotional paralysis can also stem from the weight of past experiences, such as embarrassment, bitterness, grief, disappointment, or regret. These burdens can hinder our emotional freedom and manifest as various ailments if left unaddressed. It is time to" act now" and lay aside these weights that hold us back, freeing ourselves from emotional paralysis.

Social paralysis is a unique affliction where individuals experience extreme shyness, social anxiety, or a fear of social interactions. This fear limits their ability to connect with others and participate in social activities. Some may attempt to hide their social paralysis under the guise of introversion, but it is essential to acknowledge and address this issue. We are meant to connect, not isolate. Just as Mephibosheth found himself in Lo-debar, a place of silence and isolation, some of us have been marginalized by our own fears and insecurities. The remedy is to congregate, not isolate. To break free from social paralysis, we must act now by stepping out of our comfort zones and embracing the beauty of human connection.

Two formidable adversaries can grip us with paralyzing force: unbelief and unforgiveness. These twin afflictions, while distinct, share the power to restrict our lives and hinder our growth. This chapter explores the profound impact of unbelief and unforgiveness and the liberation that awaits those who choose to act now. Aeneas, in the face of physical paralysis, exhibited remarkable faith. Upon hearing Peter's words, he wasted no time in rolling up his mat and receiving his deliverance. His unwavering belief in the power of Christ's healing touched the core of his being, and he embraced his transformation without hesitation. King David's life serves as a powerful example of forgiveness in the face of wrongdoing. Despite the animosity of King Saul, who sought to kill him, David displayed immense forgiveness and compassion. He extended this forgiveness by reaching out to help one of Saul's descendants, Mephibosheth, inviting him back to the table of fellowship.

The grip of paralysis, whether driven by unbelief or unforgiveness, is not absolute. Its power is confined because a counterforce known as resurrection exists. In our text, Aeneas was paralyzed for eight long years, but something profound occurred in the eighth year of his affliction. The number eight symbolizes resurrection, new birth, growth, and deliverance from bondage. Jesus Himself rose from the dead on the eighth day, signifying the triumph over that which binds us. In all its forms, paralysis is a conquerable foe. Just as Aeneas was liberated from his physical paralysis through faith, we, too, can break free from the chains of unbelief and unforgiveness. The power of paralysis is limited, and it can be shattered by the resurrection of faith, forgiveness, and new beginnings. Act now, for your deliverance is closer than you think.

# CHAPTER 20

# Act Now: Occupy Until I Come!

∞∞∞∞∞∞∞∞∞∞∞∞∞∞∞

*Some are so heavenly-minded that they are of no earthly good!*

∞∞∞∞∞∞∞∞∞∞∞∞∞∞∞

"But about that day or hour, no one knows, not even the angels in heaven, nor the Son, but only the Father." (Matthew 24:36), yet there have been numerous predictions and claims regarding the return of Christ or the end of the world that did not come to pass. Harold Camping, a Christian radio host, predicted the end of the world on May 21, 2011, and later revised it to October 21, 2011. William Miller and his followers believed that Christ would return on October 22, 1844, but the event became known as the Great Disappointment when it did not happen. The Jehovah's Witnesses have had multiple predictions. The Watch Tower Society, which publishes literature for Jehovah's Witnesses, made several predictions about the end of the world, including 1914, 1925, and 1975. Edgar C. Whisenant, a former NASA engineer, predicted the return of Christ on several occasions in the 1980s and 1990s. Televangelist Pat Robertson predicted that the world would end in 1982. Leland Jensen claimed that the end times would occur in the 1980s and that the city of Fergus Falls, Minnesota, was the biblical city of refuge. The Heaven's Gate cult believed that the Hale-Bopp comet signaled the arrival of a spacecraft that would take them to a higher plane of existence. They committed mass suicide in 1997.

Millions believe that Jesus will return and that the world will end in 2000. They believed that the Y2K computer bug would cause widespread chaos and the end of the world when the year 2000 began. Some interpreted the end of the Mayan Long Count calendar on December 21, 2012, as a prediction of the end of the world. Herbert W. Armstrong, founder of the Worldwide Church of God, made several predictions about the return of Christ, including 1936, 1972, and 1975. The Heaven's Gate cult leader, Marshall Applewhite, predicted that the group would ascend to a higher level via a spacecraft behind the Hale-Bopp comet. The leader of the Aum Shinrikyo cult in Japan predicted an apocalyptic event in 1997, which included a deadly sarin gas attack on the Tokyo subway. Ronald Weinland, a self-proclaimed prophet, made predictions about the return of Christ and the end of the world for 2008, 2011, and other dates. Evangelical Pastor John Hagee suggested that the "blood moon" tetrad of 2014–2015 could signify the end times. Bulgarian mystic Baba Vanga made various predictions, including a supposed end of the world in the late 1990s and another in 2020. The Universal Church and Triumphant leader, Elizabeth Clare Prophet, made several predictions about nuclear Armageddon and the apocalypse. Karl J. Smith, a self-proclaimed prophet, predicted the end of the world in 1989. Joachim of Fiore, a medieval theologian, made several predictions about the end of times, including one for the year 1260. Dorothy Martin claimed that she received messages from extraterrestrials predicting a worldwide flood on December 21, 1954. Actress Shirley MacLaine believed in the imminent return of Christ in the late 1980s. David Berg, leader of the Children of God cult, predicted the end of the world in 1973. The founder of the Jehovah's Witnesses, Charles Taze Russell, made several predictions about the end times, including one for 1914. The leader of the Unification Church, Sun Myung Moon, made predictions about the end of the world in 1988 and other dates. Romanian pastor Richard Wurmbrand predicted that Christ would return in 1979. Numerous smaller cults and groups throughout history have made predictions about the end of the world, often resulting in disappointment or tragedy for their followers.

## Last Days and the End Times

The Olivet Discourse in Matthew 24, Mark 13, and Luke 21 is a significant passage in Christian eschatology (the study of end times. These three chapters share common themes and teachings regarding the end times and the Second Coming of Christ; they also have some distinct differences in wording and emphasis. However, in each of the passages, Jesus provides a list of signs that will precede the end times. These signs include wars, famines, earthquakes, and the rise of false prophets and false messiahs. Jesus warns his followers in all three accounts that they will face persecution and tribulation for their faith. He encourages them to endure and remain faithful despite these challenges. All three passages mention the "abomination of desolation" as a significant sign, and Jesus advises those in Judea to flee when they see this sign. This shared detail highlights its importance in eschatological teachings. In all three accounts, Jesus describes the dramatic and visible return of the Son of Man (referring to himself) with power and glory. This event is central to the teaching about the end times. Jesus emphasizes the need for watchfulness and preparedness in all three passages. He compares his return to a thief coming in the night, underscoring the importance of being spiritually vigilant.

## Significant Events

Various significant events and crises have led some individuals and groups to believe that they were witnessing signs of the end of the world or the apocalypse. The bubonic plague pandemic, known as the Black Death, swept through Europe, Asia, and Africa in the 14th century, resulting in the deaths of millions of people. Many saw it as a biblical punishment and a sign of the impending end times. After the Great Fire of London in 1666, some interpreted it as a divine judgment and a precursor to the end of the world. The Napoleonic

Wars and the rise of Napoleon Bonaparte in Europe led some to believe that he was the Antichrist mentioned in the Bible and that these events signaled the end times. The unprecedented scale of destruction and loss of life during World War I (1914–1918) led to widespread speculation that it was a sign of the end times, with some associating it with biblical prophecies. The Spanish flu pandemic of 1918–1919, which claimed millions of lives globally, raised fears and speculations about the end of the world, as pandemics were often seen as divine judgments. The economic devastation of the Great Depression in the 1930s led to apocalyptic predictions and religious movements that interpreted the economic collapse as a sign of the end times. The outbreak and devastation of World War II, including the Holocaust, fueled beliefs that it represented the apocalyptic events described in biblical prophecies. The Cuban Missile Crisis, a tense standoff between the United States and the Soviet Union, raised fears of a nuclear Armageddon and prompted apocalyptic concerns. Natural disasters such as earthquakes, tsunamis, hurricanes, and volcanic eruptions have often been interpreted as signs of the end times due to their destructive power. In more recent times, concerns about climate change and environmental degradation have led some to interpret these issues as signs of impending ecological catastrophe and the end of the world. While many of these events have indeed caused immense suffering and disruption, they have not resulted in the literal end of the world as predicted by some.

## The End will Come!

The end will come, but until then, we must occupy until he comes! "God blessed them, and God said unto them, 'Be fruitful, and multiply, and replenish the earth, and subdue it: and have dominion over the fish of the sea, and over the fowl of the air, and over every living thing that moveth upon the earth'" (Genesis 1:28, KJV). This is God's foundational decree to humanity, outlining various fundamental actions, including procreation, signifying the propagation and expansion of the human population. Additionally, God's directive urges people to both inhabit the Earth and responsibly harness its resources for sustenance and growth. To "subdue the earth" is to manage the planet's resources, underscoring the importance of mindful stewardship, not exploitation. It underscores the significance of preserving and prudently utilizing these resources. To "be fruitful and replenish the earth" encapsulates God's intent for humanity to flourish, prosper, and conscientiously tend to both the Earth and its inhabitants. It underscores the cooperative partnership between humans and God in fostering and overseeing the world they have been entrusted with.

"Occupy till I come" is a phrase that comes from a parable told by Jesus Christ in the New Testament of the Bible. This phrase is found in the Gospel of Luke, chapter 19, verses 11-27, specifically in the Parable of the Ten Minas (or Pounds). In this parable, a nobleman goes away to receive a kingdom and entrusts his servants with different amounts of money (minas) before leaving. When he returns, he evaluates how each servant has managed the resources given to them. In the context of the parable, it highlights the responsibility of the servants to invest wisely and use the resources they were given by the nobleman. Likewise, it's seen as a call for believers to be active and fruitful in their lives while anticipating Christ's second coming.

As believers await the return of Jesus Christ, they can engage in several productive and faithful activities to live purposefully and align with their faith. They follow Jesus's teachings by practicing honesty, integrity, humility, and kindness in everyday interactions and striving to lead a life that reflects Christian values and principles. Engaging in regular prayer and meditation to strengthen their relationship with God, seek guidance, and find inner peace. Prayer is a way to communicate with God and express gratitude, concerns, and hopes. They regularly read and study the Bible to deepen their understanding of Christian teachings and gain insights into how to live a righteous life—engaging in acts of kindness, compassion, and service to help those in need. Volunteering at shelters, food banks, hospitals, or other community organizations to demonstrate love for others.

## How to Occupy Until Jesus Comes

It nurtures healthy relationships with family, friends, and neighbors and provides support and encouragement. It is practicing good stewardship of the environment by being mindful of one's impact on the planet and taking steps to care for and preserve God's creation. It is standing up for the rights and dignity of all people, advocating for justice and equality, addressing systemic issues such as poverty, discrimination, and oppression, and continuously striving for personal growth, self-improvement, and spiritual development. That lifestyle can include overcoming personal challenges, developing new skills, working towards self-awareness, participating in a local church or religious community, attending worship services, engaging in fellowship, and building relationships with fellow believers. Practice forgiveness and seek reconciliation in relationships where there may be conflicts or hurt feelings—being a positive influence in the workplace, community, and among friends by demonstrating Christian values and ethics. It is mentoring and guiding new believers in their faith journey, helping them grow spiritually and navigate the challenges of life.

Christians can occupy the earth by actively engaging in acts of service and charity. Occupying includes helping those in need, caring for the marginalized and vulnerable, and working towards social justice and equity. By doing so, Christians embody the values of Christ's teachings and positively impact society. Another important aspect of occupying the earth is sharing the message of the Gospel. Christians are encouraged to spread the good news of salvation through Jesus Christ and to make disciples of all nations. This can be done through evangelism, missionary work, and personal relationships to bring more people into a relationship with God. Stewardship of the environment is also considered part of occupying the earth. Christians believe God created the earth and entrusted it to humanity's care. Therefore, they are responsible for protecting and preserving the natural world, working towards sustainability and responsible resource management. Christians are called to participate in building God's kingdom on earth. This involves promoting values such as love, peace, justice, and righteousness. It includes striving for moral and ethical behavior in all aspects of life, including politics, economics, and social relationships. Christians need to maintain a strong spiritual life through prayer, worship, and fellowship with other believers. These practices not only deepen their relationship with God but also provide them with the strength, wisdom, and guidance to occupy the earth in a way that aligns with God's silicifying the earth until Jesus returns, which means actively and purposefully living out one's Christian faith in all aspects of life. It involves being a positive force for good in the world, sharing the message of salvation, caring for others, and working towards a more just and compassionate society. Ultimately, Christians believe their faith calls them to be agents of transformation and hope in a world that requires God's love and redemption.

## Do This Right Now!

For those who anxiously await the second coming of Christ, remember you shouldn't simply passively wait for the return of Jesus. Still instead, they should actively engage in good works, share the message of Christ's teachings, and positively impact the world around them. Live a life aligned with Christian values and principles, reflecting the teachings of love, compassion, and service that Jesus exemplified. Make a positive difference in the world and contribute to the betterment of society while keeping their hope and anticipation for Christ's return.

Get a good education. Buy properties. Start a family. Give back to society. Seek to achieve prosperity, success, and upward social mobility through hard work, determination, and opportunity. Regardless of your background or circumstances, it would be best if you aspired to a better life based on economic success and by accomplishing your purpose on earth. Buy and take care of your home here before you think of a home in heaven. Jesus declared: "In my Father's house are many mansions: if it were not so, I would have told you. I go to prepare a place for you" (John 14:2).

## Contemporary Examples

Stop making predictions about the apocalypse; it is unscriptural and unproductive. Learn to "occupy until he comes." Acclaimed actor Denzel Washington is not only known for his Christian faith but also for his unwavering commitment to using his platform to promote positive values and inspire others. He has spoken openly about how his faith guides his life and career, emphasizing the importance of integrity, hard work, and compassion in his roles and interactions with others. Washington's dedication to his faith is reflected in his efforts to influence the entertainment industry positively. NBA superstar Stephen Curry is not just an outspoken Christian but also a philanthropist who actively engages in efforts to impact society positively. He and his wife, Ayesha Curry, have been involved in initiatives like providing clean water to communities in need through their organization, "Nothing But Nets." Curry's faith is evident in his on-court demeanor, where he often points to the sky after making a three-pointer as a gesture of gratitude.

There are others. Known for his roles in TV series like "Growing Pains," Kirk Cameron has transitioned from a successful acting career to becoming a Christian evangelist. He has dedicated his life to spreading the message of Christianity and encouraging others to deepen their faith. Cameron's commitment to sharing the gospel and his Christian beliefs exemplifies the concept of "occupying until Jesus comes" by actively participating in the work of faith. Filmmaker and actor Tyler Perry is known for his deep Christian faith, often reflected in his work's themes of faith, redemption, and forgiveness. Through his movies, television shows, and stage plays, Perry has used storytelling as a medium to convey Christian values and messages of hope. His commitment to his faith is evident in his creative endeavors and philanthropic contributions. The former NFL quarterback Tim Tebow has consistently demonstrated his devout Christian beliefs throughout his career. Beyond his achievements in sports, he has been actively involved in various charitable and philanthropic efforts, including the "Tim Tebow Foundation," which focuses on initiatives like helping children with life-threatening illnesses. Tebow's dedication to making a positive impact on the lives of others aligns with the Christian principle of serving others to express one's faith. There are individuals from various fields, including entertainment, sports, and philanthropy, who actively live out their Christian faith while making meaningful contributions to society. They are not perfect, but their commitment to "occupying until Jesus comes" inspires many within and outside the Christian community, emphasizing the importance of faith-driven actions and values in their daily lives and endeavors.

# CHAPTER 21

# Act Now: Are you a soldier, a warrior, a conqueror, or a whiner?

In a biblical context, soldiers serve in an army or military force. They are typically associated with being part of a larger organized group, such as the armies of ancient Israel or the Roman legions. They may engage in combat, defend their nation or people, and follow orders from their superiors. Soldiers are often portrayed as individuals who are trained and equipped for battle.

Warriors in the Bible are engaging in warfare. They can include soldiers but may also encompass other individuals who participate in battles, such as tribal or clan-based warriors in the Old Testament. Warriors are brave, skilled in combat, and willing to defend their people, but they may not necessarily be part of a formal military structure.

In the Biblical sense, conquerors typically achieve victory over a city, region, or people through military conquest. They are often associated with expanding territory or establishing dominance over others. In biblical narratives, conquerors may be used as instruments of God's judgment or as part of more significant historical events.

David is often described as a warrior (for his victories in battle) and a conqueror (for his establishment of the United Kingdom of Israel).

Similarly, Joshua is a conqueror known for leading the Israelites in conquering Canaan. Conversely, Gideon is a biblical figure known for leading a small group of warriors against a more significant enemy force.

## David: The Warrior and Conqueror

David, one of the most prominent figures in the Old Testament, is known for his dual roles as a warrior and a conqueror. As a young shepherd boy, David gained fame when he bravely confronted the Philistine giant Goliath with nothing but a sling and stones. He defeated Goliath, which marked the beginning of his reputation as a skilled and fearless warrior. Throughout his life, David was involved in numerous military campaigns and battles. He served as a military leader under King Saul and later became the king of the southern kingdom of Judah.

David's most significant conquest was the establishment of the United Kingdom of Israel. After a period of strife and division between the tribes of Israel, David first became king over the tribe of Judah and later over all of Israel. He successfully united the northern and southern tribes, making Jerusalem his capital city. Under his rule, Israel experienced a period of relative peace and stability. David's reign is often called a time of conquest and consolidation of power.

## Joshua: The Conqueror

God chose Joshua to succeed Moses as the leader of the Israelites as they prepared to enter the Promised Land, Canaan. Joshua is best known for leading the Israelites in the conquest of Canaan. He played a central role in the military campaigns to capture the cities of Canaan, including the famous battle of Jericho, where the walls of the city fell after the Israelites encircled it and blew trumpets. Over time, under Joshua's leadership, the Israelites gained control of much of Canaan, fulfilling God's promise to give them the land.

## Gideon: The Resourceful Warrior

Gideon is a biblical figure whose story showcases his resourcefulness and leadership in the face of overwhelming odds. When the Midianites oppressed the Israelites, God called Gideon to deliver his people. He assembled a small, unconventional army of just 300 men. With trumpets, torches, and clever tactics, Gideon's forces defeated a much larger Midianite army. Gideon's story highlights his role as a leader of a small group of warriors who achieved a remarkable victory through faith and strategic thinking. His story is a testament to the power of faith and resourcefulness in adversity.

## Christians: Soldiers, Warriors, Conquerors

Christians are often referred to as soldiers in the context of spiritual warfare. The Bible teaches that believers are engaged in a spiritual battle against evil forces and temptations. In Ephesians 6:10–18, the apostle Paul talks about putting on the "armor of God" to stand against the schemes of the devil. As soldiers of Christ, Christians are called to defend and uphold the truth of the Gospel, righteousness, and moral values. They must resist the influences of sin and the world and remain faithful to their beliefs. Just as soldiers must endure hardship and stay disciplined, Christians are encouraged to persevere in their faith, even in the face of trials and challenges.

Warriors are often associated with the idea of being engaged in battles. In the Christian context, believers are warriors against darkness and sin. They are called to fight the good fight of faith (1

Timothy 6:12). Christian warriors are called to stand firm in their faith, boldly proclaiming the Gospel and contending for the truth. They are to be unafraid to confront the spiritual battles that may arise. The ultimate victory for Christian warriors is not achieved through physical weapons but through faith in Jesus Christ. Through His sacrifice on the cross, Christians believe they have already won the ultimate victory over sin and death.

Christians are called to be conquerors over sin and temptation through the power of Christ. Romans 8:37 states believers are "more than conquerors through him who loved us," referring to Jesus. The Bible also speaks of believers reigning with Christ in the future (Revelation 20:6). This conquering involves being faithful to Christ and participating in His eternal kingdom. Conquerors in the Christian faith trust in God's promises and believe that, through Christ, they have the strength to overcome all obstacles.

## Whiners

A whiner is a complainer or murmurer. Are you a whiner? The world is about to become much more unstable.

The Israelites were frequently complainers during their journey through the wilderness after being liberated from Egypt. They complained about various issues, including the lack of food, water, and the challenges they faced (Exodus 16:2-3; Numbers 14:2-4). In the parable found in Luke 15:11-32, the older brother complains and expresses resentment when his younger, wayward brother is welcomed back by their father. He feels that his years of loyalty have not been adequately rewarded. In Numbers 11, Moses complains to God about the burden of leadership and the people's demands.

Today, people complain about many things. When individuals have expectations that are not fulfilled, whether in relationships, work, or other areas of life, they may express dissatisfaction through complaints. High levels of stress, whether from work, personal life, or other sources, can lead people to vent their frustrations through complaining. Stressors such as tight deadlines, financial pressures, and health concerns may contribute to this. Misunderstandings or poor communication can lead to complaints. When individuals feel unheard or misunderstood, they may resort to complaining to express their frustration. Experiencing negative events, whether in customer service, daily interactions, or personal circumstances, can prompt people to voice their displeasure through complaints.

Some individuals use complaints to seek empathy, understanding, or support from others. Sharing grievances can be a means of connecting with others who may have similar experiences. Complaining can serve as a coping mechanism for dealing with stress or challenges. It may provide a temporary release of tension or frustration. In some cultures, or social groups, expressing dissatisfaction or complaining about certain issues is considered normal or expected behavior. Perceptions of unfair treatment or injustice can lead people to voice their grievances through complaints. This may occur in various contexts, such as work, relationships, or societal issues. For some individuals, complaining can become a habitual way of interacting with the world. It may be a learned behavior, or a coping strategy developed over time. When people feel a lack of control over their circumstances or believe they are powerless to change a situation, they may resort to complaining to express their frustration.

## Are you a warrior, conqueror, or a whiner?

The biblical narratives of soldiers, warriors, and conquerors offer profound insights into the qualities of strength, bravery, and faith exhibited by figures like David, Joshua, and Gideon. These stories underscore the multifaceted nature of their roles, encompassing both physical battles and the establishment of kingdoms. David, as both a warrior and conqueror, exemplifies the transformative power of faith and courage, uniting the tribes of Israel and establishing a period of peace and consolidation of power. Joshua, chosen by God to lead the conquest of Canaan, exemplifies the fulfillment of divine promises and the victorious outcomes of following God's commandments. Gideon's resourcefulness and leadership in the face of overwhelming odds showcase the impact of faith and strategic thinking in achieving remarkable victories.

Drawing parallels to the spiritual realm, Christians are likened to soldiers engaged in spiritual warfare, warriors fighting against darkness and sin, and conquerors overcoming the challenges through the power of Christ. The biblical teachings call believers to don the armor of God, stand firm in their faith, and resist the schemes of the devil. This metaphorical battle is not fought with physical weapons but with unwavering faith, righteous living, and the proclamation of the Gospel. As conquerors, Christians trust in God's promises and believe in the ultimate victory over sin and death through Christ.

In contrast to these inspiring examples, the "whiner" is highlights a negative and complaining attitude. The broader discussion on contemporary complaints sheds light on the diverse reasons people express discontent in various aspects of life. While legitimate grievances exist, a habitual or unproductive complaining attitude can hinder personal growth and resilience. As individuals navigate the complexities of life, the biblical narratives of soldiers, warriors, conquerors, and even complainers offer valuable lessons on faith, resilience, and the transformative power of one's attitude. In a world that will become more unstable, the choice between adopting the virtues of a soldier, warrior, or conqueror, versus succumbing to a whining disposition, becomes increasingly significant. The biblical narratives provide a timeless guide for individuals seeking strength, courage, and faith in their life journeys.

# CHAPTER 22

# Act Now: Change Your Will into a Trust

A compelling argument can be made in favor of the trust over a will as the superior estate planning instrument. This is not just a matter of legal preference but of providing comprehensive protection and peace of mind for you and your loved ones.

A will, also known as a "last will and testament," is a legal document that outlines a person's wishes and instructions regarding the distribution of their assets and the care of their dependents after their death. It serves as a critical component of estate planning, allowing individuals to ensure that their property and belongings are distributed according to their desires and that their loved ones are provided for. A will has several features. First, it has an executor. A will typically designate an executor, also known as a personal representative or administrator, who is responsible for carrying out the instructions in the will. This person is responsible for managing the deceased person's estate, including the distribution of assets, payment of debts, and handling other administrative tasks. Second, it specifies who will receive the deceased person's property and assets. Beneficiaries can include family members, friends, charitable organizations, or any other individuals or entities chosen by the person creating the will. Third, a will identifies the specific assets and property that are to be distributed. This can include real estate, personal possessions, financial accounts, investments, and more. It provides instructions on how these assets are to be divided among the beneficiaries. Fourth, for individuals with minor children, a will can designate a guardian who will be responsible for the care and upbringing of the children in the event of the parents' death. This is a crucial aspect of estate planning for parents. Fifth, wills may also address the payment of outstanding debts, funeral expenses, and estate taxes, specifying whether these should be paid from the estate's assets. Sixth, a will has conditions and special requests. Some wills include specific conditions or special requests, such as naming conditions for beneficiaries to meet before they can inherit or providing instructions for the distribution of sentimental items. Seventh, a will has revocability.

In most cases, a will is revocable during the creator's lifetime. This means that the person who created the will (the testator) can make changes or revoke the will entirely as long as they are of sound mind. A will must have witnesses and Legal Formalities: To be legally valid, a will usually requires the signatures of witnesses who can attest to its authenticity. Legal requirements for witnesses and notarization can vary by jurisdiction.

On the other hand, a trust is a legal arrangement that allows one party, known as the grantor or settlor, to transfer ownership of assets to another party, known as the trustee, for the benefit of a third party or multiple beneficiaries. Trusts are versatile estate planning tools that serve various purposes and can provide benefits such as asset protection, control over the distribution of assets, and privacy. There are several types of trusts, each designed to achieve specific goals. First, a revocable living Trust is a revocable living trust is created during the grantor's lifetime and can be altered or revoked by the grantor at any time. It allows for the seamless management and distribution of assets, often avoiding probate (the legal process of estate administration). After the grantor's death, the assets in the trust can pass directly to the beneficiaries without going through probate. Second, an irrevocable Trust. Unlike a revocable trust, the grantor cannot alter or revoke an irrevocable trust once it's established. Common types of irrevocable trusts include:

- Irrevocable Life Insurance Trust (ILIT): This trust is designed to hold life insurance policies and provide tax benefits by removing the policy's value from the grantor's estate.
- Charitable Remainder Trust (CRT): CRTs allow grantors to donate assets to charity while retaining an income stream for themselves or other beneficiaries.
- Qualified Personal Residence Trust (QPRT): A QPRT allows a grantor to transfer a residence or vacation home to an irrevocable trust while retaining the right to live in the property for a specified period. After that period, the property passes to the beneficiaries.
- Medicaid Irrevocable Trust: This type of trust is used to protect assets from being counted toward Medicaid eligibility for long-term care.

Third, a special needs trust (SNT) is established to provide for the financial needs of a beneficiary with a disability without jeopardizing their eligibility for government assistance programs like Medicaid or Supplemental Security Income (SSI). Fourth, a testamentary Trust. Unlike a revocable trust, which is created during the grantor's lifetime, a testamentary trust is established through the grantor's will and takes effect upon the grantor's death. It allows for the distribution of assets over time or under specific conditions. Fourth, a bypass Trust (Credit Shelter Trust) is used to maximize estate tax exemptions for married couples. They allow the assets of the first spouse to pass to the trust without incurring estate taxes, ultimately benefiting the surviving spouse and heirs. Fifth, a generation-skipping Trust (GST) transfers assets to beneficiaries at least two generations younger than the grantor, such as grandchildren. It can offer potential estate tax savings. Sixth, a dynasty Trust is created to provide for multiple generations of beneficiaries while minimizing estate taxes.

Assets in the trust can remain protected from estate taxes for an extended period. Sixth, a grantor retained annuity trust (GRAT) and grantor retained unitrust (GRUT) trusts allow a grantor to transfer appreciating assets to an irrevocable trust while retaining an income stream for a specified period. After that period, the remaining assets pass to the beneficiaries with potential estate tax savings. Seventh, a family limited partnership (FLP) or family limited liability company (LLC while not trusts are often used for estate planning purposes to transfer assets to family members while maintaining control.

## Why a trust is the more powerful and effective choice?

A trust protects your privacy and discretion. One of the most compelling reasons to opt for a trust is privacy. A trust allows your assets to pass privately to your beneficiaries without going through probate, a public legal process. Conversely, a will becomes a matter of public record, subjecting your personal and financial affairs to scrutiny by anyone who wishes to access the information. A trust shields your family from unwanted attention and ensures the confidentiality of your estate.

Choosing a trust avoids probate delays and costs. Probate is notorious for its time-consuming and costly nature. By placing your assets in a trust, you bypass the probate process entirely. This means your heirs receive their inheritances faster, without the lengthy court proceedings and hefty legal fees associated with probate. With a trust, you save your family both time and money during an already challenging period.

A trust allows for control and flexibility. A trust grants you greater control and flexibility over your assets, even beyond your passing. You can specify conditions for distributing your assets, ensuring they are used for the benefit of your beneficiaries according to your wishes. Whether you want to provide for education, healthcare, or any other specific need, a trust empowers you to do so with precision.

A trust offers protection from legal challenges. Wills are often susceptible to legal challenges, which can lead to prolonged and emotionally draining disputes among family members. Trusts offer a more robust layer of protection. They are less prone to challenges, providing greater security for your intended beneficiaries and reducing the likelihood of costly courtroom battles.

A trust allows for incapacity planning. A trust is not only about distributing your assets after death; it can also provide for managing your assets in case of incapacity. With a properly structured trust, you can ensure that your financial affairs are seamlessly managed by a trusted individual of your choosing, sparing your family the stress and confusion that can arise during times of incapacity.

Multistate and International Assets. Trust is an indispensable tool for those with assets in multiple states or abroad. It can help streamline the management and distribution of assets that are subject to varying state and international laws, ensuring a more efficient and coordinated transfer of wealth.

Both wills and trusts serve essential roles in estate planning. A trust stands out as the more powerful and comprehensive choice. It affords you privacy, control, flexibility, and protection, all while avoiding the burdensome probate process. A trust is not merely a legal instrument; it is a vehicle for preserving your legacy, protecting your loved ones, and ensuring your wishes are carried out with precision. In the complex world of estate planning, a trust emerges as the most potent tool to safeguard your assets and your family's future.

## Illustrations

Scenario 1: Person with a Will (John)

*John, a diligent man, had a will in place to outline his wishes regarding the distribution of his assets upon his passing.*

- Asset Distribution: When John passed away, his estate went through the probate process. The will dictated the distribution of his assets, but this process was subject to court oversight and took several months.
- Public Record: The details of John's will, including his assets and beneficiaries, became a matter of public record. Anyone interested could access this information, potentially compromising the privacy of his family.
- Probate Costs: The probate process incurred legal fees, court costs, and executor fees, reducing the overall value of John's estate that could be passed on to his beneficiaries.
- Limited Control: John's will provide a basic framework for asset distribution, but it does not offer the flexibility to address specific conditions or ongoing management of assets.

Scenario 2: Person with a Trust (Sarah)

*Sarah, a forward-thinking individual, established a revocable living trust as part of her estate plan.*

- Asset Management and Distribution: Sarah placed her assets into the trust during her lifetime, naming herself as the initial trustee. She appointed a successor trustee to manage the trust in the event of her incapacity or passing. Upon her death, her successor trustee seamlessly distributed her assets to the beneficiaries named in the trust.

- Avoidance of Probate: Because her assets were held in the trust, they bypassed the probate process entirely. This allowed for a faster and more efficient transfer of assets to her beneficiaries.
- Privacy: Unlike a will, Sarah's trust remained private. The details of her assets, beneficiaries, and the distribution plan were not made public, preserving her family's privacy.
- Cost Savings: Sarah's trust avoided many of the costs associated with probate, such as court fees and legal expenses. As a result, a more significant portion of her estate was available for her beneficiaries.
- Flexibility and Control: Sarah's trust provided her with greater flexibility to specify how and when her assets would be distributed. She included provisions to provide for her minor grandchildren's education and health expenses over time.

In this illustration, it's clear that Sarah, who established a trust, was better served in several key ways compared to John, who relied solely on a will. Sarah's estate planning strategy allowed for a smoother, more private, and cost-effective distribution of assets while affording her greater control and flexibility over her legacy. A trust can be a powerful tool for individuals seeking to protect their assets, ensure privacy, and provide for their loved ones comprehensively and efficiently.

In New York, various professionals and organizations can assist individuals with creating, managing, or navigating trusts as part of their estate planning and financial strategies. Here are some resources and entities that can help people deal with trusts in New York:

First, there are estate planning attorneys. Experienced estate planning attorneys specialize in creating and managing trusts. They can provide tailored advice and draft trust documents to meet your specific needs. Look for attorneys with expertise in trusts and estate law in New York. Second, there are financial advisors and planners.

Financial advisors can help individuals incorporate trusts into their overall financial plans. They can work with you to identify the most suitable type of trust based on your financial goals and circumstances. Third, there are trust companies. Trust companies in New York offer professional trust administration services. They can act as trustees or co-trustees, managing the trust assets and ensuring the trust's terms are carried out according to your wishes. Fourth, there are banks and financial institutions. Many banks and financial institutions in New York offer trust services. They can serve as corporate trustees, managing the trust assets and providing fiduciary services. Fifth, there are certified Public Accountants (CPA) in estate planning and taxation that can provide guidance on the tax implications of various trusts and help you make informed decisions about your estate plan. Fifth, nonprofit organizations and foundations in New York may offer guidance on charitable giving through trusts. They can help you establish and manage charitable trusts or foundations. Sixth is the New York State Bar Association (NYSBA), which has a section on trusts and estates. It offers resources to find qualified attorneys specializing in trusts and estates in your area. Seventh, online directories, local estate planning seminars and workshops, and Community Senior Centers all help create trusts. When seeking assistance with trusts in New York, choosing reputable and qualified professionals or organizations well-versed in the state's specific trust and estate laws is essential. Be sure to conduct due diligence, ask for referrals, and consult with professionals who can effectively address your unique needs and goals.

# CHAPTER 23

# Act Now: Use Your Powers

The power of "dunamis" in the New Testament encompasses miraculous and transformative aspects of God's power, particularly through the work of the Holy Spirit. It is seen as a force for healing, transformation, and spiritual empowerment, both in the lives of individual believers and in the mission of the early Christian community. Belief in this power is central to the Christian faith and underscores the idea that through God's "dunamis," believers can experience profound change and carry out their mission effectively. In Romans 1:16, the apostle Paul writes that the gospel is the "dunamis of God for salvation to everyone who believes," highlighting the life-changing power of the message of Christ.

Believers have power over spiritual forces. The verse "Behold, I give you the authority to trample on serpents and scorpions, and over all the power of the enemy, and nothing shall by any means hurt you" (Luke 10:19, NKJV) is often understood as a metaphorical expression of the authority and power that Christians have over spiritual forces and evil influences. It represents the idea that through faith in Christ, believers have the ability to resist and overcome the temptations and spiritual challenges they encounter in life. The believers' power through the Holy Spirit. The statement "You shall receive power when the Holy Spirit has come upon you" (Acts 1:8, ESV) is a promise made by Jesus to his disciples before his ascension.

This power is often interpreted as the empowerment of believers by the Holy Spirit to fulfill their mission of spreading the teachings of Jesus and sharing the message of salvation. It includes the power to proclaim the gospel, perform acts of kindness and love, and live according to Christian principles.

But what kind of power do you have? It's a question that transcends titles, job descriptions, and backgrounds. It's a question that goes to the core of who we are as individuals and what we can collectively achieve in this diverse and interconnected world. We bring a kaleidoscope of experiences, talents, and expertise. Each one of us possesses a unique set of skills, knowledge, and abilities. But beyond the surface, beyond our professional titles and the positions we hold, lies a deeper form of power, a power that has the potential to shape our lives and the world around us. The power of which I speak is not solely about influence or authority, nor is it limited to those in high-ranking positions. It is the power that resides within each one of us—the power of choice, the power of values, the power of impact, the power of awareness, the power of blessing, the power of example, the power of forgiveness, the power of friendship, the power of gratitude, the power of healing, the power of influence, the power of knowledge, the power of love, the power of manifestation, the power of now, the power of opportunity, the power of persuasion, the power of questioning, resilience, silence, the power of two the power of unity, the power of vision, the power of words, the power of "X', the power of the delete, the power of yearning, and the power of zeal.

**The Power of Choice.** We all have the power to make choices every single day. We can choose how we respond to challenges, treat others, and prioritize our time and resources. Our choices have a ripple effect, touching not only our own lives but the lives of those around us. The question is, what choices are we making, and how are they shaping our world?

**The Power of Values.** Our values are the compass by which we navigate our professional and personal lives. They define what we stand for, what we believe in, and what we are willing to fight for. The power of values lies in their ability to guide us towards ethical and just actions. What are your core values, and how do they influence your decisions and actions in your professional life?

**The Power of Impact.** Every action we take every decision we make, has the potential to create a positive or negative impact. As professionals, we are in positions to influence our workplaces, the communities we serve, and the wider world. What kind of impact do you want to leave behind? What legacy do you aspire to build?

**The Power of Awareness**. Beyond our choices and actions, the power of awareness is a transformative force. It's the ability to understand ourselves and our impact on the world around us. When we cultivate self-awareness, we become attuned to our strengths and weaknesses, biases, and blind spots. This awareness allows us to navigate our professional and personal interactions with greater empathy and authenticity, making us better leaders and colleagues. As we become more aware of the challenges faced by others, we can use our influence to promote inclusivity and create environments that respect the dignity and worth of every individual.

**The Power of Blessing**. The power to bless is a profound and often underestimated force. It involves recognizing the inherent value and potential in others and acknowledging their contributions. By offering blessings and encouragement to our colleagues and peers, we create a culture of positivity and affirmation. Our words and actions can uplift spirits, inspire confidence, and ignite the spark of potential in those around us. In doing so, we tap into the transformative power of kindness and support, fostering a nurturing and empowering atmosphere within our professional circles.

**The Power of Example.** Leading by example is a potent form of leadership that transcends words. The power of example lies in the way we live out our values and principles, serving as role models for others to follow. Whether it's through ethical decision-making, a commitment to hard work, or a dedication to lifelong learning, our actions set a standard for integrity and excellence. As professionals, we can inspire positive change simply by living out the values and principles we hold dear and encouraging others to do the same.

**The Power to Forgiveness.** Forgiveness is a profound and liberating power. It allows us to release the burden of resentment and find healing, both personally and in our relationships. In our professional lives, the power to forgive can mend rifts, restore trust, and create pathways to reconciliation. Extending forgiveness to ourselves and others opens the door to growth, collaboration, and the potential for more harmonious and productive workplaces.

**The Power to Develop Friendship.** Building genuine friendships is a powerful force in the professional world. The power to develop friendships extends beyond networking; it's about cultivating meaningful connections rooted in trust, mutual respect, and shared values. These friendships can foster collaboration, support, and a sense of belonging in our professional communities. When we invest in relationships built on friendship, we tap into a source of encouragement and strength that can enhance both our personal and professional lives, creating a culture of camaraderie and support.

**The Power of Gratitude.** Gratitude is a transformative force that has the potential to change our outlook on life and influence those around us. When we cultivate the power of gratitude, we not only acknowledge the blessings we receive but also express appreciation for the efforts of others. In our professional lives, expressing gratitude can foster positive working relationships, boost morale, and create a culture of recognition and appreciation. It can inspire greater dedication, loyalty, and a sense of purpose among colleagues, ultimately enhancing teamwork and productivity.

**The Power to Heal.** Healing is a profound and often overlooked power, not only in the physical sense but also emotionally and spiritually. In professional contexts, the power to heal can manifest through empathy, active listening, and a commitment to supporting and understanding colleagues facing challenges. By acknowledging the pain and struggles of others, we contribute to their emotional well-being and create an environment where healing and personal growth can occur.

**The Power to Influence.** Influence is a potent force that extends beyond positions of authority. The power to influence involves persuading, inspiring, and motivating others to take action or embrace new ideas. As professionals, we can use our influence to drive positive change, advocate for important causes, and champion innovation. By leveraging this power responsibly, we can shape organizational cultures and impact broader societal trends.

**The Power of Knowing.** Knowledge is a formidable source of power. The power of knowing encompasses what we have learned and our capacity for critical thinking and problem-solving. In our professional roles, the power to know empowers us to make informed decisions, address complex challenges, and drive progress. It involves the continuous pursuit of knowledge and a commitment to lifelong learning, enabling us to adapt to evolving circumstances and remain at the forefront of our fields.

**The Power to Love**. Love, often associated with empathy, compassion, and a deep sense of care for others, is a transformative power that transcends professional boundaries. The power to love involves fostering a genuine concern for the well-being of colleagues, clients, and stakeholders. It has the capacity to create strong bonds, inspire trust, and lead to collaboration and cooperation. By infusing our professional interactions with love and kindness, we contribute to a more compassionate and harmonious workplace, ultimately enhancing the quality of our work and relationships.

**The Power to Manifest.** The power to manifest is the ability to turn thoughts and desires into reality through focused intention and action. It involves setting clear goals, visualizing success, and taking deliberate steps toward achieving them. In the professional realm, this power encourages us to dream big, set ambitious targets, and work diligently to bring our visions to fruition. We can inspire innovation, create opportunities, and drive meaningful change within our organizations and industries by harnessing the power to manifest.

**The Power of Now.** The power of now underscores the importance of living in the present moment, fully engaged and attentive. It encourages us to be mindful of our actions and decisions, recognizing that we have the most influence in the present moment. In our professional lives, this power enables us to make the most of each opportunity, respond effectively to challenges, and savor the journey of continuous growth and achievement. We can maximize our productivity, creativity, and overall well-being by embracing the power of now.

**The Power of Opportunity.** Opportunities are windows to growth and advancement, and the power of opportunity lies in our ability to recognize, create, and seize them. It involves being open to new experiences, seeking out challenges, and turning setbacks into learning opportunities. This power encourages us to be proactive, adaptable, and resourceful. By leveraging the power of opportunity, we can unlock our potential, expand our horizons, and achieve remarkable success in our careers.

**The Power of Persuasion.** Persuasion is the art of influencing others' beliefs, attitudes, and actions through effective communication and argumentation. It is a potent power that can be used ethically to build consensus, inspire collaboration, and promote positive change. In the professional world, the power of persuasion is essential for negotiation, leadership, and advocacy. It empowers us to articulate our ideas convincingly, mobilize support for important initiatives, and foster a culture of cooperation and shared goals.

**The Power of Questioning.** Questioning is a powerful tool for critical thinking, problem-solving, and gaining deeper insights. It involves asking probing and thought-provoking questions to explore complex issues, challenge assumptions, and arrive at informed decisions. In our professional endeavors, the power of questioning encourages us to be curious, inquisitive, and analytical. It facilitates a culture of continuous improvement, innovation, and intellectual growth. By harnessing the power of questioning, we can uncover hidden opportunities, address underlying problems, and drive meaningful progress within our organizations and industries.

**The Power of Resilience.** Resilience is the capacity to withstand adversity, bounce back from challenges, and adapt to change. It is a remarkable power that empowers us to persevere in the face of setbacks, learn from failures, and emerge stronger. In our professional lives, the power of resilience equips us to navigate turbulent times, overcome obstacles, and maintain a positive attitude. It enables us to embrace change as an opportunity for growth and innovation, ultimately contributing to our long-term success and well-being.

**The Power of Silence.** Silence is a profound source of strength and wisdom. It offers the space for reflection, inner peace, and deep understanding. The power of silence encourages us to listen attentively, both to others and to our own inner voice. It fosters effective communication, active listening, and mindfulness in the professional realm. By harnessing the power of silence, we can make more thoughtful decisions, build stronger relationships, and create a culture of respect and contemplation.

**The Power of Two**. The power of two signifies the strength of collaboration and partnership. It emphasizes that we can achieve more together than we can individually. In the professional world, the power of two encourages teamwork, synergy, and complementary skills. It underscores the importance of diverse perspectives and joint efforts in solving complex problems and achieving shared goals. By embracing the power of two, we enhance our collective potential and foster a sense of camaraderie and shared achievement.

**The Power of Unity**. Unity is a force that brings people together, transcending differences and fostering a sense of belonging. It is the power to create solidarity, build consensus, and inspire collective action. In professional settings, the power of unity encourages collaboration, inclusivity, and a shared commitment to a common purpose. It enables us to address challenges and achieve transformative change as a cohesive group. By embracing the power of unity, we create environments where diversity is celebrated and collective strengths are harnessed for the greater good.

**The Power of Vision.** Vision is seeing possibilities beyond the present and imagining a brighter future. It is a power that inspires innovation, sets direction, and motivates action. In the professional realm, the power of vision drives strategic planning, goal–setting, and organizational alignment. It provides a sense of purpose and direction, guiding us toward meaningful achievements. By embracing the power of vision, we can lead with clarity, inspire others to follow, and leave a legacy of purposeful and impactful work.

**The Power of Words**. Words are potent tools that can inspire, inform, uplift, and transform. The power of words lies in their ability to convey ideas, emotions, and messages. In our professional lives, the power of words encompasses effective communication, storytelling, and persuasion. It enables us to articulate our thoughts clearly, build meaningful connections, and inspire action. By harnessing the power of words, we can foster understanding, resolve conflicts, and create a positive impact within our organizations and communities.

**The Power of "X".** The power of "X" represents adaptability, versatility, and the capacity to fill various roles and functions. In professional contexts, this power signifies the ability to pivot, embrace change, and take on diverse challenges. It encourages us to be agile and open to learning, enabling us to navigate evolving industries and roles successfully. By embracing the power of "X," we become valuable assets in our workplaces, capable of tackling a wide range of tasks and contributing to innovation and growth.

**The Power to Delete**. The power to delete is the ability to let go of what no longer serves us, whether it be outdated practices, unproductive habits, or unnecessary clutter. In our professional lives, this power encourages us to streamline processes, declutter our workspaces, and prioritize what truly matters. It enables us to create room for innovation, efficiency, and personal growth. By embracing the power to delete, we can free ourselves from distractions and focus on what drives progress and success.

**The Power of Yearning.** Yearning is a profound source of motivation and drive. It represents a deep and persistent desire to achieve something meaningful. In our professional endeavors, the power of yearning fuels our ambition, dedication, and perseverance. It encourages us to set ambitious goals, pursue excellence, and overcome obstacles. By embracing the power of yearning, we can channel our passion and determination toward realizing our dreams and making a significant impact in our chosen fields.

**The Power of Zeal.** Zeal is an unwavering enthusiasm and passion for our work or goals. The driving force propels us forward, even in the face of challenges or setbacks. In the professional world, the power of zeal inspires dedication, innovation, and a tireless pursuit of excellence. It encourages us to lead by example, infuse our work with energy and purpose, and motivate others to join us in our pursuits. By embracing the power of zeal, we become catalysts for positive change and achievement for ourselves and those around us.

Our power, regardless of our roles, can catalyze positive change, justice, knowledge, and understanding. However, this power comes with the responsibility of recognizing that our choices, driven by our values, shape our lives and society's narrative, leaving a legacy for future generations. A multitude of powers, such as choice, values, impact, awareness, blessing, example, forgiveness, friendship, gratitude, healing, influence, knowledge, love, manifestation, presence, opportunity, persuasion, questioning, resilience, silence, collaboration, unity, and vision, define our professional journeys. These powers enable us to find strength in adversity, wisdom in reflection, synergy in collaboration, purpose in unity, and direction in vision. Embracing these powers allows us to navigate our professional lives with grace, determination, and shared purpose, leading to extraordinary success and fulfillment. Additionally, the powers of words, adaptability, the ability to delete, yearning, and zeal emphasize diverse qualities and abilities that shape our professional identities. They highlight the importance of effective communication, adaptability, simplification, aspiration, and passion in achieving career excellence, inspiring others, and impacting our professional spheres.

## Know How to Use Your Powers

The Bible contains various passages and teachings that provide insights into how power should be wielded and what purposes it should serve. One key biblical principle is that those in power should see themselves as stewards of God's authority and resources. In this view, power is not for personal gain but for serving others and glorifying God. Jesus' example of servant leadership, as seen in washing the disciples' feet (John 13:1-17), illustrates the idea of using power to serve others humbly. The Bible emphasizes the importance of justice and fairness in the exercise of power. Proverbs 29:4 states, "By justice a king gives a country stability, but those who are greedy for bribes tear it down." Leaders are encouraged to act justly, protect the vulnerable, and promote equity in society. Biblical teachings often call for leaders to show compassion and mercy to those under their authority. Micah 6:8 instructs, "He has shown you, O mortal, what is good. And what does the Lord require of you? To act justly, love mercy, and walk humbly with your God." This suggests that power should be used with a compassionate heart.

The Bible encourages leaders to be humble and to avoid arrogance and pride. Proverbs 16:18 cautions, "Pride goes before destruction, a haughty spirit before a fall." Humility is seen as a virtue that prevents abuse of power. Biblical figures like Solomon are often associated with seeking wisdom from God to govern effectively. Proverbs 2:6 states, "For the Lord gives wisdom; from his mouth come knowledge and understanding." Leaders are encouraged to seek divine guidance and wisdom in their decision-making. The Bible teaches that those in power will be held accountable for their actions. Luke 12:48 states, "From everyone who has been given much, much will be demanded; and from the one who has been entrusted with much, much more will be asked." This underscores the idea that power comes with a responsibility to use it wisely and justly. Biblical leaders are often called to trust in God's guidance and providence. Proverbs 3:5-6 advises, "Trust in the Lord with all your heart and lean not on your own understanding; in all your ways submit to him, and he will make your paths straight." This trust can influence their decision-making and actions.

## Self-Interest vs. Altruism

King Solomon, known for his immense wisdom, initially sought wisdom from God rather than personal gain (1 Kings 3:5-14). However, as his reign progressed, he also accumulated great wealth and splendor. While God did bless Solomon with wealth, his accumulation of wealth and many wives eventually led him away from God's commandments, and his later years were marked by idolatry and disobedience (1 Kings 11:1-10). His story exemplifies how the pursuit of power and wealth can lead individuals away from their initial intentions and ethical values, as seen in Solomon's case.

In Luke 12:16-21, Jesus tells the parable of a rich man who accumulated great wealth but lacked a focus on God and eternal matters. He decided to build larger barns to store his surplus and said to himself that he could now relax and enjoy his wealth. However, God called him a fool and said that his life would be required of him that very night. The parable illustrates how the pursuit of personal wealth and security, without consideration for others or one's spiritual life, can lead to spiritual emptiness and consequences. In 1 Timothy 6:10, the apostle Paul warns that the love of money is the root of all kinds of evil. This verse highlights the potential dangers of prioritizing wealth and personal advantage over more virtuous pursuits. Individuals who seek power primarily to serve their self-interest, often driven by a love of money or personal gain, may find themselves ensnared in unethical or immoral behavior, as pursuing power can sometimes lead to compromising principles and values.

One of the foundational teachings of Jesus is the Golden Rule, which states, "So in everything, do to others what you would have them do to you" (Matthew 7:12). Leaders motivated by altruism are more likely to treat others with kindness, empathy, and fairness, in accordance with this principle. Jesus himself exemplified a life of service, often ministering to the needs of the marginalized and oppressed. His washing of the disciples' feet (John 13:1-17) is a powerful symbol of servant leadership and selfless service. The Bible teaches the importance of loving one's neighbor as oneself (Matthew 22:39). Leaders driven by altruism are inclined to prioritize the welfare and well-being of their fellow citizens, striving to create a more just and compassionate society.

In the Old Testament, Joseph served as a model of public service. He rose to a position of power in Egypt and used his authority to store grain during times of plenty and distribute it during times of famine, saving countless lives (Genesis 41:39–57). His commitment to the common good illustrates the potential positive impact of leaders motivated by altruism. In the book of Nehemiah, Nehemiah exemplified a strong sense of duty and commitment to public service. He played a crucial role in reconstructing Jerusalem's walls, driven by a desire to restore the city and protect its inhabitants from harm (Nehemiah 2:1–20). His leadership demonstrated a selfless dedication to the well-being of his community.

## Modern-Day Applications

In contemporary society, leaders motivated by altruism often pursue policies and initiatives that address social injustices, poverty, healthcare disparities, and environmental concerns. They prioritize the needs of vulnerable populations and work towards greater equity and inclusivity. Altruistic leaders may also engage in domestic and international humanitarian efforts to alleviate suffering and promote peace and stability. Individuals in positions of power who are motivated by altruism and a commitment to public service are seen as fulfilling a higher calling. Their actions align with the teachings of the Bible, which emphasize the importance of love, compassion, and service to others. Such leaders seek to leave a positive and lasting impact on society by working toward the betterment of the common good, reflecting the Christian virtues of selflessness and love for one's neighbor.

## Ideological or Political Beliefs

Strong ideological or political beliefs may drive people in power. They may use their power to advance and implement policies or agendas that align with their convictions, whether those are related to social justice, economic reform, environmental protection, or other issues. The Bible contains numerous examples of individuals who held strong moral convictions and used their positions of authority to advance them. For instance, the prophets of the Old Testament often spoke out against injustice and unrighteousness, aligning their actions with their beliefs in the righteousness of God's law. Prophetic figures like Isaiah, Jeremiah, and Amos used their influence to call for social justice, the care of the vulnerable, and the protection of the oppressed. Their commitment to their convictions illustrates the potential impact of leaders who prioritize the pursuit of righteousness. In the book of Nehemiah, Nehemiah combined his strong belief in God's law with his position as governor to implement social and economic reforms in Jerusalem. He challenged the exploitation of the poor and encouraged the redistribution of resources to address poverty (Nehemiah 5:1-13). King Josiah initiated extensive religious and political reforms in Judah, driven by his commitment to restoring true worship and righteousness in the nation. His leadership exemplified the impact of political leaders guided by their convictions (2 Kings 22-23).

## Modern Applications

Today, leaders with strong ideological or political convictions may advocate for policies and reforms that reflect their values and beliefs. These convictions can encompass a wide range of issues, including social justice, economic equality, environmental sustainability, and human rights. For example, leaders who prioritize social justice may work to reform criminal justice systems, promote equal access to education and healthcare, and address systemic inequalities. Those with a strong commitment to environmental protection may advocate for policies to combat climate change and preserve natural resources. While leaders guided by strong convictions can effect positive change, their actions may also face opposition and controversy. Conflicting ideologies and beliefs can lead to political polarization and gridlock, making it challenging to achieve consensus and cooperation. Leaders should be mindful of balancing their convictions with the need for inclusive and fair governance, respecting the diversity of beliefs within society. Leaders driven by strong ideological or political convictions can significantly impact society, particularly when their beliefs align with principles of justice, compassion, and righteousness. However, they also face the responsibility of seeking wisdom and guidance and fostering unity and dialogue to address the complexities and challenges that may arise from differing perspectives within their communities and nations.

## Maintaining Stability and Order

Leaders in positions of power who prioritize stability, order, and security within a society often do so with the intention of maintaining a sense of safety and predictability for their constituents. While this approach can be seen as pragmatic, it also presents certain challenges and ethical considerations. Leaders who emphasize stability typically aim to prevent conflicts, civil unrest, and disruptions to social order. They seek to create an environment where citizens can go about their daily lives without fear of violence or instability. Stability and order are often seen as prerequisites for economic growth and prosperity. When societies experience political turmoil or frequent changes in leadership, it can deter foreign investments and hinder economic development.

A stable and ordered society can foster social cohesion and a sense of unity among its citizens. People are more likely to trust and cooperate with one another when they feel secure and have confidence in their government's ability to maintain order. Leaders who prioritize stability may also seek to uphold the rule of law and protect human rights. A well-functioning legal system and law enforcement agencies are essential for maintaining order while respecting citizens' rights.

One ethical challenge associated with a strong emphasis on stability is that it can sometimes lead to the suppression of dissent and the restriction of civil liberties. In such cases, leaders may prioritize order at the expense of individual freedoms and human rights. Leaders who prioritize the status quo may resist necessary social or political changes, even when a desire for greater justice, equality, or social progress drives those changes. This resistance can hinder societal advancement. In extreme cases, leaders who prioritize stability may veer towards authoritarianism, concentrating power in their hands and limiting political opposition. This can undermine democratic principles and lead to abuses of power.

Effective leadership often involves striking a balance between maintaining stability and promoting progress. Leaders should recognize that societies evolve, and change can be necessary for addressing emerging challenges and achieving greater justice and equality. To ensure stability is achieved just and ethically, leaders should strive for inclusivity and engage with diverse perspectives within their society. Inclusive decision-making can help prevent grievances and conflicts that may arise from marginalized groups feeling unheard or excluded. Leaders who prioritize stability, order, and security play a crucial role in creating a safe and predictable environment for their societies. However, they must navigate ethical challenges related to individual freedoms, justice, and inclusivity. Effective leadership involves finding the right balance between preserving stability and promoting necessary societal changes for the greater good.

## Corporate Interests, Social Influence, and Security

In business, individuals and corporations with power often seek to maximize profits and shareholder value. Their primary purpose may be to grow their businesses, expand market share, and generate financial returns for their stakeholders. Celebrities, artists, and cultural figures wield different power, often focused on shaping public opinion, cultural norms, and trends. Their purpose may be to influence societal values, attitudes, and behaviors through their work and public presence. Governments and military leaders may use their power to protect and defend their nations, citizens, and interests. National security and defense are often paramount concerns for those in these positions.

## Power in the Church

Those who hold positions of power within the church are expected to act in accordance with principles and values that reflect the teachings of their faith, promote the well-being of the congregation, and serve as examples of Christian leadership. Sadly, many are grifters. Leaders in the church should strive to live out their faith in a way that serves as an example to others. It includes maintaining a personal relationship with God, regularly engaging in prayer and study of scripture, and demonstrating a commitment to Christian values. Church leaders should embrace a spirit of humility, understanding that their authority and power are meant to be used for the service and spiritual growth of the congregation, not for personal gain or recognition. Leaders should have a servant's heart, putting the needs of the congregation ahead of their own desires and ego. It involves actively seeking opportunities to serve and care for those they lead. Church leaders are expected to maintain high moral and ethical standards in all aspects of their lives. They should avoid actions or behaviors that would undermine their credibility and the integrity of the church. Leaders should be willing to be held accountable for their actions and decisions by their peers and the congregation. This accountability helps maintain transparency and trust.

## Compassion and Care

Church leaders, especially pastors and clergy, should provide pastoral care and support to individuals and families in times of need, offering spiritual guidance and comfort. Demonstrating empathy and compassion is essential. Leaders should be sensitive to the struggles and challenges faced by their congregants and extend care to those who are hurting. Leaders should provide sound and biblically grounded teaching and preaching to help the congregation grow in faith and understanding. Encouraging and facilitating spiritual growth and discipleship within the church community should be a priority. This involves mentoring and equipping others for leadership and service.

Leaders should work to foster unity and harmony within the congregation, resolving conflicts in a spirit of reconciliation and peace. Embracing inclusivity and welcoming all people, regardless of their backgrounds or circumstances, is fundamental to Christian values. Church leaders should actively participate in and lead congregational worship and prayer, setting an example of reverence and devotion. Leaders should seek God's guidance and direction through prayer and spiritual discernment, especially when making important decisions for the church. Leaders should oversee the financial and material resources of the church with integrity and transparency, ensuring that they are used wisely for the benefit of the congregation and the community. Church leaders should lead by example in engaging with the community, participating in outreach and mission efforts, and promoting social justice and compassion beyond the church walls. People with power in the church should act as servants of God and the congregation, guided by the principles of faith, love, humility, and moral integrity. Their actions should reflect the teachings of Jesus Christ and contribute to the church community's spiritual growth, unity, and well-being.

# CHAPTER 24

# Act Now: Despite Much Loss, You Can Win in the Fourth Quarter of Life

Develop a fourth-quarter mentality. The fourth quarter is where the stakes are often highest. It's that crucial stretch where the game can be won or lost and where resilience, determination, and a strategic mindset can make all the difference. Just as Ecclesiastes 9:11 wisely notes, "The race is not given to the swift or to the strong but to the one who endures to the end," the fourth quarter of life can be the most rewarding and transformative period if you approach it with the right perspective.

Life has a way of throwing curveballs, and the fourth quarter is no exception. It's a time when you may face significant challenges and losses – whether it's the loss of loved ones, career changes, health issues, or unfulfilled dreams. But in this period, your resilience can shine through, and you can turn the tide in your favor.

## The Miracle in the Fourth Quarter

It was a chilly autumn evening, and the championship football game had reached its critical fourth quarter. Once a powerhouse team, the Falcons found themselves trailing 21-7 against the seemingly invincible Thunderhawks. The scoreboard was merciless, and the stands were filled with disheartened fans, their hopes dwindling with every passing minute. The Thunderhawks had been dominating the game with their superior size, speed, and strategy. They'd silenced the Falcons' offense, intercepted passes, and precisely blocked kicks. It seemed like an insurmountable challenge. But a remarkable transformation was underway in the Falcons' locker room during the halftime break. Coach Mitchell, a seasoned and wise strategist, delivered a passionate speech that ignited a fire in his players' hearts.

"Men, I've seen us face tougher odds than this," he declared, his eyes gleaming with determination. "We may be down, but remember why you started playing this game. Remember the dreams you had as kids. It's not about how hard you hit but how hard you can get hit and keep moving forward." The Falcons took his words to heart, and something had changed as they stepped back onto the field. They had a vision, a shared determination to rise from the ashes of defeat. The Thunderhawks received the kickoff but couldn't make much progress against the revitalized Falcons' defense. The Falcons' defense, inspired by their coach's words, began reading plays like never before. They forced a fumble, and the Falcons' offense took over at the Thunderhawks' 30-yard line. With vision, focus, and determination, the Falcons executed a flawless drive, capitalizing on every opportunity. Quarterback Jake Harrison, under immense pressure, threw a pinpoint pass to wide receiver Mike Lawson in the end zone. Touchdown, Falcons! The score now stood at 21-14. The Thunderhawks, shocked by the Falcons' resurgence, struggled to regain their composure. The Falcons' defense, energized and relentless, forced another turnover. The Falcons' offense seized the moment, and running back Tony Sanchez bulldozed through the Thunderhawks' defensive line for a game-tying touchdown.

The stadium erupted into cheers, with fans who had given up hope now rallying behind their beloved Falcons. The score was tied at

21-21 with just two minutes left in the game. The Thunderhawks received the kickoff, but the Falcons' defense, fueled by vision and determination, held firm. With 30 seconds left, the Thunderhawks attempted a desperate pass deep into Falcons territory. The Falcons' cornerback, Sarah Miller, intercepted the pass and raced down the sideline. She was tackled just short of the end zone. With only seconds remaining on the clock, the Falcons had one last chance to win it. Coach Mitchell, with tears in his eyes, called a daring play. Quarterback Jake Harrison executed a perfectly timed quarterback sneak, crossing the goal line with the ball stretched out for the winning touchdown. The Falcons had done the unthinkable. They had risen from a certain defeat, fueled by their vision, focus, and determination. The final score: Falcons 28, Thunderhawks 21. It was a moment of triumph that would be etched in football history as "The Miracle on Fourth and Goal." The Falcons' victory wasn't just about winning a game; it was a testament to the power of belief, teamwork, and never giving up on a dream.

## In the Fourth Quarter of Life

To turn the tide of life in your favor in the fourth quarter, you should redefine success. The markers of success that may have driven you in your earlier years might no longer apply. Instead, focus on what truly matters to you now. What are your passions, values, and aspirations for this stage of life? Realign your goals with your current priorities and embrace the journey ahead with purpose.

No more should you go above and beyond the call of duty to help others when they will not lift a finger to help you! Use wisdom, or you will be used. There is no time for errors in the fourth quarter; you win or lose here. Defining success in the fourth quarter of life is a deeply personal and subjective endeavor, depending on an individual's values, aspirations, and life circumstances. Many people in their fourth quarter seek fulfillment and contentment as a primary measure of success. This may involve finding peace with one's life choices, embracing gratitude for what one has, and deriving joy from everyday experiences.

For many, legacies and impact are integral to their success stories. Their legacies are a major part of their impact on life. Some individuals define success by embarking on "legacy projects" that allow them to channel their passions and experiences into meaningful pursuits, such as writing a memoir, starting a charitable endeavor, or pursuing a long-held dream. Writing a Memoir or Autobiography is a notable legacy project. Many people choose to document their life experiences, insights, and lessons learned in the form of a memoir or autobiography. This can serve to share their unique story and wisdom with future generations. Starting a Charitable Foundation is a favorite legacy project. A common legacy project is creating a charitable organization or foundation to support a cause or community. It allows individuals to make a long-term impact by addressing issues they are passionate about. Artists, musicians, and writers may leave behind a legacy by creating a body of work that continues to inspire and influence others even after their passing. It could include creating a series of paintings, composing music, or writing a series of novels.

Other legacy projects include establishing a Scholarship Fund. Families often set up a scholarship fund to support the education of promising students in a particular field or from a specific background, which is a meaningful way to ensure that one's values and interests continue to be promoted. Many individuals embark on projects to build or restore monuments, memorials, or historical sites in their communities. This can be a way to commemorate important events or figures. For those passionate about the environment, establishing or contributing to conservation projects, reforestation efforts, or wildlife sanctuaries can be a way to leave a lasting positive impact on the planet.

Biographical writing is a good legacy project. No one will write your history better than you. Documenting the history of one's family, including stories, photographs, and genealogy, can be a valuable legacy project to pass down the family's heritage to future generations. Sharing one's knowledge and expertise by mentoring or teaching others is a form of legacy. This can involve becoming a teacher, creating educational resources, or offering mentorship in a specific field. Initiating or contributing to community projects, such as building a community center, starting a local farmers' market, or organizing cultural events, can leave a legacy in the place where one lives. Innovators and inventors often create products or technologies that shape industries and improve people's lives. These inventions can have a long-lasting impact and legacy. Finally, documenting oral histories must be considered. Let older adults narrate their lives and experiences and record their own words. Recording and preserving the stories and oral histories of individuals or communities can be a way to ensure that their voices and experiences are remembered for generations to come.

Legacy projects vary widely, but they all share the common goal of making a positive and lasting impact on the world, whether through creativity, philanthropy, education, or other means.

So, making a positive impact on others, contributing to one's community, or passing on wisdom and values to future generations is important. Health and well-being become increasingly important in the later stages of life. Success might involve maintaining physical fitness, managing health conditions, and prioritizing mental and emotional well-being. For many, the quality of relationships is a significant indicator of success. This can include nurturing deep connections with family and friends, repairing strained relationships, and fostering new bonds. Success can be linked to ongoing personal growth and self-discovery. This may involve pursuing new hobbies, learning, and embracing opportunities for personal development.

While financial success may take a different form in the fourth quarter, having a sense of financial security can be crucial. This includes managing resources for retirement, ensuring a comfortable lifestyle, and having a plan for estate planning and inheritance. Success can also be tied to spiritual or philosophical exploration. This might involve deepening one's spiritual beliefs, engaging in mindfulness practices, or seeking answers to existential questions. Some individuals view success as the opportunity to explore new horizons, travel to dream destinations, and embark on adventurous journeys they may not have had the chance to pursue earlier in life. Success can be defined by giving back to society through volunteer work, mentoring, or supporting charitable causes. The act of giving can be deeply fulfilling and purposeful. Ultimately, defining success in the fourth quarter of life is a deeply personal journey. It may involve a combination of these elements or completely unique criteria. The key is to reflect on what truly matters to you, consider your life experiences and values, and align your definition of success with the goals and aspirations that will bring you the greatest sense of fulfillment and happiness in this stage of life. Success, in the end, is about living authentically and in accordance with your own values and desires.

## Embracing Change

Change is a constant companion in the fourth quarter. It can be daunting but can also be the catalyst for growth and self-discovery. Whether it's adapting to a new phase of your career, relocating, or exploring new interests, be open to change. Embrace the opportunity to reinvent yourself and explore uncharted territories. Begin by reflecting on your interests, passions, values, and what you want to achieve in this stage of life. Consider what brings you fulfillment and happiness. Define clear and achievable goals for this phase. What do you want to learn, experience, or accomplish? These goals can be personal, professional, or a mix of both.

Embrace a growth mindset and a commitment to lifelong learning. Take up new hobbies, enroll in courses, attend workshops, and read to acquire new knowledge and skills. The idea is to live and enjoy life to the very end. And, to that end, building new social connections and networks. Join clubs, organizations, or online communities related to your interests. Meeting new people can open up new opportunities and perspectives. If you have a business idea or a passion project, consider turning it into a small business or side gig. The flexibility of your retirement years can make it an ideal time to explore entrepreneurship.

If you enjoy travel, use this time to explore new places and cultures. Traveling can be a source of inspiration and personal growth. Go to Timbuktu and beyond! And when you return, find meaning in giving back to their communities or contributing to causes they are passionate about. Volunteering or getting involved in philanthropic activities can be deeply rewarding. Prioritize your physical and mental well-being. Regular exercise, a balanced diet, and mindfulness practices can help you stay healthy and energized. Ensure your financial situation is well managed to support your lifestyle changes and new endeavors. Seek the advice of financial advisors if needed. Embrace change and be open to adapting to new circumstances. Challenges and setbacks are a natural part of any reinvention process, so resilience is important.

Success in the fourth quarter of life requires a structured plan. Develop a clear plan or roadmap for your reinvention journey. Break down your goals into smaller, actionable steps and timelines. Maintaining a positive and optimistic mindset is crucial. Be patient with yourself and stay open to the possibilities that lie ahead. As you make progress and achieve your goals, take the time to celebrate your successes and acknowledge your growth. Reinventing oneself in the fourth quarter of life can be a deeply fulfilling and liberating experience. It's a time to pursue what truly matters to you and to shape your life in a way that aligns with your values and desires. Remember that it's never too late to explore new passions, make a difference, and find renewed purpose and joy in life.

Life's fourth quarter is a time of transition, reflection, and opportunity. It is not dead-end. By embracing a fourth-quarter mentality marked by resilience, adaptability, and a focus on what truly matters, you can weather the losses and challenges and savor the victories and discoveries that await you. Remember, the race is not won by the swift or the strong alone but by those who endure, adapt, and act purposefully in this final stretch of life's journey.

Experiencing disappointment in the fourth quarter of life is a reality that some individuals may face. This disappointment can stem from a variety of factors and circumstances. It's important to acknowledge and address these feelings constructively. Here are some common reasons why individuals might feel disappointed in this stage of life:

## Distractions

Distractions can cause you to lose a game. In the fourth quarter of life, some people can become distracted with unfulfilled dreams or aspirations. They might feel unaccomplished or a failure. Unmet career goals, unrealized personal ambitions, or missed opportunities can lead to disappointment. Health issues can become more prominent as people age, and dealing with chronic illness, pain, or limitations can be emotionally and physically taxing, leading to disappointment about one's physical condition. Death or separation from loved ones, friends, and peers can come in the fourth quarter. Coping with grief and loneliness can be challenging and lead to feelings of disappointment and isolation. Strained or challenging relationships can contribute to disappointment and emotional distress, whether with family members, friends, or romantic partners. And reflecting on past decisions or actions and feeling regretful about certain choices can be a source of disappointment and self-criticism.

Social isolation and loneliness can be particularly difficult in the fourth quarter of life, especially if individuals have limited social connections or support systems. Some individuals may struggle with a sense of purpose or productivity in retirement or after leaving the workforce, leading to disappointment about how they spend their time. So, adjusting to the physical and emotional changes that come with aging can be challenging and may lead to feelings of disappointment about the loss of one's youth or former capabilities. A lack of support systems, whether emotional, financial, or caregiving, can contribute to feelings of disappointment and a sense of being overwhelmed. Thus, it is essential to address disappointment constructively in the fourth quarter of life to reach out to friends, family, or support groups to share your feelings and seek emotional support. Given your current circumstances and limitations, reevaluate your goals and aspirations to make them more attainable. Focus on self-care practices, including physical and mental well-being, to improve your overall quality of life. Embrace opportunities for personal growth and explore new interests or hobbies that can bring fulfillment and purpose. Professional help is crucial. Consider seeking the assistance of a therapist or counselor specializing in aging, grief, and life transitions.

It has been said that "if a man is not dead, do not call him a ghost." The idea is that as long as a person is alive and breathing, there is potential for them to achieve remarkable and extraordinary things. It emphasizes the inherent capacity for growth, change, and achievement that comes with life. It serves as a motivational reminder that one should not underestimate one's potential and should continue to pursue one's dreams, aspirations, and goals because life offers opportunities for incredible accomplishments and contributions. It's never too late to make positive changes and find sources of joy and fulfillment in the fourth quarter of life. While disappointment is a natural emotion, taking proactive steps to address its underlying causes can lead to greater contentment and satisfaction in this stage of life.

# CHAPTER 25

# Act Now: Abandon the Slave Narratives about You!

"Abandon the slave narratives about you" is a powerful call to challenge and overcome the harmful narratives that have been imposed on descendants of slaves. Often rooted in stereotypes and misconceptions, these narratives have had detrimental effects on individuals and communities. First, we must abandon the notion of black inferiority and the practice of racial bias. Descendants of enslaved people, many of whom are descendants of African royalty, have been told that they are inherently inferior to white people. This harmful belief has led to systemic racism and discrimination, limiting opportunities and access of black people to resources needed to level the playing field. Overcoming the internalized belief of inferiority and self-hatred, which can result from systemic racism and historical oppression, is a complex and deeply personal process. It's important to recognize that these feelings are not inherent but have been shaped by societal factors. Some steps and strategies can help individuals, particularly African Americans, address and overcome internalized racism and self-hatred. We must begin by recognizing and acknowledging the existence of internalized racism and self-hatred. Understand that these feelings are not our fault but are a result of societal conditioning.

We must remember that black people are beautiful. Black people are bright! Black people are resilient. The history of African Americans is marked by incredible resilience in the face of adversity, from the struggles of the civil rights movement to the achievements of Black leaders in various fields. Black people are among the creative geniuses of history. African American culture has made significant contributions to the world of art, music, literature, and entertainment. It has given rise to iconic figures like Maya Angelou, James Baldwin, Duke Ellington, and Beyoncé. Black people are diverse. The African diaspora is incredibly diverse, encompassing a rich tapestry of cultures, languages, and traditions. This diversity has enriched societies around the world. The history of African American activism and leadership inspires empowerment and social change. Figures like Martin Luther King Jr., Malcolm X, and Harriet Tubman exemplify the power of individuals to effect positive change. Black people have survived the unimaginable, and they are unstoppable. Despite facing immense challenges, African Americans have achieved greatness in all walks of life. Their accomplishments serve as a testament to the indomitable spirit that drives progress and innovation.

Our liberation from the traumas of slavery begins with therapy. Professionals can provide guidance and a safe space to explore and address emotions and inherited flaws. We must actively challenge negative thoughts and beliefs about ourselves. For example, if a black man catches himself thinking negatively, ask he should ask himself, where do these thoughts come from? They are based on reality. We must use the positive affirmations from Scripture to counter negative self-talk. We must repeatedly affirm our worth, value, and capabilities. Over time, positive affirmations can reshape our self-perception. It is a shame but a fact that many black people do not know their history or culture. This is not entirely their fault. The erasure of our history and culture has been a major task of white supremacy. Learning about the achievements and contributions of African Americans throughout history can foster a sense of pride and identity.

Black people should prioritize self-care and mental health. Engage in activities that promote well-being, such as meditation, exercise, or hobbies that bring joy. We must consider counseling or therapy specifically focused on addressing internalized racism and self-esteem issues. Therapists can provide strategies tailored to your unique experiences and challenges.

There is a desperate need for community and mentorship in the black community. Many little black boys who seek out mentors and role models within your community cannot find a trustworthy individual to confine. As a group, we must understand that overcoming internalized racism is a process that takes time, so we should be patient with ourselves and persistent in our efforts to challenge and heal from deeply ingrained beliefs. Overcoming internalized racism and self-hatred is a personal journey, and the process differs for everyone. Seeking support and engaging in self-reflection can be powerful steps toward healing and reclaiming a positive self-image. Additionally, the broader society must continue to work toward dismantling systemic racism to prevent its perpetuation.

## Criminalization and Stereotyping

Some narratives unfairly portray African Americans as more prone to criminal behavior. This stereotype has contributed to racial profiling, biased policing, and disproportionate incarceration rates among African Americans. Studies have consistently shown that African Americans are more likely to be stopped by law enforcement officers during traffic stops compared to white individuals. For example, the Stanford Open Policing Project found that black drivers are about 20% more likely to be stopped than white drivers. The stop-and-frisk policy disproportionately targeted black and Hispanic individuals in cities like New York. Data revealed that many stops involved these communities despite lower rates of contraband discovery among them.

Research has shown that African Americans are disproportionately subjected to the use of force by police officers. A study published in the Proceedings of the National Academy of Sciences found that black men and boys face a significantly higher risk of being killed by police compared to their white counterparts. African Americans are more likely to be arrested for certain offenses, even when the rates of criminal activity are similar across racial groups. This indicates a bias in law enforcement practices.

The United States has one of the highest incarceration rates in the world, and African Americans are disproportionately represented in the prison population. Despite comprising only about 13% of the U.S. population, African Americans comprise a significantly higher percentage of the incarcerated population. African Americans often receive harsher sentences for the same crimes as white individuals. The Sentencing Project reports that black men are nearly six times more likely to be incarcerated than white men. Mass incarceration disrupts African American families, as many black children grow up with parents who are incarcerated. This can have long-term social and economic consequences for these families and communities. Criminal records can limit employment opportunities for African Americans, perpetuating economic disparities and contributing to cycles of poverty. African American students are disproportionately subjected to suspension and expulsion in schools. It can contribute to a higher likelihood of involvement in the criminal justice system later in life. These statistics illustrate the deeply rooted issues of racial bias and systemic racism within the criminal justice system. The disproportionate rates of stops, arrests, use of force, and incarceration among African Americans highlight the urgent need for reform and greater accountability in law enforcement. Efforts to address these disparities include advocating for policy changes, implementing bias training for law enforcement officers, and promoting transparency in policing practices. Recognizing and challenging harmful stereotypes and narratives is crucial in achieving a more equitable and just criminal justice system.

## Intellectual Limitations

One of the deeply troubling "Big Lies" perpetuated during the era of slavery was the notion that slaves were ineducable. This false belief served as a convenient rationalization for denying African Americans the right to education and the opportunity to acquire knowledge. Enslavers feared that an educated enslaved population would be more aware of their oppression and more inclined to seek freedom and equality. Consequently, efforts to suppress education among African Americans were rampant. Slaves caught learning to read or write often faced severe punishments, as education was viewed as a threat to the institution of slavery itself.

Furthermore, as a means of control and manipulation, some enslavers redacted a version of the Bible specifically for enslaved individuals. This "Slave Bible" excluded significant portions of the text and passages that emphasized freedom, liberation, and equality while retaining verses that appeared to endorse servitude and obedience. By presenting a distorted religious narrative, this manipulation sought to convince African Americans that their enslavement was not only sanctioned by earthly authorities but also by divine will. This insidious use of religious texts further reinforced the harmful narrative that African Americans were inherently subservient and contributed to the perpetuation of their oppression. These harmful narratives about the supposed intellectual inferiority of African Americans, combined with the deliberate suppression of education, have had long-lasting effects. They have created self-doubt and limited access to quality education, which is essential for personal development and empowerment. It is vital to recognize the historical context in which these narratives emerged and actively work to dismantle the systemic barriers to education and personal growth that continue to impact African Americans today.

## Dependency Myths

There has been a narrative that African Americans are overly reliant on social welfare programs. This narrative ignores the historical and systemic barriers to economic mobility and perpetuates negative stereotypes. The narrative that African Americans are overly reliant on social welfare programs oversimplifies a complex issue and ignores the historical and systemic factors that contribute to economic disparities. It is essential to recognize and address the structural barriers to economic mobility that persist and work toward creating more equitable opportunities for all individuals and communities, regardless of their racial or ethnic backgrounds. Debunking this myth is a step toward a more accurate and fair understanding of the challenges faced by African Americans in pursuit of economic well-being.

## Colorism

Within the African American community, colorism is another issue. Some narratives suggest that lighter skin is more desirable, leading to discrimination and bias against those with darker skin tones. It can harm self-esteem and contribute to division within the community. Colorism has historical roots dating back to the era of slavery. Lighter-skinned slaves were sometimes favored by enslavers and given preferential treatment, perpetuating the belief that lighter skin was superior. This division has persisted over generations. The media, including advertising, entertainment, and fashion industries, has often perpetuated and reinforced the preference for lighter skin. Lighter-skinned individuals are often overrepresented in media and held up as beauty standards, while those with darker skin tones are underrepresented or portrayed less favorably. The preference for lighter skin can deeply affect the self-esteem of individuals with darker complexions. They may internalize feelings of inadequacy, unattractiveness, or inferiority, which can have long-lasting psychological effects. Colorism can create divisions within the African American community. Lighter-skinned individuals may experience privileges and opportunities that are denied to those with darker skin tones. This inequality can foster resentment and tension within the community.

Colorism also influences beauty standards, as individuals may feel pressured to conform to certain ideals of beauty associated with lighter skin. This can lead to the use of skin-lightening products or cosmetic surgeries to achieve a desired complexion. Colorism intersects with other forms of discrimination, such as racism, sexism, and classism. Dark-skinned African American women, for example, may face compounded biases based on both their race and gender. Challenging colorism within the African American community and society at large involves promoting a more inclusive definition of beauty that embraces diversity in skin tones. Celebrating and affirming the beauty of all complexions is crucial for healing and unity. Advocating for diverse representation in media and the fashion industry is essential. When individuals with darker skin tones are portrayed positively and prominently, it can challenge harmful beauty standards and promote self-acceptance. Raising awareness about the harmful effects of colorism and educating individuals on its historical roots can empower them to confront biases and challenge stereotypes. Colorism is a deeply ingrained issue that affects individuals' self-esteem, relationships, and overall well-being within the African American community. Addressing this issue requires both individual and collective efforts to challenge biases, redefine beauty standards, and promote self-acceptance, unity, and inclusivity. Recognizing that beauty comes in all shades is vital to healing the divisions caused by colorism.

## What should a black girl say to herself when told she is ugly?

When a black girl is told she is ugly, it can be a hurtful and damaging experience. She needs to build a strong sense of self-esteem and self-worth.

## Positive Affirmations for Black Girls

**I am beautiful**. Beauty comes in all shapes, sizes, and shades, and I am beautiful just the way I am.

**Others do not define my worth**. The opinions of others do not determine it.

**I am proud of my heritage.** Embrace and celebrate your heritage, culture, and the unique qualities that make you who you are. Your identity is a source of strength and beauty.

**My inner beauty shines brightly. I** understand that true beauty radiates from within. Your kindness, compassion, intelligence, and resilience make you truly beautiful.

**I Love and Accept Myself.** Treat yourself with the same kindness and respect that you offer to others.

**I am Confident.** Confidence is your powerful shield against hurtful words and negativity.

**I Surround Myself with Positivity.** Choose to be around people who uplift and support you. Surrounding yourself with positivity can boost your self-esteem.

**I Rise Above Negativity.** Rise above negative comments and stereotypes. Remember that these opinions are not a reflection of your true worth.

**I Define My Own Beauty Standards.** Reject society's narrow beauty standards and create your own. Beauty is subjective, and you have the authority to define what is beautiful to you.

**I Am Strong and Resilient.** Recognize your strength and resilience in the face of adversity. Your ability to overcome challenges is a testament to your inner beauty.

**I Focus on Self-Improvement.** Continuously work on personal growth and self-improvement, not conforming to others' standards but becoming your best version.

**I Support Others.** Lift up other girls and women who may be experiencing similar negativity. Building each other up strengthens collective self-esteem.

**I Seek Help When Needed.** If negative comments affect your mental health and self-esteem, don't hesitate to seek support from friends, family, or a mental health professional.

## Cultural Appropriation

African American culture has often been appropriated and commodified by others, while the contributions and innovations of African Americans are sometimes overlooked or minimized. Cultural appropriation refers to the act of borrowing or adopting elements of one culture by members of another culture, often without understanding or respecting the cultural significance behind those elements. African American culture, including aspects of music, fashion, dance, and language, has frequently been appropriated by mainstream culture and commercialized for profit. The appropriation of African American culture has sometimes led to the exploitation of cultural products and practices. For example, the music industry has commodified and commercialized African American musical genres like jazz, blues, and hip-hop, which have deep roots in African American history and struggle, often without adequate compensation or recognition for the original creators.

Despite their substantial contributions to various fields, African Americans have faced a historical pattern of being overlooked or under-credited. It has occurred in areas such as scientific innovations, sports, literature, and art. For instance, inventions and innovations by African Americans have frequently been overlooked in favor of other narratives. African American culture has been a source of cultural capital, often sought after for its perceived coolness or trendiness. It can lead to a superficial or shallow appreciation of cultural elements without understanding their historical or social significance.

In some cases, African American contributions have been erased or whitewashed from history. For example, the role of African Americans in the civil rights movement may be minimized in favor of a more simplified narrative that overlooks their leadership and sacrifices. Cultural appropriation and the overlooking of contributions can profoundly impact African Americans' identity and self-esteem. It can reinforce feelings of invisibility and devalue the cultural significance of their heritage.

While appropriation is problematic, it is important to recognize that cultural exchange can be enriching and positive when conducted respectfully and with an understanding of cultural contexts. It is essential to distinguish between appropriation and genuine cross-cultural exchange that promotes understanding and appreciation. Addressing the appropriation of African American culture and ensuring that the contributions and innovations of African Americans are recognized and celebrated is a matter of cultural respect, social justice, and historical accuracy. It requires ongoing efforts to promote cultural awareness, educate about the historical context of African American contributions, and challenge instances of appropriation and cultural erasure. Ultimately, a more equitable and inclusive appreciation of African American culture benefits society by fostering a deeper understanding of the diverse tapestry of American culture and history.

## Single-Story Narratives

The media and popular culture have sometimes portrayed African Americans in one-dimensional ways, focusing on stereotypes such as the "angry black person" or the "thug." These single-story narratives limit understanding and perpetuate harmful biases.

The media and popular culture significantly shape societal perceptions and attitudes toward various racial and ethnic groups, including African Americans. Unfortunately, these platforms have often resorted to one-dimensional and harmful portrayals of African Americans, perpetuating stereotypes that have real-world consequences. The focus on stereotypes such as the "angry black person" or the "thug" can limit understanding and contribute to the reinforcement of harmful biases. The "Angry Black Person" Stereotype portrays African Americans as excessively angry or aggressive, often in response to issues of racial injustice. While anger in response to systemic racism is entirely justified, reducing the entire African American community to this stereotype oversimplifies the community's range of emotions and experiences. It can lead to dismissing legitimate concerns and grievances, stifling meaningful dialogue and progress. The "Thug" Stereotype depicts African American men as dangerous criminals or troublemakers. This portrayal is misleading and dehumanizing, as it suggests that African American individuals are inherently predisposed to criminal behavior. It can lead to racial profiling, biased policing, and unjust treatment within the criminal justice system. The perpetuation of these stereotypes can limit educational and employment opportunities for African Americans. Teachers, employers, and law enforcement personnel may harbor unconscious biases based on these stereotypes, leading to discriminatory practices.

African Americans exposed to these one-dimensional portrayals can internalize negative self-perceptions. The constant barrage of negative stereotypes can contribute to feelings of self-doubt, reduced self-esteem, and a sense of alienation. Single-story narratives can also reduce empathy and solidarity among different racial and ethnic groups. When individuals are exposed to only negative portrayals of African Americans, they may fail to see the common humanity and shared experiences that connect all people. Conversely, the media has often underrepresented the diversity of African American experiences. A wide spectrum of experiences within the African American community, including achievements, successes, and everyday life, are often overlooked in favor of sensationalized narratives. Media outlets have a responsibility to challenge and move beyond these harmful stereotypes. Promoting more diverse and nuanced portrayals of African Americans can help break down these biases and promote a more accurate and fair understanding of the community. Diverse representation in media, including film, television, and news media, is crucial for counteracting stereotypes. When African Americans are portrayed in multidimensional roles, it challenges preconceived notions and promotes empathy and understanding.

Portraying African Americans in one-dimensional ways through harmful stereotypes has real-world consequences, from limiting opportunities to perpetuating biases and discrimination. Media and popular culture need to recognize their role in shaping public perceptions and take steps to promote more inclusive, accurate, and respectful portrayals of African Americans and other marginalized communities. By doing so, they can contribute to a more equitable and empathetic society.

Narratives that suggest African Americans are solely responsible for their economic disparities ignore the systemic barriers and discrimination they have faced. These narratives undermine efforts to address economic inequality. Challenging and dismantling these detrimental narratives is crucial to achieving racial equity, justice, and social progress. It involves embracing a more inclusive and accurate portrayal of African American experiences and contributions, acknowledging the resilience and strength of the community, and working collectively to overcome the legacy of discrimination and prejudice.

# EPILOGUE

You stand at the crossroads of fate!
Ready to journey to a promised land?
A clarion call, bold and true,
ACT NOW! It's time for you.

Elevate your focus, cast away your haze,
In a world of distractions, seek purpose anew.
With unwavering resolve, let your compass guide you,
Through life's twists and turns, let purpose be your ride.

Aspire to greatness, dreams untold,
In the treasure of your heart, there's a story to unfold.
Set audacious goals, pursue them with might,
You are equipped for greatness; reach for the heights!

Utilize your power for a divine purpose,
You are a source of light, and your gifts will shine.
In a world that yearns for a guiding star,
You are a vehicle of light!

Initiate a plan, both body and soul,
Nourish your being and make yourself whole.
Your health is a resource; it is a gift to adore,
Fulfill your purpose; serve and explore!

Embrace ACT NOW; it's a transformative decree,
It's a catalyst for change,
For in the ACT, as we boldly proclaim,
Lies the power to transform, to ignite the flame.

The time is upon you; don't let it pass by,
In the depths of your heart, let your purpose fly.
Remember, my friend, as you stand at this door,
ACT NOW to create a transformation that will last forever!

# ABOUT THE AUTHOR

Born into this world with a purpose as unique as a rare gem, Linton Thomas emerged like a belated gift, meticulously wrapped in the exquisite ebony of his existence. He arrived bearing a profound passion for God, enveloped by an unwavering commitment to serve the divine. With a rich tenure of over three decades in academia and spiritual vocation, he has unfurled a holistic approach to life that echoes the luminaries of our time, making his presence felt like the subtle tremors of a seismic shift.

Linton Thomas is a man of unyielding courage, unwavering integrity, unmatched intensity, and unceasing inquiry. He stands as a bulwark in defense of the Faith, melding profound theoretical insights with the crucible of practical application. His journey through the halls of education is a testament to his unrelenting pursuit of knowledge and growth, as he proudly boasts degrees from esteemed institutions, Jamaica Theological Seminary, Hofstra University, the College of St. Rose, and Concordia University, Chicago. In him, one witnesses the embodiment of the illustrious motto of RABALAC: "The Utmost for the Highest."

Beyond the written word, beyond the confines of authorship and motivational speaking, Linton Thomas is a dedicated servant of the divine, a visionary luminary who guides others toward the light, and a vibrant champion of the Christian Faith. His life's narrative is a fascinating journey that leaves an indelible mark upon the hearts and minds of all fortunate to cross his path.

Printed in the United States
by Baker & Taylor Publisher Services